POPEYE
THE SAILOR

The 1960s TV CARTOONS

by FRED M. GRANDINETTI

Popeye the Sailor: The 1960s TV Cartoons
© 2024 Fred M. Grandinetti. All Rights Reserved.

No part of this book may be reproduced in any form or by any means, electronic, mechanical, digital, photocopying or recording, except for the inclusion in a review, without permission in writing from the publisher.

Popeye and related characters © King Features Syndicate.

Published in the USA by:
BearManor Media
4700 Millenia Blvd.
Suite 175 PMB 90497
Orlando, Florida 32839
www.bearmanormedia.com

Hardcover: ISBN 978-1-62933-851-4
Paperback: ISBN 978-1-62933-850-7

Printed in the United States of America.
Cover Illustration by David Hudon.
Book design by Brian Pearce | Red Jacket Press.

Table of Contents

Introduction 5
POPEYE'S ROOTS 6
The Sailor Sails into Theaters and on The Small Screen 9
POPEYE GETS MADE FOR TELEVISION 16
Producer Al Brodax 18
The Studios 22
    Jack Kinney 22
    Gerald Ray 23
    Larry Harmon 23
    Gene Deitch 23
    Halas and Batchelor 25
    Paramount Cartoon Studios 25
The Quality 27
Popeye's Success on Television 34
Segar's Characters Make Their Animation Debut! 43
Make Way for Brutus! 47
The Voices 52
THE TELEVISION CARTOON SPIN-OFFS 58
EPISODE GUIDE 78
    Cartoons Produced by Larry Harmon 79
    Cartoons Produced by William L. Synder
    and Supervising Director Gene Deitch 86
    Cartoons Produced by Gerald Ray 102
    Cartoons Produced and Directed by Jack Kinney 108
    Cartoons Produced by Paramount Cartoon Studios 160
About the Author 227

Introduction

When my brother and I were in grade school, we watched *Popeye and The Three Stooges* early in the morning on WPRO. This was a television station located in Providence, Rhode Island. My brother always complained the program ran more Popeye than The Three Stooges. A half-hour consisted of one Three Stooges short followed by a Popeye theatrical film or four television cartoons starring the one-eyed sailor.

This was my first introduction to the Popeye cartoons produced exclusively for the small screen by King Features Syndicate. As a child, I remember not particularly pleased Olive Oyl ate Popeye's spinach so often and had to save her boyfriend from The Sea Hag.

The varying quality of the cartoons was something I didn't notice at such a young age. This little boy was just thrilled there was so much more of Popeye to watch. I was later exposed to these same cartoons on Rex Trailer's Boomtown program, which aired weekend mornings on WBZ-TV. During the mid-1970s, I was home sick from school; I watched an early morning broadcast of the television cartoons on WSBK-TV. This particular bloc of Popeye television cartoons happened to be the poorest in terms of animation. From this point on, I studied each television cartoon and was puzzled why some were of excellent quality and others unwatchable.

Many of the cartoons were animated so terribly they have given the entire series a horrible reputation. Hopefully, this book will allow readers to understand the cartoon's origins and appreciate better films in the series.

Popeye's Roots

Cartoonist Elzie Crisler Segar created many of the characters who appeared in the Popeye television cartoons produced by King Features Syndicate. He was born on December 8, 1894, in Chester, Illinois, and began his apprenticeship in the entertainment industry at the age of 12. Segar worked as a motion picture projectionist, house painter, and drummer. He took an 18-month W.L. Evans correspondence course in cartooning. After completing the course, he went to Chicago where R.F. Outcault, then doing *Buster Brown*, got him a job working on the strip *Charlie Chaplin's Comic Capers* in 1916. The following year Segar started a strip called *Barry the Boob*, featuring a nutty soldier in the European War. In 1919 Segar joined the staff of King Features Syndicate and created *The Thimble Theatre*. Initially, the strip starred Olive Oyl and her family: Castor Oyl, her pint-sized brother; Cole Oyl, her father; and Olive's boyfriend, pickle-nosed Ham Gravy. The strip's stories were similar to vaudeville routines and later focused on the get-rich schemes of Castor Oyl. Segar was always adding new characters, and when each served its purpose, they vanished. Popeye himself was an unexpected hit who first appeared on January 17, 1929. Having bought a ship, Castor decided he needed a crew and met a stranger on the pier. He asked Popeye, "Hey, are you a sailor?" "Ja think I'm a cowboy?" came the reply, and a legend was born. The lore of Chester, Illinois, claims the character of Popeye was influenced by town resident Frank "Rocky" Fiegel. Fiegel was described as "strong, tall, always a winner in a fight."

Other characters Segar created included J. Wellington Wimpy, Swee'pea, King Blozo, Alice the Goon, Poopdeck Pappy, Eugene the Jeep, Rough House, Geezil, and Bluto.

With Popeye on board, the strip was syndicated to hundreds of newspapers, and Segar received thousands of fan letters. King Features Syndicate licensed his characters to six hundred manufacturers, radio, and animated cartoons. Unfortunately, during all of this success, Segar became ill with spleen and liver disease. He passed away on October 13, 1938, but other cartoonists and writers continued the comic strip:

Doc Winner (cartoonist) and Tom Sims (writer), 1938 to 1939

Bela "Bill" Zaboly (cartoonist) and Tom Sims (writer), 1939 to 1954 (daily), 1939 to 1958 (Sunday)

Bela "Bill" Zaboly (cartoonist) and Ralph Stein (writer), 1954 to 1958 (daily)

Bud Sagendorf (cartoonist and writer), 1958 to 1986 (daily), 1958 to 1994 (Sunday)

Bobby London (cartoonist and writer), 1986 to 1992 (daily)

Hy Eisman (cartoonist and writer), 1994 to 2022 (Sunday)

Randall Keith Milholland (cartoonist and writer) 2022 to present (Sunday)

The televison-cartoon version of Brutus made his debut in the daily strip by Bobby London on July 23, 1991.

The Sailor Sails into Theaters and on The Small Screen

Thimble Theatre had been a favorite of Max Fleischer, the man behind Fleischer Studios. He produced animated cartoons featuring Koko the Clown, Bimbo, and the popular Betty Boop for Paramount Pictures. Max decided to make an animated film featuring Popeye and finalized the arrangements with King Features Syndicate. Fleischer decided to test audience's reaction to the one-eyed sailor by featuring him in a Betty Boop film. This 1933 cartoon, called *Popeye the Sailor*, featured a newspaper headline announcing, "Popeye a movie star…the sailor with a sock accepts a movie contract." The success of this *Betty Boop* cartoon led to his own series of theatrical cartoons. From 1933 to 1942, Popeye cartoons were produced by The Fleischer Studios. In 1942 Fleischer was taken over by Paramount's Famous Studios. Famous Studios was known for eventually improving Olive Oyl's looks. The studio gave her a more attractive facial design and bust. By the time the last *Popeye the Sailor* theatrical film was released in 1957, the spinach-loving sailor had appeared in 234 animated productions. The series ceased production when Paramount Pictures realized they could reissue the same cartoons to theatres for ten years (until 1967). They would make more money reissuing older Popeye cartoons to theatres than creating new ones. Besides, Paramount wanted to cash out by selling their film library for television syndication. The black and white animated films by The Fleischer Studios are held in high esteem. The animated films by Famous Studios remain one of the longest-running in television syndication.

Broadcasting Magazine's June 11, 1956 edition reported Associated Artists Productions acquired from Paramount Pictures the library of 234

Popeye the Sailor cartoons. A.A.P.'s President, Eliot Hyman, announced the films would be offered for sale to television stations. The cost of the library was estimated at 1.5 million. A two-page advertisement appeared in the August 22, 1956 issue of *Variety*, stating, "Build up your whole schedule...program the winner and all-time favorite. He's loaded with 234 cartoons that will wallop your ratings sky high! And 114 of them are in COLOR, at no extra charge. Get that big boost in business-grab POPEYE. He's packed with pulling power and selling power." The advertisement was decorated with images of Popeye, Olive Oyl, Bluto, and Swee'pea. The cartoons were an instant hit on television stations across the country. Fred Tower, Vice President of WPIX Channel 11, sent a letter to Mr. Robert Rich of Associated Artists Productions, dated October 9, 1956. It stated:

> Dear Bob,
> Popeye's made a clean sweep in New York! The spinach-eating sailor topped all six competing stations, averaging all seven days of the week. You know, of course, that our Monday-Friday Popeye strip has sold out over a month before the first telecast. It's certainly been proved quickly that the charter sponsors knew a good thing when they bought it. The Popeye half-hours pulled a 7-day ARB September average of 5.6, against 4.7 for the next highest station. The Mon.-Fri. average was 6.0, with a non-duplicated cumulative rating of 3.9. Among the programs Popeye overpowered were Million Dollar Movie, *Hopalong Cassidy*, *Gene Autry*, *The U.N. Handicap*, *Wild Bill Hickok*, *Annie Oakley*, *Captain Video*, and *Sky King*. We confidently believe that Popeye ratings will grow even larger — after all, this was the first week on the air.

Lew Arnold of KTLA, Paramount Television Productions, also sent a letter to Mr. Robert Rich dated November 6, 1956.

> Dear Bob,
> That sailor man of yours certainly has the kind of muscle power it takes to beat the competition in the Los Angeles area. Our ratings have quadrupled when Popeye took over. Our ARB average for 7 to 7:30 pm, Monday-Friday last month, before Popeye took over, was 1.8. In October, thanks to Popeye, the ARB average rocketed to 8.4 — more than four and one-half times as high! On Wednesday, for instance, Popeye drew a rating of 11.2, topping all six competing channels and beating *Background to*

Danger, Carveth Wells, Kit Carson, Man Called X, Public Defender, and *Vagabond*. And check this Popeye's non-duplicated cumulative rating for the week is 20.5 — the highest of all programs (both national and local) in "competition-tough" Southern California, from sign on to 7:30 pm, Monday through Friday... and equally important, Popeye reaches the whole family — nearly 40%, ADULTS!

The January 30, 1957 edition of *Variety* noted Popeye's show on WPIX, N.Y. hit a December American Research Bureau average of 13.6, making it the number two syndicated show in New York topped only by *Highway Patrol*. WPIX initially aired Popeye from 6 to 6:30 pm, Monday through Friday, Saturdays at 5:30 pm, and Sundays at 4:30 pm. A two-page advertisement appeared in *Variety's* March 20, 1957 issue announcing Popeye cartoon programs earned "a resounding rating of 16.2 on a weekly average regardless of station, time-period or competition." Below is a listing of Popeye's rating success in ten cities:

WBZ-TV, Boston, 20.7
WBEN-TV, Buffalo, 14.4
WBNS-TV, Columbus, 13.9
KBTV, Denver, 23.3
WTVJ, Miami, 15.9
WPIX, New York, 14.9
WPRO-TV Providence, 19.5
KRON-TV San Francisco, 10.6
KFDX-TV, Wichita Falls, 13.6
WFMJ-TV, Youngstown, 20.0

It was announced on May 27, 1957, Famous Studios, the animation wing of Paramount Pictures, was reported to be on the sales block. One of the parties interested was Associated Artist Productions. The press release for this sale noted, "A.A.P has Paramount's *Popeye* cartoons, all 234 of them. They have proven to be one of the local programming sensations of the season. It was speculated that A.A.P. may want to produce some new Popeye's." In the November 11, 1957 edition of *Broadcasting Magazine,* additional Popeye cartoons' possible production was explored further. A.A.P. officials noted the production of new cartoons would be "slow and meticulous." They would be concerned with quantity, cost of production and a method of distribution. Ultimately

A.A.P. did not produce any further adventures of the sailor man, but his ratings remained high throughout the remainder of the 1950s. *Variety* published a listing of the top twenty national syndicated shows in their December 3, 1958 edition. Popeye finished in 9th place broadcast in 18 major markets with an audience share of 11.7. *Popeye* remained a rating's winner after United Artists Associated purchased the cartoons from Associated Artists Productions. The May 20, 1964 edition of *Variety* reported the theatrical Popeye cartoons aired in 191 U.S. markets with 152 representing "renewals."

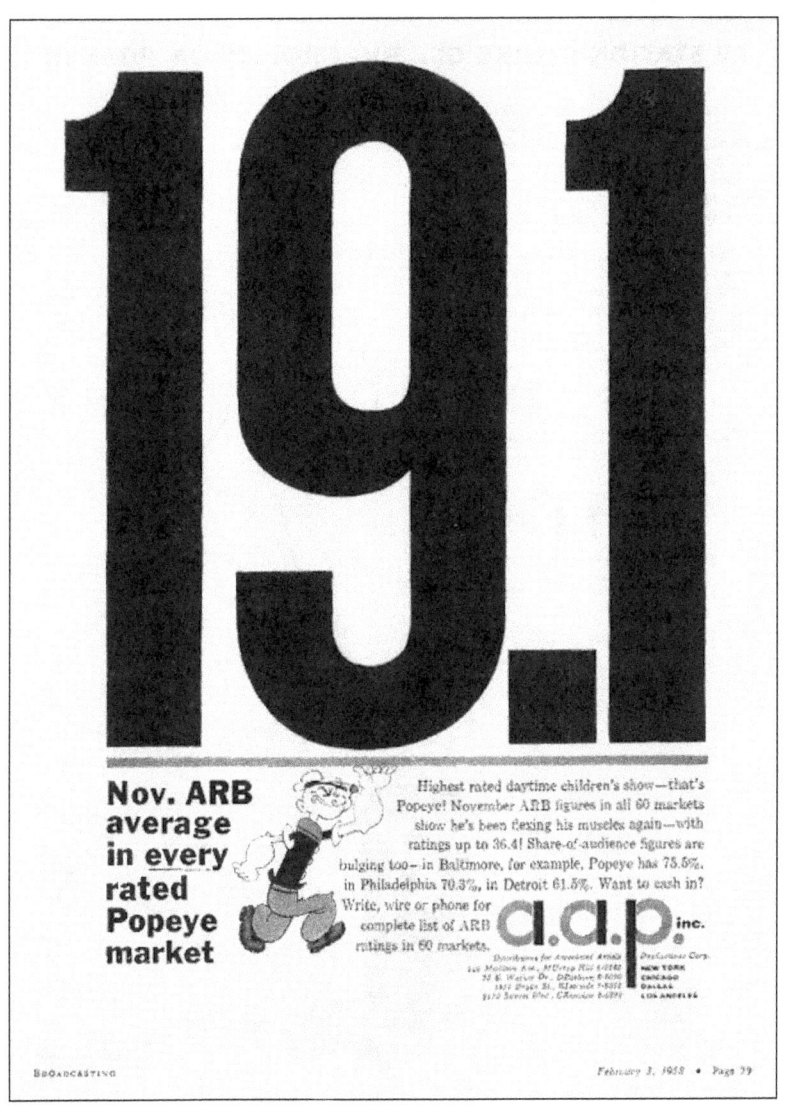

An advertisement from Broadcasting *Magazine from February 3, 1958 stating the Popeye theatrical cartoons, syndicated by A.A.P. became the highest rated daytime children's show.*

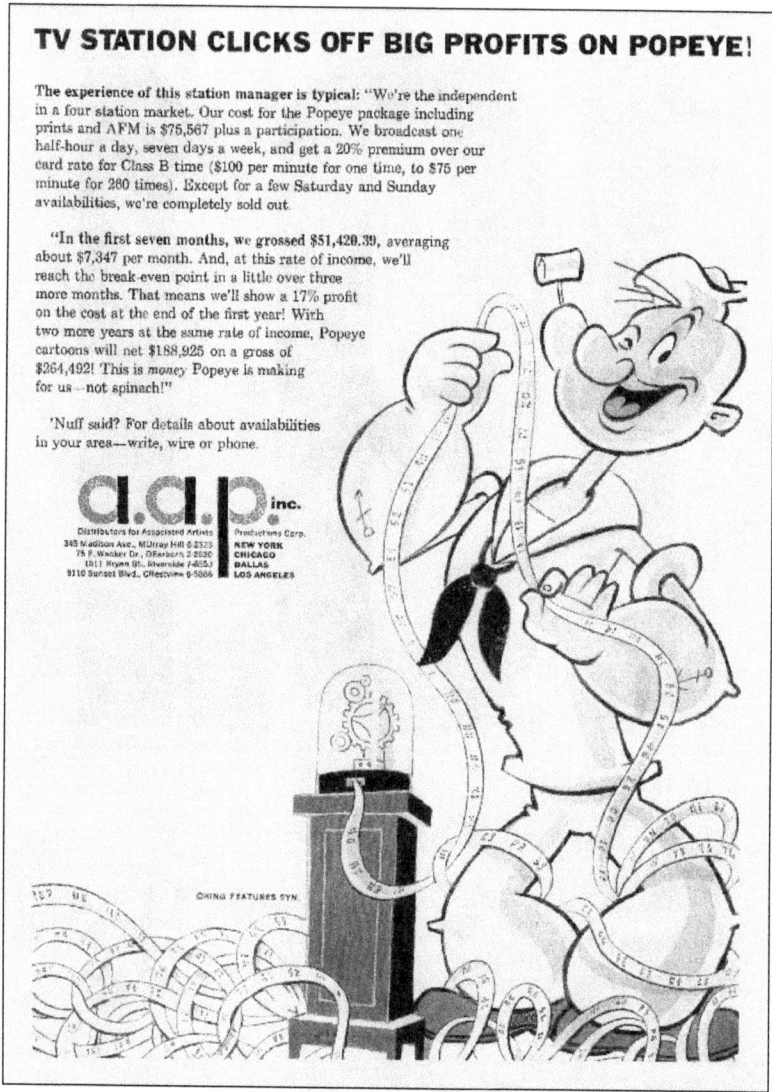

The June 9th, 1958 edition of Broadcasting *Magazine promoted the big profits television stations were earning with the theatrical Popeye cartoon series.*

The Popeye theatrical films became perennially popular favorites as evidenced by the advertisement in Broadcasting Magazine's February 16th, 1970 edition. The drawing of Popeye was by cartoonist, Bela "Bill" Zaboly, who illustrated the sailor's daily and Sunday comic strip adventures from 1939 through 1958. His artwork was also seen on Popeye related merchandise.

Popeye gets Made For Television

King Features Syndicate licensed to Paramount Pictures rights to use their characters in the theatrical cartoons. Consequently, the Syndicate was involved with Paramount and received compensation when the theatrical films were sold to Associated Artists Productions. King Features Syndicate also received royalty payments for all the Popeye-related licensed products due to the sailor's television exposure. They were not contractually involved with any payment associated with A.A.P. when the firm sold the cartoon series to numerous television stations.

In the June 10, 1959 edition of *Variety*, it was announced: *Push Popeye in King Features TV Formed by Hearst.*

"The Hearst Corp. has formed a new division of King Features Syndicate Special Service which will produce and market filmed television shows based on King Features properties. Al Brodax, for many years in the tele department of The Williams Morris Agency, has resigned the percentery to go with the new subdivision, to be known as King Features Television Production. On the immediate agenda is the production of a new Popeye animated cartoon. New features based on the King Features cartoon property will be made as soon as the contracts are set."

Producer
Al Brodax

Al Philip Brodax was born on February 14, 1926, in Brooklyn, New York, and attended Midwood High School. At the age of eighteen, he enlisted in the U.S. Army serving in World War II. He was awarded the Purple Heart, the Combat Medical Badge, and three battle stars after being wounded in action. Beginning in 1950, Brodax worked in program development for the *William Morris Agency*. He was a writer for *Pulitzer Prize Playhouse, Celanese Theatre, Suspense,* and *Omnibus*. Along the way, he co-produced, for Broadway, *Winesburg, Ohio*, which ran only 13 weeks. After finishing with *Popeye*, Brodax produced television cartoons based upon comic strips syndicated by King Features. *The King Features Trilogy* debuted in 1963 and consisted of 150 cartoons. *Snuffy Smith, Beetle Bailey,* and *Krazy Kat* each had fifty episodes produced. This series was not nearly as successful as *Popeye*. After seeing The Beatles perform on *The Ed Sullivan Show*, Brodax approached their management with the idea of producing an animated cartoon series featuring the famous foursome. The ABC network premiered *The Beatles* on September 25, 1965. The show, consisting of 39 episodes, was a huge success. Later, Brodax was the producer and co-screenwriter for the feature film *Yellow Submarine*. From 1969 to 1980, he worked as a freelance producer, writer, lyricist, and director. He supervised the animation for ABC's *Make a Wish* and *Animals, Animals, Animals*. In 2004 Brodax released his memoir, *Up Periscope Yellow: The Making of Beatles' Yellow Submarine*. He resided in Weston, Connecticut, where he was the head of *Brodax Film Group*, a television and production company. He passed away on November 24, 2016, at the age of 90.

One of the official announcements for the new Popeye series was published in *Variety* on August 26, 1959. The headline simply read: *New Popeye Cartoons* and explained King Features Syndicate had started production on "208 Popeye animated cartoons to be produced for library syndication." Al Brodax is producing half the films in New York, and Jack Kinney is producing the other half in Hollywood. Each episode being five and a half minutes in length. Eventually, Brodax hired six studios to produce a minimum order of 208 Popeye cartoons (which ultimately ended up totaling 220). Neither Brodax nor King Features Syndicate knew how long the sailor's popularity would last on television. Consequently, it was a wise business move to hire several animation studios, with each churning out as many cartoons as possible.

The availability of new Popeye cartoons was welcomed with enthusiasm across the United States. By September 19, 1960, the following television stations had purchased the completed films:

    Altoona, PA — WFBG
    Albany-Schenectady-Troy, N.Y. — WTEN
    Albuquerque, N. M. — KOAT
    Asheville-Greenville-Spartanburg, S.C. — WLOS
    Atlanta, GA — WSB
    Bakersfield, Calif. — KLYD
    Baltimore, MD — WBAL
    Bangor, ME — WLBZ
    Bay City Saginaw, Mich. — WNEM
    Billings, MT. — KGHL
    Binghamton, N.Y. — WNBF
    Birmingham, Ala. — WAPI
    Bismarck, Minot, N.D. — KFYR
    Boise, Idaho — KBOI
    Boston, Mass. — WBZ
    Bristol, Va.-Johnson City, Tenn. — WCYB
    Buffalo, N.Y. — WKBW
    Cape Girardeau, Mo. — KFBS
    Chicago, Ill. — WBBM
    Cincinnati, Ohio — WCPO
    Cleveland, Ohio — KYW
    Columbus, Ohio — WBNS
    Colorado Springs, Colo. — KKTV
    Dallas-Ft. Worth, Texas — WBAP
    Denver, Colo. — KBTV
    Detroit, Mich. — CKLW
    Duluth, Minn. — WDSM
    Eugene, Ore. — KVAL

Fort Wayne, Ind. — WKJG
Fresno, Calif. — KFRE
Grand Rapids-Kalamazoo, Mich. — WOOD
Green Bay, Wisc. — WBAY
Greenville, N.C. — WNCT
Holdrege-Kearney, Neb. — KHOL
Honolulu, Hawaii — KHVH
Huntington-Charleston, W. Va. — WSAZ
Jacksonville, Fla. — WFGA
Kansas City, Mo. — KMBC
Lebanon, Pa. — WLYH
Los Angeles, Calif. — KTLA
Lubbock, Texas — KDUB
Miami-Ft. Lauderdale, Fla. — WTVJ
Minneapolis, Minn. — WTCN
New Haven, Conn. — WNHC
New Orleans, La. — WWL
New York City, N.Y. — WPIX
Norfolk, Va. — WVEC
Omaha, Neb. — KMTV
Orlando, Fla. — WDBO
Peoria, Ill — WEEK
Philadelphia, Pa. — WFIL
Phoenix, Ariz. — KPHO
Pittsburgh, Pa. — WTAE
Portland, Ore. — KGW
Richmond, Va. — WRVA
Roanoke, Va. — WSLS
Rochester, N.Y. — WROC
Sacramento, Calif. — KCRA
St. Louis, Mo. — KMOX
Salt Lake City, Utah — KUTV
San Antonio, Texas — KENS
San Diego, Calif. — KFSD
San Francisco, Calif. — KPIX
Seattle-Tacoma, Wash. — KING
Sioux Falls, S.D. — KELO
Spokane, Wash. — KREM
Syracuse, N.Y. — WSYR
Steubenville, Ohio — WSTV

Tampa, Fla. — WTVT
Temple, Texas — KCEN
Toledo, Ohio — WSPD
Washington, D.C. — WTTG
Wichita-Hutchinson, Ks. — KTVH
Yakima, Wash. — KNDO
Youngstown, Ohio — WKBN

The Studios

Jack Kinney

Al Brodax informed me Jack Kinney was given most of the cartoons to produce because "he was a well-respected Disney animator." His long career in animation began with the Walt Disney Studios in 1931. Kinney's Disney credits include *Santa's Workshop* (1932), *The Band Concert* (1935), and *Moose Hunters* (1937). He directed shorts featuring Donald Duck and several with Goofy. Kinney left Disney during the late 1950s and was hired by Brodax, in association with Format Films, to supply one hundred and one *Popeye the Sailor* cartoons for King Features Syndicate. At this same time, Kinney also worked on several *Mr. Magoo* and *Dick Tracy* television cartoons for UPA. Kinney's first Popeye cartoon, *Barbecue for Two*, was one of two pilot films produced to sell the entire series to television stations. This is the only episode in the entire group where Popeye and Olive resembled their strip and comic book counterparts. Popeye wore his dark shirt, red collar sporting black stripes, blue pants, and captain's hat. Olive Oyl retained her homely facial appearance wearing a long-sleeved red shirt, flowery collar, and elongated shoes. When The Fleischer Studios drafted Popeye into the navy, he began sporting a white sailor's suit. Eventually, Famous Studios gave Olive Oyl a more attractive design. She wore a clump of hair on her forehead, a pretty face, a short-sleeved shirt, high heels, and (in some theatrical cartoons) breasts! Kinney went back to what appeared on the printed page for *Barbecue for Two*. When the series officially went into full-speed production, he put Popeye back in his navy whites. Olive's attire from *Barbecue for Two* remained, but her hairstyle and facial design resembled the Famous Studios period.

Gerald Ray

Reportedly Gerald Ray began his early training at UCLA, Chouinard Art Institute, and Disney Studios. According to film historian Barry Grauman, Ray worked originally as an animator for UPA. By the end of the 1950s, he worked with Jay Ward on his *Fractured Fairy Tales* cartoons. Ray was associated with the formation of Val-Mar Studios, an animation unit from Mexico. In 1960 the studio became known as Gamma Productions. Ray was also involved with Shull Bonsall's Creston Studios/TV Spots. During his time with TV Spots, viewers watched Ray's most memorable animated series, *King Leonardo and His Short Subjects*. Al Brodax contracted Ray and Creston/TV Spots staff to supply ten episodes in the *Popeye the Sailor* series. His credits also include *Calvin and the Colonel*, *Beetle Bailey*, *Krazy Kat*, and *Cool McCool*. Scenes from Ray's Popeye cartoons were used for publicity photos and press announcements.

Larry Harmon

Larry Harmon studied at the University of Southern California and wanted to be a gynecologist. He found himself going into one show business job after another. According to an article from *TV Guide* circa 1966, he was a movie actor, TV producer, director, scriptwriter, composer, musician, talent agent, voice specialist, and puppeteer. In 1956 he bought the TV rights to Bozo the Clown from Capitol Records. Bozo had been an enormous recording star for the record label, but his audience was dwindling. Harmon began producing Bozo the Clown animated cartoons aired in a live Bozo's circus format. Harmon franchised this format to television stations across the United States and abroad. By the mid-1960s, virtually every station had a local Bozo show. For those who didn't, Harmon produced 130 episodes of *Bozo the Clown*. These were taped from the WHDH-TV studios in Boston, Massachusetts, and syndicated. In some markets, these episodes aired well into the 1990s. Harmon's studio produced eighteen Popeye the Sailor cartoons for television.

Gene Deitch

William L. Snyder was one of the first Americans to do business in post-war Eastern Europe. He imported European films through his production company, Rembrandt Films, founded in 1949. He began his association with Gene Deitch, the former head of UPA Studios, to produce cartoons in Prague. These included entries in MGM's *Tom and Jerry* series.

In the July 6, 1960 edition of *Variety*, a story was published titled *A Two-Continent Cartoonery*. It stated, "Upsurge of cartoon production for TV necessitated a two-continent cartoon cartoonery operation, according to William L. Snyder of Rembrandt Films. Rembrandt has a deal with King Features for the production of new *Popeye* cartoons. The two Continent operation finds Rembrandt doing the storyboards and soundtrack in the U.S. and animation and shooting in Europe. Snyder said that doing the animation and shooting in Europe initially was motivated by cost savings. But it's no longer less expensive, he stated, adding that there just isn't enough cartoon talent around the U.S. to meet the demand, and even the European pool is being severely taxed. King Features, under its Popeye program, has a policy of parceling out production. Rembrandt will do 16 episodes, with episodes due to coming in starting next month."

The Wall Street Journal reported on the production of foreign-made cartoons on June 11, 1962. The newspaper stated, "Rembrandt operates through studios in London, Milan, Rome and a state-owned studio in Prague, Czechoslovakia. King Features Syndicate is now distributing to U.S. Television stations 28 five-minute Popeye cartoons produced in England, Italy, and Yugoslavia. Al Brodax, director of television for King Features, says the foreign-made Popeye's cost less than $14,000 each compared with the $15,000 cost of similar Popeye cartoons made recently in the U.S. Mr. Brodax says the foreign-made Popeyes contain "substantially more animation" than the American-made cartoons. Full animation requires a great number of drawings with varied details to give viewers the impression of life-like movement. But to cut costs, many American producers are using fewer detailed drawings; often several seconds pass with only a character's mouth or eye moving."

Gene Deitch told animation historian Jerry Beck of his experience with Popeye: "I did a whole slew of ersatz Popeye films directly for King Features Television (Al Brodax). I had mixed feelings about it, as Segar's newspaper strip was always my number one favorite as I grew up in the 1930s and '40s, reading *Thimble Theatre* every single day as they were originally published. I hated the Fleischer cartoons as they reduced a masterpiece I loved to a cliché formula and completely lost the marvelous Segar style and character models. I did insist to Brodax that we at least bring into our serial as many as possible of the great supporting characters of the strip, such as Wimpy, Eugene the Jeep, The Sea Hag, Alice the Goon, etc. We had a chokingly small budget. I desperately needed the work at the time, so I took it on and did my best with the storylines I was given by Brodax to get as close as I could to the Segar feel. It was not easy with the money we had, and the inexperienced international crew (Czechs, Italians and Croations). It was fun working with Jack Mercer and Mae Questel, who actually recorded their lines half a world away from each other. I certainly don't regret doing the Popeye serial."

Halas and Batchelor

This was a British animation company founded by John Halas, a Hungarian émigré, and his wife, Joy Batchelor. In 1936 Halas ran a small animation unit that created commercials for theatrical distribution. Joy Batchelor replied to Halas' advertisement for an assistant. Halas and Batchelor were founded in 1940 and produced approximately 70 animated propaganda short films for the British Ministry of Information during World War II. The team produced the first British animated feature, *Handling Ships*, in 1945. Its best-known animated series include *Foo Foo*, *DoDo*, *The Kid from Outer Space*, *The Lone Ranger*, and *Popeye the Sailor*. The December 1, 1960, edition of Britain's *Television Today* reported on the team's plans for Popeye:

HALAS AND BATCHELOR LAND
BIG AMERICAN CARTOON ORDER

"Successful cartoon-making production company Halas and Batchelor Films, have landed a contract to produce a new series of Popeye films for America. Six cartoons, all in colour will be made for the American's Rembrandt Films. They are intended for both television and cinema. John Halas said, "We are going to give the films a more up-to-date treatment." For, while the films will feature Popeye and his old friends Bluto, Olive Oyl and Wimpy, they will be presented in the world of today — instead of 1905. Popeye will now be taking journeys into space or traveling on luxury liners. First of these six cartoons is in current production and is expected to be delivered to New York before the end of the year."

Paramount Cartoon Studios

In 1956 Paramount Pictures assumed complete control of Famous Studios, becoming Paramount Cartoon Studios. Although Popeye's theatrical career ended in 1957, the studio continued to produce other animated series for theatrical distribution. These included cartoons featuring *Jeepers and Creepers*, *The Cat*, *Honey Halfwitch*, and *Swifty and Shorty*. None achieved the overwhelming success Popeye brought Paramount Pictures. Brodax contracted Paramount Cartoon Studios to produce the second pilot for King Features Syndicate's new Popeye series and another sixty-two cartoons. Paramount's initial entry in the series, *Hits and Missiles*, featured Olive Oyl as she appeared in the Famous Studios cartoons. Olive was tall, wearing a short-sleeved shirt and high heels. Once the pilot was completed, Popeye's girlfriend kept her modern hairstyle but wore her clothes from the original comic strip. Brodax later hired Paramount to contribute films for *The King Features Trilogy* (1963). These were cartoons featuring long-time comic strip favorites: Beetle Bailey, Barney Google, Snuffy Smith, and Krazy Kat. Under the title, *Comic Kings*, some of these cartoons were released theatrically in 1962.

The Quality

Unfortunately, several of the Jack Kinney-produced Popeye cartoons are poorly animated. Based on the observation of these particular cartoons, critics unfairly paint the series, as a whole, in a bad light. Kinney's scripts feature several funny gags and puns. In *After the Ball Went Over* (1960), Popeye and Brutus engage in a ping pong match. Popeye says to Olive, "Fat boy doesn't have a chance. If I gets in trouble, I can always use my spinach gimmick" and "Ya knows I always win in these stories." Popeye packs a ball with explosives to win but ends up caught in an explosion. Olive asks Popeye if there is something special he'd like, and his response, "Yeah, a new writer to writes me spinach back in the script." *Popeye the Lifeguard* (1960) features the sailor admired by several bathing beauties. Olive Oyl is jealous, and Popeye consoles her by declaring, "No more pretty girls for me, Olive…only you!" Olive gives the viewing audience a sorrowful look. In *Golden Type Fleece*, Popeye, as Jason the Argonaut, searches for the Golden Fleece. After dealing with several obstacles, he brings back golden fleas! In *Fashion Fotography* (1960), Olive Oyl wants her photo taken to appear in a fashion magazine. After several beatings subjected to Popeye, Brutus, and Olive Oyl, Alice, the Goon paints a bizarre-looking portrait. *Wimpy's Lunch Wagon* (1960) has Brutus forcing a Juke Box into an eating establishment. Popeye ends up consuming spinach leaves from a submarine sandwich to deal with the musical problem. *Frozen Feuds* (1960) takes place in Alaska, where Alice the Goon is pining for her true love, Popeye. To keep the Goon happy, the sailor gives her a picture of himself. The picture is actually a television set where Alice can watch him anytime she wants. *Spinach Shortage* (1960) depicts Brutus causing a demand for Popeye's favorite vegetable. Desperately the sailor tries several times to break into one of Brutus's spinach warehouses. *Coffee House* (1960) has Olive Oyl becoming a beatnik and falling for Brutus, who serenades her with "Ode to an Onion!" Olive was under Brutus's spell in *Popeye's Hypnotic Glance* (1960), which included a hypnotized

Alice the Goon! *I Yam Wot I Yamnesia* (1960) featured a case of mixed-up personalities. Though delightful, the scripts couldn't overcome the terrible animation. This was a distraction to anyone over the age of thirteen (when I discovered many artistic mistakes). The Kinney cartoons' quality, including the character's designs, depended upon who was billed as animation director. The worst cartoons were under the directorial leadership of Hugh Fraser. *Popeye and the Giant* (1960) includes stock footage from other Kinney cartoons. The opening scene of Popeye walking with flowers and Brutus laughing at a window is pulled from *Ballet De Spinach*. This cartoon features repeated scenes and nonsensical dialogue to match unnecessary lip movements. *Time Marches Backwards* (1960) depicts animation as if you were watching pieces of paper being flipped. Olive Oyl's dialogue is mainly a continuous loop of her screaming. *Old Salt Tale* (1960) includes The Sea Hag's short sleeve attire becoming long in a close-up scene. At this cartoon's conclusion Olive develops an eyeball under her nose. Additionally, Popeye's swimsuit becomes his white uniform in less than a blink of an eye! *Popeye The Popular Mechanic* (1960) has the sailor's pipe disappearing and reappearing in a couple of scenes. Stock footage of Brutus laughing at the window from *Ballet De Spinach* makes another appearance in this cartoon. *Popeye's Tea Party* (1960), *Camel Aires* (1960), *Invisible Popeye* (1960), *Rip Van Popeye* (1960), *Mississippi Sissy* (1960), and *Double-Cross Country Feet Race* (1960) are all credited to Fraser featuring scenes with clumsy animation. There are a few, under his direction, which can be viewed without too much displeasure: *Aztec Wreck* (1960), *Popeye's Used Car* (1960), *The Day Silky Went Blozo* (1960), *Popeyed Columbus* (1960), *Popeye in Haweye* (1960) and *Popeye's Fixit Shop* (1960). Animation director, Osmond Evans, is credited to the tolerable *Popeye's Picnic* (1960) and unwatchable *Timber Toppers* (1960). *Timber Toppers* features close-up scenes of Brutus laughing pulled from other Kinney cartoons. At least the animators were good enough to make sure Brutus's clothes' colors matched his new scenes in the stock footage. Some prints of *Popeye the Fireman* (1960) credit Rudy Larriva as animation director, but it marks the shoddy animation of Osmond Evans. Larriva is credited to some of the best-animated cartoons in the series: *Jeep Tale* (1960), *Private Eye Popeye* (1960), *Popeye the White Collar Man* (1960), *Paper Pasting Pandemonium* (1960), *The Square Egg* (1960), *Popeye's Cool Pool* (1960), *Popeye and Buddy Brutus* (1960), *Popeye and The Polite Dragon* (1960), *Bottom Gun* (1960), *Skyscraper Capers* (1960), *Popeye's Pet Store* (1960) and *Skinned Divers* (1960). Animation director, Harvey Toombs, is credited to generally good animated entries, including: *Pest of the Pecos*

(1960), *Popeye in the Grand Steeple Chase* (1960), *Popeye the Piano Mover* (1960), *Bell Hop Hop Popeye* (1960), *Tiger Burger* (1960), *Little Olive Riding Hood*(1960), *Popeye the Lifeguard* (1960), *Madam Salami* (1960), *Spinachonare* (1960), *Popeye's Car Wash* (1960), *Bird Watcher Popeye*(1960) and *Around the World in Eighty Ways* (1960). Ken Hultgren's credit as animation director started off shaky with the choppy looking *Sea Hagracy* (1960) but greatly improved with:*Popeye and The Magic Hat* (1960), *Popeye and the Spinach Stalk* (1960), *The Green Dancin' Shoes*(1960), *Jeep, Jeep* (1960), *The Black Knight* (1960), *The Golden Type Fleece* (1960), *The Blubbering Whaler* (1960), *Ballet De Spinach* (1960), *Popeye Revere* (1960) and *I Yam Wot Yamnesia* (1960). The flaw in Hultgren's cartoons is the use of repeated scenes in the same film. For example, in *Jingle Jangle Jungle* (1960), an overgrown plant repeatedly grabs Brutus and kisses him over and over again. Ed Friedman and Volus Jones' well-animated efforts include: *Weather Watchers* (1960), *Olive Drab and the Seven Sweapeas* (the name Swee'pea being misspelled in the title credit) (1960), *Coach Popeye* (1960), *The Super Duper Market* (1960), *Popeye's Folly* (1960), *Wimpy's Lunch Wagon* (1960), *Westward Ho-Ho* (1960), *Popeye's Hypnotic Glance* (1960), *Battery Up* (1960) *Out of this World* (1960), *Uncivil War (1960)* and *Popeye's Service Station* (1960). Eddie Rehberg's cartoons are noted for annoyingly abrupt scene changes. In *Frozen Feuds* (1960), Wimpy, waist up, is shown his food bill, which quickly cuts to him looking for his wallet. The scene jumps to Wimpy, sitting in a chair, writing out several I.O.U.s. *Blinkin Beacon* (1960) mainly consists of quick scene jumps that are a determent to the entertaining script involving The Sea Hag's attempts to rob a gold shipment. Rehberg's more acceptable contributions in the series include: *The Golden Touch* (1960), *Forever Ambergris* (1960), *Lighthouse Keeping* (1960), *Popeye's Museum Piece* (1960), *Popeye and the Herring Snatcher* (1960), and *The Glad Gladiator* (1960). Borderline entries are *Popeye's Pizza Palace* (1960), *Popeye DeLeon* (1960), *After the Ball Went Over* (1960), and *Popeye's Corn-Certo* (1960). Other animation directors, for Jack Kinney, were: Alan Zaslove's *Down the Hatch* (1960) and *Spinach Shortage* (1960), Hal Ambro's *Plumber's Pipe Dream* (1960), Phil Duncan's *Fashion Fotography* (1960), and Murray McClennan's *Popeyed Fisherman* (1960). In Kinney's cartoons, both Wimpy and Brutus had their own theme music. Wimpy's had a lazy, laid-back tune while Brutus was "Blow the Man Down" originally heard for Bluto in the theatrical films.

    The cast's character designs were rustic in Gerald Ray's cartoons, but the scripts quite funny. They harkened back to the unexpected moments in the Fleischer Studios' theatrical Popeye films. In *Where There's a Will*

(1960), Brutus is furious he has been left only one can of spinach in a will. He beats up Popeye, and the sailor falls to the ground. The bully tosses the can off-camera, and the spinach-eating theme plays. Brutus looks at the audience and says, "*Whoops*, I shouldn't have done that!" Popeye leaves Wimpy to watch over a batch of hamburgers while he saves Olive Oyl in *Egypt Us* (1960). After saving his girlfriend, Popeye begins to sing his theme song but realizes he has left Wimpy alone with their lunch. Popeye and Olive race back and find Wimpy has consumed all of the hamburgers. The moocher sings, "It's bad to be tardy to a hamburger party says Wimpy the Burger Man (his shirt buttons pop off similar to the "toot"! "toot!" sound of Popeye's pipe). *The Last Resort* (1960) features Toar, who was a monstrous caveman created by E.C. Segar for his *Thimble Theatre* comic strip. He is played for laughs in this cartoon teaming up with The Sea Hag. The pair plan to flood the market with three-dollar bills, but Popeye, Olive Oyl, and Wimpy stumble upon their scheme. This cartoon's ending alludes to nuclear testing as Olive wants to visit "the atomic approving grounds." That line certainly wasn't written for the children in the audience! *Jeopardy Sheriff* (1960) has Poopdeck Pappy telling "whoppers" to Swee'pea but proves his mettle when he stops a gang of bank robbers. After the cartoon, the old man sings, "I may tell a whopper, but I am the popper of Popeye the Sailor Man!" Pappy fires off his guns as if Popeye was tooting on his pipe. In *Popeye's Junior Headache* (1960), Olive Oyl's niece Deezil beats the tar out of Popeye while he babysits the brat. This cartoon's plot is reminiscent of the theatrical cartoons when an animal or insect got the better of Popeye. *Baby Phase* (1960) has Popeye dreaming Swee'pea has become a world famous juggler! It is unfortunate Gerald Ray only contributed ten cartoons as his crew had a fondness for Popeye.

The character designs in Larry Harmon's cartoons were very simplistic, especially in the studio's first entry *Muskels Shmuskels* (1960). Although Popeye's opened eye look initially occurred in the color Famous Studios theatrical films, this was common in Harmon's episodes. A recurring animation error concerned Brutus or Popeye's sleeves. In brief moments Brutus's and Popeye's short-sleeved shirts would become long sleeve! This happened to Brutus in *Dead-Eye Popeye* (1960) and *Foola-Foola Bird* (1960). It happened to Popeye while skiing in *Ski Jump Chump* (1960). In Harmon's Popeye's, the character's necks would often jerk forward when speaking, and blasts of smoke would billow from Popeye's pipe when he was angry. The fast-paced scripts mainly concentrated on the rivalry between Popeye and Brutus. The more enjoyable of the eighteen cartoons Harmon's studio produced are: *Caveman Capers* (1960), when

Popeye explains to Olive Oyl how his family got started eating spinach; *Ace of Space* (1960): Popeye uses his "spinach rays" to stop an alien from kidnapping Olive Oyl; *Foola-Foola Bird* (1960): Brutus competes with Popeye and Olive Oyl to capture a rare loony bird; *Uranium On The Cranium* (1960): Popeye and Olive look for uranium. Still, Brutus tries to stop them dressed as a gorilla, and *Crystal Ball Brawl* (1960): Popeye inherits a crystal ball which can foretell the future! Brutus attempts to steal it but must battle both Popeye and Wimpy for its possession!

The cartoons under the directorship of Gene Deitch featured eerie and haunting background scores. Deitch's twenty-eight Popeye cartoons varied in animation quality. There was undoubtedly movement, but the character designs were too simplistic, though not necessarily for the entire cartoon. In *Hag Way Robbery* (1960), Olive Oyl is carrying baby Swee'pea, but the lad has no arms! Olive Oyl's white collar around her neck kept switching from a flowery to circular look in *Swee'pea Soup* (1960). *Sea No Evil* (1960) was a fast-moving cartoon marred by simplistic character designs for Popeye, Olive Oyl, and Brutus. When Popeye uses his arms to swim a little boat ashore, it's supposed to be moving, yet the background remains static. Yet despite these animation setbacks, the stories are quite imaginative. In the aforementioned *Hag Way Robbery*, The Sea Hag kidnaps Eugene the Jeep. To stop Popeye, she slaps "spinach" labels on the cans in his ship. When the sailor needs his strength, he keeps opening cans containing hamburgers, baby food, and olives! *Voice From the Deep* (1960) also features The Sea Hag and her plans to convert an inhabited island into a resort for criminals. Popeye visits the ocean floor and discovers tiny sea creatures in *The Lost City of Bubble-Lon* (1960). After having a heated argument, Popeye joins the Foreign Legion in *Insultin' the Sultan* (1960). Once Popeye has rescued Olive Oyl from a marrying-minded Sultan, the pair start their argument all over again! *There's No Space Like Home (1960)* features a rare moment when Brutus feeds Popeye his spinach. The sailor's muscles proceed to stop tiny aliens from creating havoc at Olive Oyl's costume party. Olive welcomes becoming a queen but loses interest when she discovers the groom is an ugly Goon in *Goon with the Wind* (1960).

Deitch's Popeye, animated by Halas and Batchelor, features excellent animation and imaginative storylines. Popeye sniffs what he thinks is shaving lotion, but it's a potion that causes people to punch him in *Potent Lotion* (1960). *The Billionaire* (1961) has a wealthy Popeye handing out a million dollars to his pals (and Brutus). Olive uses her money to make herself beautiful and ends up a blonde with curves! Popeye laughs at her new look, which causes Olive's new facial look to crack and fall off. Popeye remarks, "Don't be sad, Olive. I likes ya ugly!"

Have Time Will Travel (1961) and *Intellectual Interlude* (1962), while both credited to Gene Deitch, feature animation styles not typical of his other entries. In *Have Time Will Travel,* Popeye and Olive are transported back to caveman days. The pair encounter a dinosaur the sailor calls "Oscar" because he looks like someone from Brooklyn. Popeye and Olive share the same dream of the sailor becoming a genius in *Intellectual Interlude.*

Personnel who worked on the Popeye theatricals were involved with the sixty-three television cartoons produced by Paramount Cartoon Studios. Seymour Kneitel directed the films with music by Winston Sharples, both experienced working on the one-eyed sailor. Writers and animators Martin Taras, Gerry Dvorak, Irving Dressler, WM B. Pattengill, Dante Barbetta, Morey Reden, Jim Logan, and Jack Mercer (the voice of Popeye) contributed their talents to the cartoons. Many consider Paramount's entries to be the best of the entire series. Although the animation was produced on a limited budget, most of Paramount's efforts are top-notch. While the scripts did not lack humor, they were more adventurous with their plots. *The Spinach Scholar* (1960) features a cute story where Popeye's attempts to get an education prove very embarrassing. Spinach gives the sailor brainpower to succeed in Kindergarten, which pleases Olive Oyl. In *Psychiatricks* (1960), Brutus disguises himself as Prof. Ed Shrinker to cease Popeye's unnecessary fighting. This leads to flashbacks from the sailor's youth, where he battles Brutus as a baby and a school-aged bully. The Sea Hag wants to destroy a whale that swallowed The Sea Man's Orphanage Treasury in *Moby Hick* (1960). She enlists Popeye's aid by telling him the whale is a "monster" and "drowns poor sailors' lads." Swee'pea eats Popeye's spinach and saves the sailor after winning competitions against Brutus's bully boy in *The Baby Contest* (1960). In *Mirror Magic* (1960), Popeye is a child destined to grow up and rule the little kingdom of Muscle Lona. *Hamburgers Aweigh* (1961) depicted The Sea Hag plotting to steal Popeye's hamburger cargo. She casts a spell over Wimpy to aid her. The ol' witch impersonates Olive Oyl to get back a gold coin, with three wishes on it, given to Popeye by mistake in *Popeye's Double Trouble* (1961). In this cartoon, as in others featuring The Sea Hag, Olive eats the spinach to defeat the witch. Popeye is not allowed to hit a woman no matter how wicked she is! *County Fair* (1961) features Popeye and Brutus as farmers competing in different contests. The last event is the spinach-eating contest and the test to prove its strength. Before consuming the spinach, Brutus shakes Popeye's hand, saying, "Let's keep this contest fair." Once the brute has Popeye's hand, he flings him away. Brutus looks right at the viewing audience and remarks, "You didn't think I was gonna play fair with that runt and take a chance against his spinach." Brutus eats Popeye's spinach but tosses what's left on the plate in the sailor's direction. Popeye eats the remains and defeats Brutus, singing, "Brutus was beaten because he was cheatin' says Popeye the Farmer Man!" As with the television cartoons produced by Gerald Ray, many of Paramount's Popeye's ended with a song related to the film's plot. Paramount's writers reviewed Segar's *Thimble Theatre* daily and Sunday comic strips. *Poppa Popeye* (1960), *The Valley of the Goons* (1960), *Me Quest for Poopdeck Pappy* (1960), *It Only Hurts When They Laugh* (1960), *Wimpy the Moocher* (1960), *What's News* (1960), and *Myskery Melody* (1961); each originated from the comic strip page.

Popeye's Success on Television

On January 1, 1960, the Popeye television cartoons, produced by King Features Syndicate, went on the marketplace. The March 16, 1960 edition of *Variety* reported the series chalked up $2,785,344 in sales to forty-six markets. By September 21, 1960, the number of stations buying the cartoons rose to seventy-five. On November 1, 1961, it was reported the films were broadcast in Venezuela, Canada, Australia, the Philippines, Japan, and Brazil. They were also in the process of being dubbed in Spanish. With the Spanish sale, King Features Syndicate sold the series to a total of seven countries outside of the United States. This brought the syndicate's international gross sales to $500,000. By early 1962 the series had been sold to Beirut, Lebanon, and one hundred and twenty-five television stations in the United States.

The June 10, 1964 edition of *Variety* featured a bold headline which announced *Popeye's $20,000,000 Gross* declaring, "Popeye cartoons now occupy the Ft. Knox of video cartoon land." By the time this article was published, the television Popeye cartoons had grossed "some $6,000,000 in syndication." The theatrical version, on television screens since 1956, "grossed about $14,000.000." Many television stations ran both the theatrical and television cartoons "for the kiddie viewers." Popeye out grossed any cartoon series in syndication, and both series, theatrical and made-for-television, accounted for 454 episodes, the largest number for any one TV cartoon star. By August 5, 1964, the television Popeye cartoons aired in 137 markets.

In 1965 the Popeye television cartoons were up for renewal by the television stations that initially purchased the series. By the summer of that same year, King Features Syndicate reported Popeye racked up more than $1,500,000 in renewals. Originally stations were broadcasting black and white prints of the cartoons but were switching to color.

An advertisement for WPIX-11 published on January 17, 1963, in *Variety*, declared the television cartoons delivered 897,400 kids per average telecast and 38.0% share of the audience from November 5 through December 2, 1961. The July 28, 1965 edition of Variety reported: "Popeye Has Muscles, Renewals in 68 Markets." While King Features Syndicate reported Popeye racked up more than $1,500,000 in renewal sales, the mark was passed with the resigning of KMOX-TV, St Louis. Though three markets dropped the series, King crossed the street and sold the television cartoons to the competition. This happened in Dallas, Miami, and Salt Lake City. Additionally, the article reported the series was placed on the market five years ago and is now reaching a basically new audience of boys and girls.

When Gold Key Entertainment acquired the syndication rights to the series, the film's popularity remained high. According to Robert Lloyd, VP and National Sales Manager for Gold Key, in the September 12, 1988 edition of *Backstage*, it was reported, "Popeye cartoon series has now been sold in 47 of the top 50 markets. Popeye is the second-highest-rated syndicated cartoon series in both the February and May Nielsens," said Lloyd. "The show has been an enormously successful product, and it continues to grow."

The television Popeye's continued to air in the United States on independently owned television stations well into the 1990s. They continue to air internationally, have been broadcast on MeTV and all the episodes can be found on Popeye's Official YouTube page.

Broadcasting *Magazine's April 4th, 1960 edition featured a full-page advertisement announcing the sale of the new Popeye cartoon series to television stations since January 1, 1960.*

Although many stations aired both the theatrical and television cartoons, this advertisement from January 22, 1962 edition of Broadcasting Magazine *promotes the success the "New Popeye Cartoons" were having on WPIX-11.*

Advertisements from Broadcasting *Magazine during 1965 produced by King Features Syndicate promoting the television stations renewing their contracts to broadcast the cartoons.*

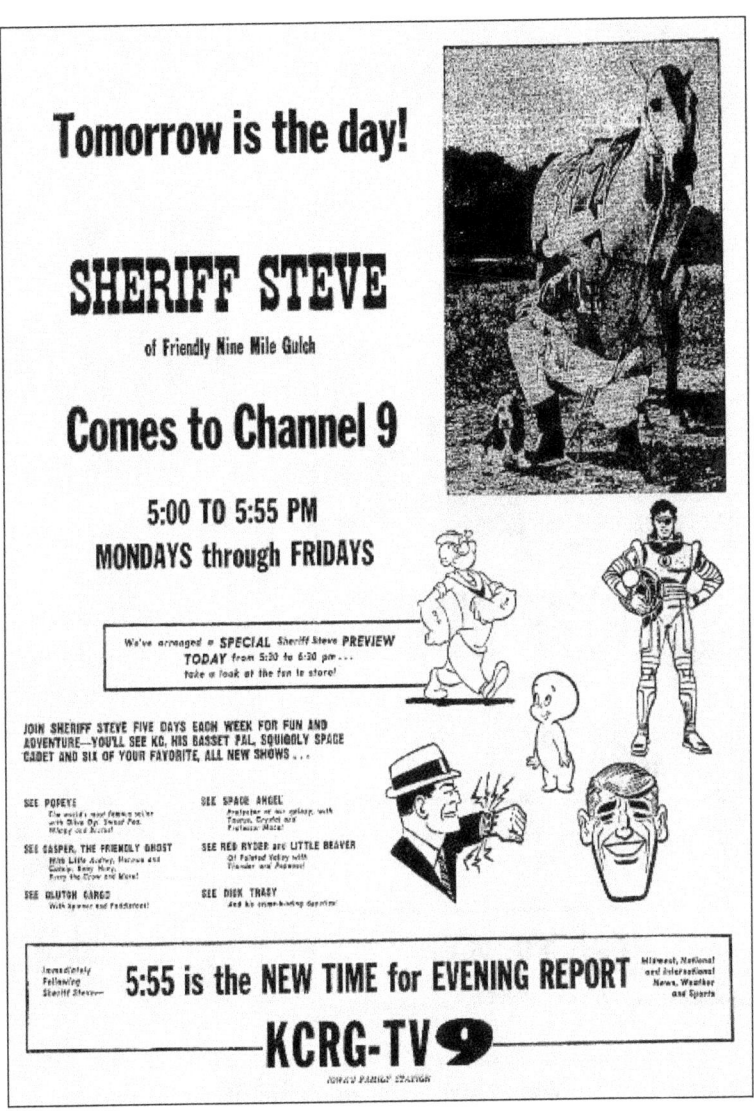

Iowa's KCRG-TV Channel 9 Sheriff Steve *program included the new Popeye cartoons to his line up which also featured* Casper the Friendly Ghost, Clutch Cargo, Space Angel *and* Dick Tracy.

 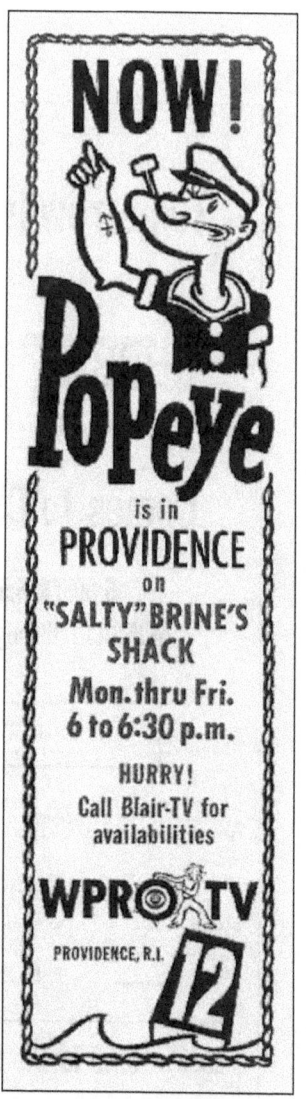

LEFT: *A newspaper advertisement from September 17, 1962 spotlighting the addition of "All New Popeye Cartoons" to* Sheriff Steve Fun Show.

RIGHT: *Following Salty Brine's Shack, WPRO TV in Providence R.I. aired a half hour of* Popeye and the Three Stooges *weekday mornings. The program usually consisted of one Popeye theatrical followed by a* Three Stooges *short or four television adventures of the spinach-eating sailor.*

LEFT: *Despite complaints from parents about the violence in children's programming stations earned high ratings combining Popeye cartoons with* The Three Stooges.

RIGHT: *WBAP-TV 5, from Forth Worth, Texas broadcast "New Popeye Color Theatre" Monday thru Friday at 5:30PM. The advertisement features the comic strip design of Popeye at the top right and the television versions of Popeye, Brutus, Olive Oyl and Wimpy.*

A press release for The "New Popeye Color Theatre" *pictured Jack Hicks of WBAP-TV 5 was published on October 2, 1960 in The* Fort Worth Star-Telegram.

The made for television Popeye cartoon series was still being offered for syndication in 1970. This full-page advertisement was published in the April 13, 1970 edition of Broadcasting *Magazine.*

Segar's Characters Make Their Animation Debut!

As the television cartoons were produced by King Features Syndicate, which distributed the *Popeye* comic strip, they used characters pulled straight from the funny pages. Olive Oyl, Wimpy, Swee'pea, and Poopdeck Pappy were all creations of E.C. Segar. These supporting players appeared several times in the theatrical cartoons. Others, who populated the comic strip, made their animation debut in the television productions.

The Sea Hag

The Sea Hag is often billed as the last witch on earth and is a pirate who sails the Seven Seas in her boat, *The Black Barnacle*. She made her comic strip debut in 1929 and has plagued Popeye with her schemes to bring back piracy ever since. Unfortunately, because she is a woman, Popeye can't sock her, and this is often left to his girlfriend, Olive Oyl. Although she was a fixture in both the strip and comic books, her wide recognition came from her numerous television cartoon appearances. Segar's character design was a tall, flesh-colored, skinny older woman wearing a necktie, black hood, and dress. She was redesigned for the television cartoons with her chin elongated and skin colored green. This visual design certainly captured her character as an evil ol' witch. The Sea Hag is often aided in her schemes by her pet vulture. As in the print medium, Olive Oyl often engages in fisticuffs with The Sea Hag. This is, of course, after she eats Popeye's spinach! The Sea Hag menaced Popeye in the following cartoons: *Hag Way Robbery* (Gene Deitch, 1960), *Voice From the Deep* or *See Here Sea Hag* (Gene Deitch, 1961), *Which is Witch* (Gene Deitch, 1961) *Tooth Be or Not Tooth Be* (Gene Deitch, 1962), *The Last Resort* (Gerald Ray, 1960), *Sea Hagracy* (Jack

Kinney, 1960), *Private Eye Popeye* (Jack Kinney, 1960), *Little Olive Riding Hood* (Jack Kinney, 1960), *Jeep-Jeep* (Jack Kinney, 1960), *Popeye and the Giant* (Jack Kinney, 1960), *Popeye and the Spinach Stalk* (Jack Kinney, 1960), *Olive Drab and the Seven Sweapeas* (Jack Kinney, 1960), *Blinkin Beacon* (Jack Kinney, 1960), *The Green Dancin' Shoes* (Jack Kinney, 1960), *The Glad Gladiator* (cameo appearance, Jack Kinney, 1960), *The Golden Touch* (Jack Kinney, 1960), *Hamburger Fishing* (Jack Kinney, 1960), *Popeye's Folly* (Jack Kinney, 1960), *Old Salt Tale* (Jack Kinney, 1960), *The Golden Type Fleece* (Jack Kinney, 1960), *Sweapea Thru the Looking Glass* (Jack Kinney, 1960), *The Black Knight* (Jack Kinney, 1960), *Uncivil War* (cameo appearance, Jack Kinney, 1960), *Popeye's Testimonial Dinner* (Jack Kinney, 1960), *Mobey Hick* (Paramount, 1960), *Voo Doo to You, Too* (Paramount, 1960), *Spinach Greetings* (1960), *Gem Jam* (Paramount, 1960), *Aladdin's Lamp* (Paramount, 1961), *The Leprechaun* (Paramount 1961), *Hamburgers Aweigh* (Paramount, 1961), *Popeye's Double Trouble* (Paramount, 1961), *Kiddie Kapers* (Paramount, 1961), *Myskery Melody* (Paramount, 1961), *The Cure* (Paramount, 1961), *A Poil for Olive Oyl* (Paramount, 1961), *Strange Things are Happening* (Paramount, 1961) and *A Mite of Trouble* (Paramount, 1961).

Rough House

Since 1931 Rough House has been plagued by Wimpy's attempts to mooch hamburgers from the gullible chef. Often Segar, and his successors Tom Sims and Bela Zaboly, would devote an entire Sunday strip showcasing Wimpy's genius in obtaining hamburgers from Rough House without payment. Segar's version of Rough House was a muscular-looking fellow with wisps of hair under his nose and who donned a chef's hat. This character design was pretty much left intact when he made his debut in the television cartoons. He appeared in the following television cartoons produced by Paramount Cartoon Studios: *Quick Change Ollie* (1960), *The Valley of the Goons* (1960), *Wimpy the Moocher* (1960), *Robot Popeye* (1961), *The Wiffle Bird's Revenge* (1961) and *Boing Boing Gone* (1961).

King Blozo

King Blozo was often concerned with his subjects' welfare while ruling various kingdoms since his comic strip debut in 1931. His ruling methods are often dubious and ineffectual, but he welcomes Popeye's help upon the sailor's visits. King Blozo is best known for his penchant for worrying, worrying, and worrying. The King's character design, from the comic strip, was pretty much kept intact when transferred to animation. King Blozo was a skinny fellow with a big nose and long white beard. He appeared in the following cartoons: *Swee'pea Soup* (Gene Deitch, 1960), *The Day Silky Went Blozo* (Jack Kinney, 1960), *Popeye's Testimonial Dinner* (Jack Kinney, 1960), and *Incident at Missile City* (Paramount Cartoon Studios, 1960).

Alice the Goon

Alice the Goon initially gave children nightmares when this hairy, hulking monster first appeared on December 10th, 1933, in the comic strip. Parents would tell their children to behave, or the Goon would get them. Alice took orders from The Sea Hag until Popeye saved her Goon child. Later she donned a dress and flowery hat to become Swee'pea's babysitter. Alice appeared in the following television cartoons: *Old Salt Tale* (Jack Kinney, 1960), *Hypnotic Glance* (Jack Kinney, 1960), *Fashion Photography* (Jack Kinney, 1960), *Frozen Feuds* (Jack Kinney, 1960), *The Golden Touch* (Jack Kinney, 1960), *Popeye the Ugly Ducklin* (Jack Kinney, 1960) and cameo appearances in *Uncivil Wars* (Jack Kinney, 1960) and *The Glad Gladiator* (Jack Kinney, 1960). Members of the Goon family, whose facial designs looked different from Alice, appeared in *Goon with the Wind* (Gene Deitch/William Snyder, 1960) and *Which is Witch* (Gene Deitch/William Snyder, 1961). Paramount Cartoon Studio's *Valley of the Goons* (1960) featured a tribe of the creatures. *The Cure* (1961) and *Strange Things are Happening* (1961), also from Paramount, featured male Goons who served The Sea Hag.

Eugene the Jeep

Technically, Eugene did not make his animation debut in the television cartoons, instead in the theatrical films produced by the Fleischer Studios. However, he only appeared in two films (and a cameo appearance in one). Eugene was more prominently featured in the cartoons produced by King Features Syndicate.

The Jeep first appeared in the comic strip on March 16, 1936. He is a cute-looking creature from another dimension with spots, a big nose, and a thin tail. When he is angry, his tail sends out electricity. He worked his magic in the following cartoons: *Hag Way Robbery* (Gene Deitch/William Snyder, 1960), *Jeep-Jeep* (Jack Kinney, 1960), *Private Eye Popeye* (Jack Kinney, 1960), *Popeye's Museum Piece* (Jack Kinney, 1960), *Popeye and the Magic Hat* (Jack Kinney, 1960), *Popeye and the Spinach Stalk* (Jack Kinney, 1960), *Azteck Wreck* (Jack Kinney, 1960), *Jeep Tale* (Jack Kinney, 1960),

Swea'pea Through the Looking Glass (Jack Kinney, 1960), *The Golden Touch* (Jack Kinney, 1960), *Popeye's Testimonial Dinner* (Jack Kinney, 1960), *Voo Doo to You Too* (Paramount, 1960) and *Myskery Melody* (Paramount, 1961).

Professor O.G. WotaSnozzle

The scientist who produced so many outlandish creations first appeared in the comic strip, *Sappo*, created by E.C. Segar on May 8, 1932. *Sappo* was published above *Thimble Theatre* on Sundays for several years. This short man with a long white beard was given a black gown and graduation cap when he appeared in the television cartoons. His most frequent role in the films was sending Popeye back through time via a huge machine he created. WotaSnozzle appeared in the following cartoons: *Swee'pea Soup* (Gene Deitch/William Snyder, 1960), *Child Hood Daze* (Larry Harmon, 1960; in this particular cartoon, his beard was trimmed, and he was minus his trademark gown and graduation cap), *Time Marches Backwards* (Jack Kinney, 1960), *Out of This World* (Jack Kinney, 1960), *Popeye's Museum Piece* (Jack Kinney, 1960), *Popeye's Tea Party* (Jack Kinney, 1960), *Invisible Popeye* (Jack Kinney, 1960), *The Square Egg* (Jack Kinney, 1960), *The Black Knight* (Jack Kinney, 1960), *Popeyed Columbus* (Jack Kinney, 1960) and *Strange Things are Happening* (Paramount Cartoon Studios, 1961). In the cartoons, the Professor's name is spelled WottaSnozzle.

The Wiffle Bird

Originally known as Bernice, the Wiffle Hen, this yellow bird can grant wishes when its head feathers are rubbed. First seen in the *Thimble Theatre* comic strip in 1928, the hen was a present to Olive Oyl's brother, Castor. Later Popeye used the hen's magical abilities to save himself from a barrage of bullets. In the television cartoons, it was referred to as "The Wiffle Bird" and appeared in the following cartoons: *Quick Change Ollie* (Paramount, 1960), *Hamburgers Aweigh* (Paramount, 1961), *Giddy Gold* (Paramount, 1961) and *The Wiffle Bird's Revenge* (Paramount, 1961).

Toar

Toar was a muscle-bound caveman who first appeared in the comic strip on February 7, 1935, as an enemy of Popeye. He drank from a pool which made it impossible for him to die of old age. Later he and Popeye became great friends. Toar popped up in one of the television cartoons,

The Last Resort (Gerald Ray, 1960), working with The Sea Hag. They planned to flood the marketplace with phony three-dollar bills. Although a monstrous menace in the strip, he was portrayed in this cartoon as the witch's bumbling assistant.

Two new characters were created for the television cartoons. Roger was a cute-looking talking dog who appeared in two episodes, both produced by Gene Deitch/William Snyder: *Canine Caprice* (1962) and *Roger* (1962). Olive's pint-sized niece, Deezil, terrorized Popeye in *Popeye's Junior Headache* (Gerald Ray, 1960), became Swee'pea's playmate in *Coach Popeye* (Jack Kinney, 1960), and was told a colorful bedtime story in *The Mark of Zero* (Paramount, 1961).

Make Way for Brutus!

People have always been perplexed by the mystery of Bluto/Brutus. In a Viewer's voices column written by John Crook for *TV Data Services*, a reader asked:

> Please help settle a bet. What is the name of the big bad brute in the Popeye cartoons? I say it is Brutus, but my husband says Bluto. Did the same character have two different names?

> Crooks' reply: *No, but you two still can kiss and make up. Alex McNeil, author of Total Television, reports that in the vintage theatrical shorts of Popeye, the burly guy is named Bluto. When more than 200 new cartoons were produced in the early '60s, Popeye faced a villain named Brutus, who bears a striking resemblance to Bluto but is not literally the same character.*

Dick Kleiner, in his syndicated column, *Ask Dick Kleiner*, was asked:

> Please settle a vehement argument between my boss and myself. What is the name of the character who is the big, burly archrival of Popeye in all of the Popeye cartoons? My boss insists it's Bluto, and I am equally sure it's Brutus. My job could be riding on your answer.

> Kleiner replied: *I think you'll find the unemployment office somewhere in City Hall. Bluto is the bully who always got bopped by Popeye.*

A married couple from Victoria, B.C. asked the "In Focus" column published in *The Index-Journal* from Greenwood South Carolina:

> Recently my husband and I watched the "Popeye" movie starring Robin Williams. At one point Olive Oyl is engaged to Popeye's rival, Bluto, but on Popeye cartoons I have heard this character referred to as Brutus, as well. My husband doesn't agree with me. Are Brutus and Bluto the same character?

> The newspaper's response was: *Popeye's No. 1 nemesis has been known by both names over the years. He was introduced in the original comic strip as "Bluto the Terrible" and would go on to challenge the Sailor Man in hundreds of animated shorts produced by Max Fleischer. In subsequent inferior cartoon incarnations produced for TV during the 1960's and 70's, he was also referred to as Brutus.*

The "Graffiti" column, published in *The Independent* located in Long Beach, California, was asked by a family in Long Beach:

> Our family is having an argument about the Popeye comic strip. What is the name of Olive Oil's suitor who is also Popeye's arch enemy — Brutus or Bluto?

> The paper's response was: *Brutus is the brute who still tries to interfere with Popeye's romance with Olive Oyl according to a spokesman for King Features Syndicate in New York. The comic strip, which originally was called Thimble Theatre, was started by Elizie Segar in 1919 and is now drawn by Bud Sagendorf.*

King Features Syndicate's initial publicity for the television cartoons promoted Brutus as a new character for Popeye to battle. However, except for a bigger stomach and minus a white sailor's uniform, he looked very much like Bluto from the color theatrical cartoons produced by Paramount Pictures. Also, Bluto sounded exactly like Brutus, which has led people to believe they are the same, albeit with different monikers.

Bluto first appeared in the comic strip on September 12, 1932. He menaced Popeye only once under E.C. Segar's guidance. Max Fleischer featured the brute in Popeye's first animated film, and he became a regular in the theatrical cartoon series produced by Paramount Pictures. On March 27, 1957, Ralph Stein, who was writing the daily *Popeye* comic strip, revived Bluto. Stein portrayed him as a Pirate often encountering Popeye during his criminal activities. Cartoonist Bill Zaboly's rendition of the brute was similar, minus the sailor's uniform and muscular legs, to Famous Studio's Bluto.

King Features, naturally, wanted to use Bluto for their television cartoons. Paramount thought Bluto was a creation of the Fleischer Studios forgetting he originated in a comic strip syndicated by King Features. Apparently, King Features also forgot the character's roots. To rectify the problem, Al Brodax substituted Brutus (named after Caesar's assassin) for Bluto.

Due to King Features Syndicate's conflict with Paramount Pictures the comic books had Popeye battling a lot of bearded giants resembling Bluto. Beginning in 1957 these bearded bullies either went nameless or were called "Swab," "The Big Guy That Hates Popeye" or "Sonny Boy." These stories were written and drawn by Segar's assistant, Bud Sagendorf. "Sonny Boy" was the moniker used more often, and he was the son of the wicked Sea Hag.

It is unknown why Sagendorf had to use nameless characters in the comic books while Ralph Stein was allowed to call him Bluto in the daily strip. However, comic strips are written far in advance. Possibly Stein had his adventures already submitted for publication before the conflict over his name arose. Or no one was paying attention as to what was going on in Popeye's daily comic strip adventures.

When Sagendorf took control over both the daily and Sunday comic strip in 1958 (though his work was not published until 1959), Popeye encountered several bearded bullies without names. By 1962 the name Brutus was being used in the Sunday strip and comic books. In 1963 the name made its debut in the daily comic strip. Sagendorf said of the Bluto/Brutus situation, "When King Features bought back all of the early animated things, Paramount Studios claimed they owned the name Bluto. If King Features had been a little bit smarter, they would have seen that Segar used it long before the animation."

Bobby London, who took over the daily *Popeye* comic strip from Bud Sagendorf in 1986, wrote a hilarious story that parodied the whole Bluto/Brutus dilemma. In 1991 the original version of Bluto returned to the comic strip only to find "Goofy-Lookin' Clowns" imitating him and calling themselves Brutus! During this story, pretty much all of the various versions of Popeye's enemy appeared. London's *The Return of Bluto* has been reprinted in *Thimble Theatre Presents Popeye, Classic Newspaper Comics Volume Two: 1989-1992* by IDW Publishing (October 2014). While attempts have been made to establish Bluto and Brutus as twin brothers, many people still assume they're the same character.

Brutus was originally billed as a "new" character for Popeye to face. However, he looked a lot like the 1950's version of Famous Studios' Bluto without the sailor suit. Unlike Bluto, Brutus had a protruding stomach. The fact Jackson Beck voiced both Bluto and Brutus certainly had audiences speculating they were the same brute.

One of the monikers for Popeye's bearded foe prior to being named Brutus was "Sonny Boy". He is pictured here from Dell Comic Album #7 (1959). *Art by Bud Sagendorf.*

The Sea Hag calls for "The Big Guy That Hates Popeye" (formerly known as Bluto) in Popeye #40, June 1957. *Art by Bud Sagendorf.*

The Voices

Jack Mercer

Born as Winfield B. Mercer on January 31, 1910, he was the son of vaudeville and Broadway performers. Mercer also appeared on Broadway and legitimate stage productions. He started his work with animated cartoons as an inbetweener at The Fleischer Studio. Mercer recounted how he won the role of Popeye's voice in a February 14, 1979 interview: "I was working at Fleischer's as an inbetweener. The animator would do the extremes of the action, and the inbetweener filled in the rest. For my own amusement, I'd do the voices of the characters I was doing, chickens, and so on. They'd introduced Popeye about this time with someone else doing the voice. Well, somebody heard me doing Popeye and suggested I audition for the part. I didn't think I could do it. But I kept trying, and one night at home, I hit this peculiar tone, way down, and I said, My God, I've got it. This was a time when prizefighting was popular, and Popeye was a hard character. I wanted a tough guy, but I didn't want him belligerent. The first guy who'd done the voice, William Costello, he was kind of gruff. I lightened it up a bit, made him sort of a comedian rather than tough sailor." Mercer helped to shape Popeye's personality, particularly when it came to ad-libbing. In the early days, the voice people would work with the film, which led to a good deal of ad-libs. In that context, Popeye developed his peculiar way of thinking out loud. In later years the ad-libs decreased when the voices were prerecorded.

Mercer made his debut as the voice of Popeye in the Fleischer cartoon, *King of the Mardi Gras* (1935). He was replaced in several films produced by Famous Studios by Harry Welch when Mercer was drafted. Upon his return, he continued to voice the sailor in the television cartoons produced by King Features Syndicate and for Hanna-Barbera's *All-New Popeye Hour* (1978-1981) and *Popeye and Olive Comedy Show* (1981-1983).

Also, he provided the voice of J. Wellington Wimpy, Poopdeck Pappy, and Popeye's nephews. Mercer stated in an interview he was the voice of Bluto in the Fleischer cartoons. He found it too difficult switching back from Popeye to Bluto. He did provide Brutus's voice in one of the King Features Television cartoons, *Sea No Evil* (Gene Deitch/William Snyder, 1960). His voice was also utilized in several animated cartoons originating from Paramount Pictures. Mercer supplied all of the voices for Trans-Lux' *Felix the Cartoon* series. His voice can be heard in early entries *of The Mighty Hercules*. Mercer's voice could also be heard on several children's records. He also voiced the one-eyed sailor in television commercials which included spots for Soaky toys and Dr. Pepper.

Mercer also provided several scripts to the *Popeye* series: *Deputy Dawg*, *Milton the Monster*, and animated films produced by Paramount Pictures. Jack Mercer passed away on December 7, 1984, at the age of 74.

Mae Questel

Mae Questel was born on September 13, 1908, to an Orthodox Jewish family who didn't want her to pursue a career in the entertainment field. However, she later studied drama at Columbia University and belonged to the American Theatre Wing. At age seventeen, she was living in the South Bronx and won a local contest. The contest concerned finding a girl who resembled Helen Kane, a famous singer known as the "Boop-Ooop-A-Doop Queen." She was signed by an agent and started performing in the Vaudeville circuit. She billed herself as "Mae Questel-Personality Singer of Personality Songs." In her act, she performed outstanding vocal imitations of Maurice Chevalier, Eddie Cantor, Fanny Brice, Marlene Dietrich, Mae West, and Helen Kane. She also supplied voices of different animal and baby songs for radio shows.

Max Fleischer heard Mae's "boop-oop-a-doop" routine and hired her to provide Betty Boop's voice in 1931. She was the character's voice until 1937, when the studio moved from New York to Miami, Florida. She reprised her Betty Boop role in *Who Framed Roger Rabbit* (1988). In 1933 Questel began her long association providing the voice of Olive Oyl. She had to quit doing the voice when the Fleischer Studios moved to Miami, Florida but returned to the role in 1944 when Famous Studios in New York were producing the series. On at least one occasion, Questel filled in for Jack Mercer as Popeye, reportedly in the film *Shape Ahoy* (Famous Studios, 1945). As Questel recalled, the gentleman who was supposed to play Popeye developed mike fright, and she stepped in. The technicians were able to lower her voice giving Popeye a nasal but familiar sound. Questel's vocals could also be heard in the *Casper the Friendly Ghost* series. She was also the voice of Little Audrey. For the King Features Television cartoons, in addition to Olive Oyl, Questel was also the speaking voice for baby Swee'pea. She provided a menacing tone for The Sea Hag. She was also the lead character's voice in the CBS children's series *Winky Dink and You*.

Questel was an actress whose film roles included: *It's Only Money* (1961), *Funny Girl* (1968), and *National Lampoon's Christmas Vacation* (1989). She became known as Aunt Bluebell in a popular series of paper towel commercials. She passed away on January 4, 1998, at the age of 89.

Jackson Beck

Jackson Beck was called in a 1990 profile, "a wrinkled old rooster from the radio days with a lot of sock left in his cock-a-doodle-doo." He was born in Manhattan on July 23, 1912. His father, Max Blank, was a silent film actor. Beck's first radio show was *Myrt and Marge* in 1931. He called radio, "elemental theater." Beck said of radio, "Acting had to be bravura, black and white-simple, pure heroes and heroines, all virgins. You knew when you picked up the script that you were going to be a hero or villain by the name of your character. The hero was always John Noble. You avoided recognizable locales because there might be somebody from there who'd sue. So the heroines always came from Greendale or Fort Mudge."

Beck became involved with the *Superman* radio series playing a South American gaucho, Alfredo, on February 18, 1942. The following year he became the show's narrator. During more than sixty years on the air, his accomplishments included impersonating Stalin and other world leaders on *March of Time*. He was the voice of *The Cisco Kid*, heard in two Woody Allen films and countless television commercials. Beck said of his commercial work, "My job is to sell a carload of whatever the hell it is to clean out the supermarket shelves and get replenished. People like me are responsible for thousands of jobs, because if we don't sell that merchandise, the company goes to hell." He served as pitchman for various products, including Combat Roach Killer, Kellogg's Sugar Frosted Flakes, Little Caesars Pizza, Pepsi-Cola, and many toy products.

He began his association with Popeye in 1944, voicing Bluto for Famous Studios' *The Anvil Chorus Girl*. In addition to providing Bluto's voice in the *Popeye* series, his vocals could be heard in other animated cartoons produced by Paramount Pictures. When King Features put their

Popeye television cartoons into production, Beck voiced Brutus and the films' supporting players. While providing Brutus's vocals, Beck was also heard on the cartoon series, *King Leonardo and His Short Subjects* (1960-1963). He provided the voice of kind King Leonardo and the wicked criminal gangster Biggie Rat.

Despite his rough exterior, Beck demonstrated his kind heart. On my non-profit cable access series, *Drawing With Fred,* I teach the audience how to doodle cartoon characters. I asked Beck if he would provide a little bit of Brutus's voice for my program. He agreed, and I sent him the script, blank cassette tape, and money. Beck sent me back the cassette tape but returned the money. His kindness truly touched me.

Beck passed away at the age of 92, leaving behind a tremendous body of work.

Mrs. Virginia Mercer, the wife of Jack Mercer, provided a partial recording schedule for Mercer, Questel, and Beck in 1960:

3/8 — Gene Deitch, *3 cartoons*

3/14 — Charles Shows (Larry Harmon), *5 cartoons*

3/15 — Charles Shows (Larry Harmon), *5 cartoons*

3/21 — Jack Kinney, *7 cartoons*

3/22 — Jack Kinney, *9 cartoons*

3/24 — Jack Kinney, *7 cartoons*

4/21 — Seymour Kneitel (Paramount), *4 cartoons*

5/5 — Jack Kinney, *8 cartoons*

5/6 — Jack Kinney, *8 cartoons*

5/13 — Gene Deitch, *4 cartoons*

5/16 — Charles Shows (Larry Harmon), *5 cartoons*

5/17 — TV Spots (Gerald Ray), *5 cartoons*

6/6 — Seymour Kneitel (Paramount), *2 cartoons*

Jackson Beck (left) spars with Jack Mercer (right) for the hand of Mae Questel.

Jack Mercer provided the voices for all of the characters in the Felix the Cat television cartoon series. He was a versatile voice artist and writer.

The Television Cartoon Spin-Offs

The President's Council on Physical Fitness took note of Popeye's tremendous popularity on the small screen. *The Daily Captial News* reported on May 11, 1963, "Curley Howser, host of *Showtime*, read a letter from Popeye on the air the other day in which the famous cartoon hero said he's gone into a month of vigorous training during which he'll eat no spinach to show just how strong exercise alone can make him." A live act was developed featuring physical fitness exercises starring Herb Messinger as Popeye and Brett Pearson portraying Brutus. The duo's performance toured several locations entertaining both children and adults. The live Popeye took a fitness test before a public gathering on May 25, 1963. The sailor's fitness routine consisted of pull-ups, sit-ups, and squat thrusts prescribed by the President's Council on Physical Fitness. The campaign was being carried by other television stations throughout the country and coordinated by King Features Syndicate, who distributed the *Popeye* cartoons. The exercises were also utilized in the *Popeye the Sailor* comic book series published by Gold Key Comics. During this same period, Popeye was encouraging Wimpy to exercise in the Sunday comic strip by Bud Sagendorf.

The live Popeye act was discussed in the *Star-Gazette's* August 13, 1963 edition from Elmira, New York written by Jim Scovel.

TOT FINDS POPEYE ACT TOO REAL

"Where's dat Popeye?" shouted Brutus, thumping his rubber club on the studio floor. That's when the first small child started to cry. She was one of four juveniles clustered round-eyed before a WSYE-TV camera filming the comic combo Monday. They're at the county fair today through Monday. Small wonder the child was scared. Brutus was big, loud and hairy. It did him no good to ad-lib quickly that he "liked little girls". This one, yelling, was carried discreetly from the room.

Then, like the U.S. Cavalry, Popeye bounded onstage. "All me friends is here," he shouted hoarsely as Brutus exited. The remaining children gasped. One waved timidly. "Do I likes spinach?" said the one-eyed sailor man. "Of course I likes spinach. How do you thinks I gets me muskles?" The kids loved it. After the show, they hung around, staring in timid fascination. They even got to Brutus. Except for the one little girl. Her mother brought her back into the studio. One glimpse of the big fellow and she cut loose once more. "One of my fans," Brutus said resignedly in his dressing room. He took off his blue shirt, his false whiskers and a bulky white object that went around his stomach to give him Brutus's waist line.

Popeye took off a rubber face mask, thus getting rid of squint eye and big jaw. He took off the rubber puffed-up elbow length coverings that gave him his bulbous forearms. Thus uncovered, Brutus became George Quinn, a tall, pleasant-faced chap who looks more like Li'l Abner than Brutus. Popeye became a short, pleasant-faced chap named Herb Messinger, producer and owner of the act.

They've been doing it for two years. They're at the fairgrounds after a stint in Pittsburgh and are on their way from here to the Pacific Exposition in Vancouver. Both Quinn and Messinger have other irons in the show business fire. Quinn recently finished a serious movie with actress Viveca Lindfors. Messinger is lining up a couple of new television comic shows. Both like the Popeye and Brutus act. Why? "Kids," said both young actors. "They're the most receptive. They believe in the show. You don't have to pretend with them. They're the greatest audience."

"One last question," said the interviewer to Popeye. "Do you really like spinach?"

"Yes," Messinger said promptly. "I likes spinach." Not a muscle twitched when he said it.

King Features Syndicate celebrated Popeye's 35th birthday with the television stations that aired their cartoons. *Broadcasting* magazine announced in their December 2, 1963 edition:

Popeye invites all you swabs in the business to enjoy his beautiful 35th birthday.

This week of January 13-19 is Popeye's Birthday Week. It marks the 35h anniversury of the world debut of Popeye. And we're going to celebrate big. The stations listed nearby, all of whom play the Popeye TV cartoons, are going to throw swinging parties on their Popeye shows during birthday week. And they'll be running special promotion on this extra special event for a week in advance. We're providing the goodies. On these Popeye TV parties, the program's emcees will introduce the brand-new Popeye's Birthday Song, dedicated to children everywhere who are going to celebrate their own birthdays in the coming year. If you advertise a product "dedicated to children everywhere," the Popeye TV birthday parties give you an especially wonderful setting in which to tell about it. Just contact the swinging stations nearby. Go Popeye! Happy Birthday, everybody.

The programs that participated in Popeye's Birthday celebration were:

Old Skipper Show, Albany, N.Y.
Uncle Roy's Morning Cartoons, Albuquerque, N.M.
Popeye and Big John, Altoona, PA.
Deputy Howie and Popeye and Popeye Theater, Bakersfield, CA.
Herb's Happy Show, Billings, MT.
Popeye and the Admiral, Binghamton, N.Y.
The Popeye Show, Birmingham, AL.
Mr. Bill's Theater, Boise, IDAHO
Clubhouse Four, Boston, MASS.
Looney Tunes Club, Bristol, VA.
The Sheriff Steve Show, Cedar Rapids, IOWA
Clown Carnival, Charlotte, N.C.
Breakfast House, Chicago, ILL.
The Comedy Hour, Cincinnati, OHIO
The Uncle Pete Show, Clarksburg, W. VA
Blinky, Colorado Springs, COLO.
Big Ten Cartoons, Corpus Christi, TEXAS
Popeye Theater, Denver, COLO.
Popeye and Pals, Detroit, MICH.
Bozo and His Pals, Duluth, MINN.
The Cap'n Shipwreck Show, Eugene, ORE.
Flippo Jr. and Popeye, Fresno, CA.
Popeye Theater, Grand Rapids, MICH.
Bozo the Clown, Greenville, N.C.
Barker Bill Show, Norfolk, VA.
Captain Honolulu, Honolulu, HAWAII
Mr. Cartoon Show and Popeye and His Pals, Huntington, W. VA.
Popeye and Janie. Indianapolis, IND.
Popeye's Pals, Jacksonville, FLA.

Showtime, Jefferson City, MO.
The Bar-12 Ranger Show, Jopling, MO.
Popeye's Pier 5 Club, Los Angeles, CA.
Popeye and Gus Show, Lubbock, TEXAS
Funhouse, Memphis, TENN.
Popeye Playhouse, Miami, FL.
Dave Lee Show, Minneapolis, MINN.
Sitting Duck Cartoon Theater, Mobile, AL.
Admiral Jack, New Haven, CONN.
Let's Have Fun, New York, N.Y.
Sally Starr's Popeye Theater, Philadelphia, PA.
It's Wallace, Phoenix, AZ.
Popeye n' Knish, Pittsburgh, PA.
Bozo and The Captain Five Show, Raleigh, N.C.
Sailor Bob and Friends and Popeye and Friends, Richmond, VA.
The Cactus Joe Show, Roanoke, VA.
Popeye and The Three Stooges, Rockford, ILL.
Circle Five Ranch, Saginaw, MICH.
Marshall J, San Francisco, CA.
The Stan Boreson Show, Seattle, WASH.
Countdown with Kaptain Taltower, Shreveport, LA.
Captain Eleven, Sioux, Falls, SD.
The Cap'n Cy Show, Spokane, WASH.
Uncle Otto's Country Store, Springfield, ILL.
Kartoon Karnival and Popeye's Porthole, Springfield, MO.
S.S. Popeye, St. Louis, MO.
Elmer Duffy's Clubhouse, St. Thomas, V.I.
The Mary Ellen Show, Tampa, FL.
Popeye and Friends, Washington, D.C.

Hundreds of manufacturers produced products based on both the comic strip and animated versions of the sailor and his crew due to their immense exposure on the small screen. *Broadcasting Magazine* published a brief article acknowledging this in their February 5, 1962 edition:

POPEYE NEWSLETTER PUBLISHED BY KING

The television division of King Features Syndicate is publishing a monthly newsletter titled, "The Popeye Pipeline." It is being distributed to 3,500 executives at stations, advertisers' agencies, department stores, chain stores, and jobbers who are involved in the telecasting, advertising, or merchandising of the KFS cartoon program. The newsletter provides the latest information on merchandising of the program, the way local stations are scheduling and promoting the show, lists of advertisers participating in sponsorship.

In addition to *The Popeye Pipeline,* a 1962 merchandising catalog was published by King Features Syndicate. King Features stated in this catalog:

Production has just been completed on 220 new Popeye cartoons, made specifically for TV. They have been sold, as of this writing, to 125 TV Stations. Add the stations already playing the 234 original Popeyes, and you have at least one Popeye program in virtually every market in the U.S.

Here now is still another service to the Popeye trade, the first catalog of Popeye merchandise. Over 100 items are described in the following pages.

Though using the character designs from the television cartoons, some companies elected to color Popeye's white sailor's uniform blue. Other products mixed the TV designs of Olive Oyl, Brutus, and The Sea Hag with Popeye wearing his comic strip attire. Here is a listing of items using the television versions of the cast:

Popeye Musical Toys and Popeye Police-Set Pull Toy by American Pre-School

Popeye Paints by American Crayon

Popeye Blackboard by Bar-Zim Toy Mfg. Co.

Popeye and Sea Hag Halloween mask and costumes by Collegeville Flag & Mfg. Co.

Popeye Cartoon Kit by Colorforms (1966 edition)

Popeye Goes Swimming by Colorforms

Popeye Holster Set by J. Halpern Co.

Popeye Songs about Safety Record Album by Golden LP Record

Popeye Songs of Health by Golden Record

Popeye Records, Stories from TV scripts by Peter Pan Records

Popeye 12 inches tall Bendy Toy by Lakeside

Popeye Super Flex and *Mini-Flex* by Lakeside

Popeye Dancing Toy by Lakeside

Popeye and Olive Oyl Push Button Puppets by Kohner

Popeye Sparkle Paint Set by Kenner Products Co.

Popeye Coloring, Activity and Sticker Fun books by Lowe, Inc.

Popeye Cartoonist Stamp Set by Lido Toy Co.

Popeye, Olive Oyl and Brutus Pez Dispenser Set by Pez-Hass, Inc.

Popeye Candy by Phoenix Candy Company.

Popeye Magic Putty by M. Shimmel Sons

Popeye Bubble n' Clean by Woolfoam Corp.

Popeye Carnival by Toymaster Products

Popeye Plastic Cup and Bowl by Deka

Popeye and Brutus Soaky bottles by Colgate-Palmolive

Popeye Doozies by Kenner Products Co.

Popeye's Inflatable Sofa by Venetianaire

Popeye's Inflatable Chair by Venetianaire

Popeye Slate Set by Rosebud Art

Popeye the Sailor Battle Fleet by Larami Corp.

Popeye Sun-Eze by Tilmans

Popeye Tricky Walker by Jaymar

Popeye Blow Ups by Lakeside

Popeye Cylinder Cookie Jar by McCoy

Popeye 48" High Puncho by Coleco

Popeye Spinach Arcade Game by Holgate

Popeye Jumbo Trading Cards by Dynamic Toy (these cards used the television cartoon versions of The Sea Hag and Brutus. The other character designs were from the comic strip)

Popeye Train Set by Larami

Popeye Board Game by Parker Brothers

Popeye Card Game by Parker Brothers

Popeye Knockdown-Knockout Boxing Game by Harmony Toys

Popeye 8mm Home Movies by Americom

Popeye Flip Show Action Features by Payton-this toy featured scenes from the television cartoons: *Hits and Missiles, Azteck Wreck, The Green Dancin' Shoes, Mobey Hick,* and *Sneaking Peeking*

In 1984 Media Home Entertainment released a series of videotapes featuring Popeye, Beetle Bailey, Krazy Kat, Barney Google and Snuffy Smith, and Cool McCool television cartoons produced by King Features Syndicate. These 1984 releases were *Popeye and Friends in Outer Space, Popeye in the Wild West, Popeye; Travelin on About Travel,* and *Popeye and Friends in the South Seas.*

Popeye in Outer Space was reissued in 1988 and warranted a review in *Billboard* magazine's July 30th, 1988 edition:

> This collection of six cartoon shorts features not only Popeye, Olive Oyl and Bluto but several other King Features characters as well, including Krazy Kat, Barney Google, and Cool McCool. The running theme in each is space travel or beings from outer space. For example, viewers are treated to a look at Popeye's family life in the 21st century, a demolition of classic bug-eyed aliens by Popeye and Bluto, and Olive's rescue from some kidnapping spaceman — all, of course, with help from the old spinach can. As cartoon entertainment, this presentation is only fair. The animation is static, the colors bland and the storylines boring. This is for the young viewers, who probably won't understand the dialog and therefore can't be harmed by its nonsensical quality. Popeye is still an enormously popular character, and the rock bottom price will probably make this tape a strong sell-through item. But this collection in no way represents the best of King Feature's Popeye cartoons.

Oddly none of the Popeye television cartoons produced by Paramount Cartoon Studios, generally regarded as the best in the series, were used on these videos. There were undoubtedly episodes produced by Paramount which featured the themes utilized on these tapes. Perhaps this is why the reviewer noted, "this no way represents the best of King Features' Popeye cartoons." Also, the reviewer mistook Brutus for Bluto.

In 2013 Warner Home Video released on DVD *Popeye the Sailor, The 1960's Classics.* All of the episodes produced by Paramount Cartoon Studios are featured as well as cartoons from Gerald Ray. A total of seventy-two episodes.

Popeye the Public Service Man

A few of the Popeye television cartoons were public relations conscious. *Spare Dat Tree* (Jack Kinney, 1960) dealt with tree conservation while *Tooth Be or Not Tooth Be* (Gene Deitch/William Snyder, 1962) concerned the ways to keep your teeth healthy. The Forest Service of the U.S. Agriculture Department and state forestry groups ordered 32 color prints of a segment called *Popeye in the Woods* (Jack Kinney, 1960) produced by King Features Syndicate. *Popeye in the Woods* has the sailor and Wimpy on a camping trip. Wimpy starts a dangerous fire which is put out by Popeye's spinach power. The sailor then gives pointers to Wimpy (and the audience) on how to prevent forest fires.

UnCivil Wars (Jack Kinney, 1960) has Popeye telling Swee'pea about unsafe driving techniques. This cartoon was sent to various school systems due to its educational theme. The original version for television concluded with Swee'pea speeding off on his bike. Popeye looks at the audience and says, "Well ya can't learns them too young, arf, arf, arf, arf, arf, arf!" It was decided, when screened for public service purposes, the original ending would be replaced with Popeye singing a safety song. Utilizing animation by Paramount Cartoon Studios, Popeye sings, "Know when ya starts driving, cause safety keeps thriving, says Popeye the Sailor Man, toot! toot! Unfortunately, today's standard television version does away with Popeye's song but keeps the Paramount animation. Popeye's vocal over Paramount's animation is "Well, ya can't learns them too young, arf, arf, arf, arf, arf, arf." The animation is totally out of sync with the dialogue.

In 1971 the television cartoon version of Popeye was animated by Myron Waldman for a safety film, produced by Abe Goodman, which was distributed to school systems across the country. In the film, combining animation with live-action, Popeye instructs people on different street safety procedures. Myron Waldman (April 23, 1908-February 4, 2006) was an animator for the Fleischer Studios. There he worked on *Popeye, Betty Boop, Raggedy Ann, Superman,* and the motion picture, *Gulliver's Travels.* Waldman moved over to Famous Studios and worked mainly on the *Casper the Friendly Ghost* series. He later worked on the *Out of the Inkwell* and *Milton the Monster* series for television.

The safety film was titled *Look Where You Are Going*, and Jack Mercer was once again the voice of Popeye singing:

> *I'm Popeye the Sailor Man, beep, beep*
> *I'm Popeye the Sailor Man, broom, broom*
> *I'm very discreet what I does with me feet*
> *I'm Popeye the Sailor Man, beep, beep, broom, broom.*

King Features Syndicate's letter to school systems explained the film's contents:

> Operating on the philosophy that the best way to teach children is to talk up to their level and be amusing, this film shows youngsters the basics of sidewalk safety. Shot on the busy streets of New York, with Popeye as the lecturer, real groups of city school children are shown that Policemen are their friends and around to help them. Each traffic sign has a different shape and different meaning, which should be followed for the child's safety. Children are shown the proper ways to cross streets, individually and as a group, as well as the proper way to ride a bicycle on the road. In the most dramatic and graphic portion of the film, utilizing a New York City Police car and a doll-replica of one of the girls in the group, Popeye shows what can happen to a child crossing improperly with an oncoming car going 40 mph. Popeye leaves the children smiling with a review of all his lessons and the warning to "Keeps the eyes peeled at the sign."

Herb Messinger played Popeye and Brett Pearson portrayed Brutus at various parks to promote Popeye's Physical Fitness Campaign.

The images of Brutus and Popeye in this newspaper advertisements came from the cartoon I Bin Sculped *(Gerald Ray, 1960).*

Payton's Popeye Flip Show Action Features *(1961) featured scenes from the television cartoons. Scenes for "Look Ma, I'm Dancing" was culled from* The Green Dancin' Shoes *(Jack Kinney, 1960).*

The Samuel Lowe company produced a number of Popeye coloring and activity books from the late 1950's through the mid 1960's. The television cartoon version of Popeye is being colored in by the comic strip design of Swee'pea on the cover of the Popeye Color By Number *book (1964). The print versions of Olive Oyl and Wimpy are on the upper right while the television rendition of Brutus is at the lower left.*

Golden Record's Popeye's Songs of Health, Safety, Friendship and Manners *(1961) featured the characters on the cover as they appeared in the television cartoons produced by King Features Syndicate.*

Little Golden Record's Popeye Songs of Health *78 RPM Record depicted the television versions of Popeye and Swee'pea on the cover.*

Colgate-Palmolive's Popeye Soaky toy from the 1960's put the popular animated television character in his sailor's uniform.

The television versions of Popeye, Wimpy and Olive Oyl graced McCoy's 11" x 6" cookie jar produced in 1965.

Popeye and Swee'pea, looking as they stepped out of one of the television cartoons produced by Gerald Ray, fish on the cover of Hasbro's Popeye Paint and Crayon Set *originally sold during the 1960's. Inside the set were drawings of the characters as they appeared in the comic strip from the 1950's.*

Dynamic Toy Company produced a series of colorful jumbo trading cards featuring Popeye and his crew in 1962. The television versions of the Sea Hag and Brutus were featured on cards which were illustrated by King Features Syndicate's bullpen artist, Joe Musial.

Nintendo revived the 1960's television designs of the Popeye cast for a series of products based on the popular video game which populated various arcade centers.

The television version of Brutus gets slugged by Popeye who is wearing his comic strip attire from Kenner Toy's Sparkle Paints *set produced in 1966.*

Part of the box art from Kenner Toy's Popeye Sparkle Paints *featured Brutus and Popeye as they were seen in King Features Syndicate's television cartoons.*

Due in part to the sailor's popularity from his cartoons produced for television, King Features Syndicate issued a Popeye merchandise catalogue for retailers in 1962. Note how it's the small screen's design of Popeye which graces the publication's cover rather than his newspaper counterpart. Inside featured products depicting both the animated cartoon and print designs of Popeye's cast of characters.

Episode Guide

Cartoons Produced by
Larry Harmon

DIRECTED BY Paul Fennell. ARTISTS: Tom Baron, C.L. Hartman, Z.T. Jablecki, Lou Scheimer, Ervin Kaplan, George Rowley, Jean Blanchard, Hal Sutherland, Cal Dalton, and Frank Onaitis. WRITER: Charles Shows. MUSIC: Gordon Zahler. EDITOR: Dan Milner.

Muskels Shmuskels (1960)
Popeye and Olive Oyl witness the feats of Brutus the Strongman. When Popeye challenges his strength, the rivalry is on. Olive tells Popeye, "No more fighting," which leaves the sailor at a disadvantage. Brutus gives chase to Popeye and pours cement on the sailor. Luckily, underneath Popeye's sailor's hat is his spinach. He sucks the vegetable through his pipe and beats up Brutus. Although not called by name, Castor Oyl is the man who gives Brutus a gun. The character designs in Larry Harmon's initial outing are simplistic, and throughout most of the cartoon, Popeye is minus his tattoos. Popeye's pipe appears and disappears as well. When the spinach-fortified sailor breaks free of the cement, a frightened Brutus says "oops" but in Popeye's voice.

Hoppy Jalopy (1960)
Popeye competes in a road race with his jalopy against Big Daddy-O Brutus's Spumoni Special. Brutus refers to Popeye's jalopy as "instant junk" and kidnaps Olive Oyl. Brutus pulls various tricks to ensure a victory, but Popeye squeezes spinach juice into his jalopy's tank, which supercharges it. Popeye and Brutus end up in a tunnel. When they emerge, Olive is in the front seat while Brutus is attached to the back of Popeye's jalopy. Popeye slams Brutus's trunk over his head at the cartoon's conclusion. A fast-paced film with a simplistic animation style.

Dead-Eye Popeye (1960)

In Gully Gap Suicide, McBride is menacing Olive Oyl until Popeye comes to her rescue. The sailor becomes the town's sheriff and has to deal with the McBride Boys. They lock Popeye in jail, who breaks free thanks to "these ten-gallon hats holds a lots of spinach." One of the McBride boys shoots at Popeye, who catches the bullets in his hand then tosses them into his mouth. Popeye fires the bullets back through his pipe, and his opponent loses his pants, revealing red-striped underwear. A powerful punch by Popeye ends the gun battle. Olive attempts to kiss Popeye as a reward but smooches a horse instead. The horse turns beet red, causing Popeye to exclaim, "That's a horse of another color." Although we see a lot of Popeye's two opened eyes in this cartoon, his tattoos, for the most part, have returned. During the scene where The McBride Boy is kicking Popeye in the rear, his short-sleeved blue shirt becomes long-sleeved. In the very next scene, the sleeve is short once more. The voice of the white-bearded old prospector sounds a lot like Bozo the Clown. Larry Harmon provided the voice of Bozo in the clown's television cartoons produced by his animation studio.

Mueller's Mad Monster (1960)

A short, bald scientist with a red mustache, calling himself Mad Mueller, creates a monster he calls Irving. Popeye and Olive Oyl end up visiting the scientist while trying to find shelter during a rainstorm. Irving makes a play for Olive despite Mad Muller saying to him, "Irving, be a good boy, Irving." Popeye challenges Irving to a fight that gets very fierce. Olive asks Mueller to stop the fight by making some spinach. The scientist whips up a bottle of spinach juice which Olive gives to Popeye. Popeye's muscles expand, and one punch turns Irving into a junk pile. This saddens Mueller, who says, "My poor monster, he has gone all to pieces." Popeye rebuilds the creature who Olive calls "Alvis." Alvis looks like a sophisticated dark-haired, green-faced creature with eyelashes. Olive kisses him, and they both get a shock treatment courtesy of Popeye throwing the power switch. A fun, fast-paced cartoon featuring Popeye's ever prominent two opened eyes.

Caveman Capers (1960)

Popeye and Olive Oyl have a picnic which consists of "spinach burgers," "spinach soup," "filet o' spinach," and "spinach ice cream." This leads into a story where Popeye explains to Olive the origin of his spinach diet. The sailor says it began "a million years ago with me great, great, great gran'pappy, pre-hysterical Popeye." Caveman Popeye and Brutus both want cave girl Olive for themselves. They attempt to claim Olive as property by clubbing her on the head. After a few rounds of head knocks, Olive screams, "Hold it, fellas, hold it! Why don't you settle this like gentleman, fight it out!" Battles ensue until Brutus pins Popeye with a boulder the injured caveman can't budge. Popeye fears he will starve to death, but he notices a dinosaur eating leaves. Popeye chews on the leaves, which gives him muscles. "I am gonna call this stuff spinach cause it looks like spinach," Popeye exclaims. Upon freeing himself from the weight of the boulder, Popeye saves a captured Olive from Brutus! After Popeye's story, Olive says, "You know Popeye that club bit wasn't such a bad idea." She then bonks Popeye over the head with a club. Olive winks at the audience and says, "It's one way to get a man!" A fun cartoon.

Bullfighter Bully (1960)
In Mexico, Popeye and Olive Oyl encounter El Diablo, the world's greatest bullfighter. Olive adores "big brave bullfighters." Popeye calls him a "bullfightin' bully." Popeye doesn't want to see the fight as he puts it, "I can't stands ta see no bulls bullied." Popeye gets involved with the bullfight when El Diablo's first match is with a baby cow. El Diablo decides to fight Popeye and uses a sword revealing the sailor's blue and black striped underwear. When a fierce bull attacks El Diablo, he uses a screeching Olive as his shield. Popeye eats his spinach and turns the bull into steaks. The sailor flattens El Diablo with one punch to his face. Popeye gets kissed by the baby cow, who he thinks is Olive. The sailor says, "Ya sure kisses sweet Olive, ohhh." Popeye's kindness towards animals is emphasized in this cartoon.

Ace of Space (1960)
Popeye and Olive Oyl are taking a drive when an announcer on the radio says, "Ladies and gentleman, a special news bulletin! A few moments ago, a flying saucer was reported flying south over North Dakota." The flying saucer zooms near Popeye and Olive. The alien inside is ordered to "bring back one of the people." The alien captures Olive, who he thinks is "beautiful." Popeye snags the ship with a rope, and when he asks for Olive back, the alien squirts him with "motor oil." The alien pulls Popeye into his ship, and the gibberish-sounding creature shoots Popeye with a ray gun. Popeye says, "I'll gives ya me famous spinach rays!" Green-colored rays shoot out of the sailor's pipe, which causes the alien to float out of the spaceship. Popeye takes control of the spacecraft and sees the alien in his car singing in gibberish. A cute cartoon.

College of Hard Knocks (1960)

Professor Brutus sees Olive Oyl coming his way and says, "Here comes my star pupil, Olive Oyl, with that silly sailor Popeye again." Popeye says, "Ooh, I hates him to pieces." With that, Professor Brutus humiliates Popeye with a series of educational tests. For example, Brutus demonstrates the law of pressure by squeezing a tube of toothpaste on Popeye's face. Olive says, "Oh, Popeye, are you taking a pasting?" Brutus sends Popeye to the floor with an anvil and chases after Olive. Popeye pulls out the spinach, and his sailor's hat turns into a graduation cap. Popeye uses his fists to educate Brutus by punching him back and forth against a wall. Finally, he wallops Brutus out of the building. Olive is so pleased with Popeye's newfound education she gives him a diploma. It turns out to be a marriage license, and a distressed Popeye says, "I needs me spinach." Popeye's sailor hat initially turns into a gray graduation cap but becomes white when he places Brutus on the ground. Then it goes back to being gray. The animation seems more limited in this entry of the Harmon series.

Abominable Snowman (1960)

Popeye and Olive Oyl visit her Uncle Sylvan at The Explorers Club. This leads to Popeye, Sylvan, and Olive going after the abominable snowman. They end up at "Mighty Mount Idiot," home of the beast. Popeye meets a tiny hairy green creature called Harry, who claims to be the abominable snowman. Popeye says, "You're only a little runt." Harry replies, "I've been sick." Popeye realizes he will be the laughing stock at the Explorer's Club if he brings back this pint-sized snowman. Harry suggests Popeye buy "one of our stuffed abominable snowmen." Popeye takes it and gives Harry an all-day spinach sucker in return. Harry licks the sucker and develops muscles. An entertaining cartoon, but Harry is voiced in one style, yet when he says, "An all-day spinach sucker," it's in a different tone of voice.

Ski Jump Chump (1960)

Gorgeous Pierre challenges Popeye to a race on skis. At the beginning of the race, Pierre uses a rope to trip up Popeye. The sailor smashes headfirst into a tree and pulls out his favorite drink, spinach juice. Popeye gains in speed, and Pierre says, "I must use strategy; I will cheat." The two skiers begin brawling and land in a tree stump containing a sleeping bear. The trio emerges from the stump, with the bear winning the race. Pierre cries, "I was robbed! I was robbed!" While Popeye says, "Like Napoleon said, ya can'ts win 'em all." Upon finishing his last remark, Popeye's ski attire turns into Napoleon's uniform. In two scenes, Popeye's short-sleeved shirt becomes long while he skis down the mountain. Another cartoon from Harmon's studio where the animation looks more limited.

Irate Pirate (1960)
Popeye shows Olive Oyl his collapsible boat, and they encounter The Jolly Roger's vessel. The Captain of the Jolly Roger calls himself "the romantical pirate" and ties up Olive. He then sends sharks to attack Popeye. Roger puts Popeye at the end of a rope and keeps dipping him near a shark's mouth. Popeye exclaims, "I has had enough, and enough is too much!" He pulls out his spinach can and says, "Ah, nothing like strained spinach to tickle the tonsils." Popeye clobbers both the shark and Roger. Roger loads a cannon and fires it at Popeye. Popeye catches the cannonball and hurls it back at Roger, causing a big explosion. The explosion takes care of Roger but also does damage to Olive. The charred-looking lass says to Popeye, "Oh, Popeye let's go ashore, sailing is so boring." A delightful cartoon with Olive getting a little payback for her flirting.

Foola Foola Bird (1960)
The National Bird Watcher's Society offers one million dollars to anyone who can find a genuine Foola Foola bird. Popeye says to Olive Oyl, "I knows where the last of the Foola Foola Birds is. On a Foola Foola Island!" Popeye and Olive get to the island without realizing Brutus has overheard about the million dollars. The trio hunts down the bird, but he's a tricky one. Popeye tries to tie the bird up, but it's the sailor who ends up in knots. Brutus grabs the bird and says, "Can't you see how attached he is to me, we're inseparable!"

With that, the bird pecks Brutus's head until he's set free. Brutus catches Popeye in a trap that suspends him from a tree. In the process, his can of spinach falls to the ground. Popeye says to the Foola Foola Bird, "Hands me me spinach, pal." The bird gives Popeye his spinach, and he literally dives into Brutus's kisser. The brute bangs into a tree and is hit by several coconuts. Popeye and Olive sail home but think they've left the bird on the island. Popeye says, "Well anyway, we gots rid of Brutus." Then the bird shows up with a dazed Brutus in his beak. A fun adventure with an amusing cartoon creature. While Brutus is hiding in the bushes, waiting to steal the bird from Olive, he's wearing a long-sleeved blue shirt. It's still long-sleeved when he grabs the bird but becomes short for the remainder of the cartoon.

Uranium on the Cranium (1960)

Popeye, looking at a map, says, "Double Cross Island is between Pastrami Point and Bagel Bay in the sandwich islands." Popeye and Olive Oyl are after uranium on Double Cross Island, but Brutus is on their trail. Brutus dresses up as a gorilla to scare Popeye and Olive off the island. Brutus, still dressed as the gorilla, finds the uranium and battles Popeye. Popeye says to the disguised Brutus, "Er, pardon me, mister gorillie, but yer zipper is unzipped. Oops, ya dropped yer head!" Popeye then encounters a real gorilla who fights Brutus. While the pair brawl, Popeye eats his spinach and grabs the head of both the gorilla and Brutus. The sailor says, "And now let's put our heads together." Popeye bangs the pair's heads into each other. Popeye and Olive now own a uranium mine. At the cartoon's conclusion, Brutus is shown pushing the gorilla in a wagon full of uranium. The laughing beast munches on a banana.

Two-Faced Paleface (1960)

In the desert, Popeye digs for gold because his nose twitches when he gets near it. As Popeye puts it, "Me nose knows." Sure enough he discovers gold, and Brutus finds out. The brute decides to go into his Indian routine, claiming the land belongs to his tribe. "Gold belongs heap big chief pain in the neck," the phony Indian tells Popeye. To prove he's a real Indian, he chops the hair off of Popeye's head. This scares Olive Oyl, and the pair take off until they see the Indian wearing polka dot shorts! Popeye uses Olive's lipstick and a feather to disguise himself as an Indian. Claiming to be from the "Cha-Cha-Cha" tribe, the two fake Indians feud. Popeye ends up tied to a pole, and Brutus pulls out a lighter. As he lights the fire, Brutus says, "I'll give you an Indian hot-foot." Popeye eats his spinach, breaks free, and punches Brutus into the air. When the bearded Indian crashes to the ground, he offers Popeye a peace pipe to smoke. However, the pipe is loaded with gun powder which explodes when Popeye takes a few puffs. The fake Indian is given Popeye's pipe to smoke which has a mightier explosion that blows off his disguise. Popeye says, "That ain't no injun, that's ol' Brutus!" Olive says, "And the gold is ours!"

Childhood Daze (1960)

Brutus, Olive Oyl, and Popeye witness Professor Wottasnozzle's invention, which he calls his "automatic youth machine." The Professor demonstrates his machine by putting into it an "old chicken." He presses a few buttons, and the old chicken becomes a little egg which hatches a "baby chicken." Popeye volunteers to be a human test case, and Brutus presses a button that turns him into a baby. "This is one way to get rid of Popeye for good," Brutus says. Popeye becomes a little baby and kicks Brutus. The brute turns baby Popeye into a white-colored basketball and throws him into a hoop. Baby Popeye starts bawling and tells Olive, "I wants some baby food!" Olive gives the crying tyke some strained spinach which turns him back to his normal age. Popeye punches Brutus into the youth machine and presses a button, turning him into a baby. Baby Brutus wears a diaper but retains his full beard. When Popeye tickles baby Brutus's chin, the infant chomps down on his finger!

Sheepish Sheep-Herder (1960)
Popeye receives a telegram which states, "Rustlers ruining me ranch, signed Poopdeck Pappy, Double Cross Ranch." The sailor arrives at the ranch to aid his Pappy, Popeye's twin, other than having a white beard and red hat. Pappy explains his sheep are being stolen. He tells his son, "You and me are gonna catch those sheep-stealing varmints." The sheep stealer manages to snatch one right under Popeye's nose. When the crook uses a helicopter to snare more, Popeye blasts it out of the sky. When Poopdeck Pappy shaves off his whiskers, the sheep stealer says, "I'm seeing double; I've flipped my lid." He bounces right over a cliff, and a little sheep smacks him in the rear with its hoofs. When Poopdeck Pappy says, "Ta-ta, bon voyage," it's in Popeye's voice.

Track Meet Cheat (1960)
Popeye and Olive Oyl are in the audience when Brutus, the athlete, says, "And now for a new world's record in the pole vault." When Olive admires Brutus's feats, Popeye challenges him. Naturally, Brutus sabotages Popeye's efforts to show what he can do. Brutus uses the hammer throw and tosses Popeye into the stands with a thud. When Olive asks him, "Oh, Popeye, does it hurt much?" the injured sailor says, "Only when I laughs Olive, arf! arf! arf…*oooh!*" Nearby, Wimpy is selling spinach burgers. He asks Popeye, "Spinach burgers, sir, enriched with vitamins, minerals, and mustard both." Popeye chomps down on the burgers, and Wimpy says, "Not all of them, sir, I'll help you eat them." The spinach burgers revive Popeye's muscles, and he heads towards Brutus. He shows Brutus the "high jump" by punching him skyward. Brutus lands into Popeye's hand, who demonstrates the "hammer throw" by tossing him out of the field. When Popeye and Olive look up, they see a sailor statue erected in his honor in an athletic pose. A fun cartoon with the added touch of seeing a firing tank in Popeye's muscle while he flexes.

Crystal Ball Brawl (1960)

Popeye receives a telegram from Wimpy which states, "You are the sole heir to your uncle's Abra-Ka-Dabra's estate. Upon hearing the news, Popeye faints! Wimpy offers to go with him to the estate and carry his money. It turns out Popeye's uncle was magical and left him his crystal ball. Popeye explains, "He could looks into that ball and sees what's gonna happen tomorrow!" Wimpy gets wealthy after taking advantage of a stock tip provided by the crystal ball. Brutus overhears what's happening and attempts to steal the ball for himself. Brawling ensues among Popeye, Wimpy, and Brutus. Popeye dives face first into a large bush. The bush turns out to be spinach, and Popeye kicks Brutus skyward and catches the Crystal Ball. The cartoon concludes with Wimpy and Popeye looking into the Crystal Ball. They see Brutus sitting on a cloud saying, "What did I do wrong?" The animation in this cartoon and *Track Meet Cheat* are a couple of notches above the rest in Larry Harmon's series.

Cartoons Produced by William L. Synder and Supervising Director Gene Deitch

Unfortunately, the copyright dates on some of these cartoons were miswritten in Roman Numeral form. These films are listed in what usually is their broadcast order.

Sea No Evil (1960)

Popeye and Olive Oyl are relaxing, at sea, on a boat called "Miss Olive." While they slumber, an underwater thief steals the equipment on Popeye's boat. Popeye discovers what's happened and says to Olive, "Wow, it looks like everything fell overboard, Olive!" Popeye swims ashore to a boat, motors and supplies store run by Brutus. Brutus sells Popeye's missing supplies back to him. He says to Popeye, "That will be five hundred bucks, chump, *er* chum." Popeye sets out back to the ocean with the new supplies, but Brutus steals them once again. Upon seeing Popeye in his store once, more Brutus says, "Well, my old chump — *err* chum is back again!" Popeye buys back his equipment with the addition of a skin-diving suit. Popeye catches an underwater Brutus attempting to steal his equipment. Brutus cuts a rope on a boat lynch which crashes a vessel on Popeye. The bearded brute tries to get away on a speed boat with Olive in tow. Popeye grabs a can of spinach out of the ship's galley and chases after Brutus. Using water skis and borrowing a fisherman's pole, he snags Brutus. Upon snaring the boat, Popeye says, "I gots me self a big one." A couple of punches, and Brutus is anchored to the damaged speed boat pulling Popeye and Olive ashore. Popeye sings, "I'm strong to the finich 'cause I eats me spinach, I'm Popeye the Sailor Man." When Popeye swims his boat to shore, two scenes are the same, and the background doesn't move in either. The character designs are very simplistic, but the film itself is very fast-moving with a clever plot. Jack Mercer provided the hulking voice of Brutus.

Interrupted Lullaby (1960)

Popeye reads the *Morning Star*'s front page, stating, "Million Dollar Baby! Baby inherits fortune. Olive Oyl named guardian. Sweet Pea today becanie (yes, that's the way it's spelled) the recipient of a million dollar. Left to him by his Great Granfather." Popeye says, "Now he wonts never have to worry about his future. It couldn't have happened to a nicer baby." Brutus reads the same news and says, "What's a baby going to do with a million bucks. It'll be a shame to let all that money go to waste. And I know just the guy who can use it." Brutus stages a few kidnap attempts to capture Swee'pea at Olive's house. He finally succeeds with Popeye in pursuit. Popeye and Brutus battle it out in a cabin. While Popeye gets bopped about, Swee'pea sees a red can and reads the label out loud, "S-p-i-n-a-c-h. Popeye!" The baby feeds the spinach to Popeye, who charges back at Brutus. The kidnapper gets socked into a cornfield where he is hung like a scarecrow. Popeye then puts Swee'pea to bed. When a returning Olive asks if anything happened while she was away, Popeye says, "What could happen, Olive? Just a quiet afternoon for me and li'l Swee'pea." While some scenes in this cartoon feature a simplistic animation style, others are a bit more detailed. This doesn't distract from this exciting cartoon featuring haunting instrumental music.

From Way Out (1960)

Popeye and Olive Oyl visit a short, bald-headed, red-mustached professor who shows them his "space magnet." The professor explains, "If there is anything out in space made out of metal, my magnet will pull it in. Un I can examine it." The professor pulls in a belt buckle, space gun, and "space scooter." A pint-sized Martian with a mean streak comes to reclaim his property. The back of his black jacket reads, "Martian Maulers." Popeye attempts to be friends with the creature, but the sailor ends up giving him a spanking. The Martian calls in his gang, saying, "Big earth daddy wants a rumble." The gang appears and terrorizes Olive and the professor. Popeye pulls out his spinach, and the magnet opens the can. Popeye now takes on the gang by knocking each off their motor scooter. Out of the damaged scooters, he creates a container that the Martian gang falls in. Popeye then flings the container through space but not before saying, "You boys come back and visit us again after ya learns some manners." Popeye raises his arms in a victory pose, singing, "I puts them in place way out there in space, I'm Popeye the Sailor Man!"

Seeing Double (1960)

Olive Oyl sees a fur stole in the window for two thousand dollars, calling it "gorgeous." Popeye says, "Yeah, and so's the price. C'mon, I'll buy ya a gorgeous hamburger." Meanwhile, the head of a criminal gang is showing his henchmen a newly-created mechanical man. The machine looks just like Popeye, and bullets can't stop it. The robot Popeye proceeds to rob a bank, injuring a night watchman. The night watchman describes his attacker to the police stating, "He was wearing a sailor's uniform and smoking a corncob pipe." With other descriptive information, the policeman draws a picture of Popeye. The real sailor man is promptly arrested and thrown in jail. Olive visits him crying, "Oh Popeye, Popeye, Popeye! It's all my fault. You broke into that bank to buy me a mink stole." At the same time that Popeye's in jail, a jewelry store is robbed by the sailor's look-a-like and his gang. Popeye breaks out of jail and captures the gang but still has to deal with his mechanical double. Popeye is bopped around and says, "This calls for spinach!" Popeye splatters the mechanical man into tinier versions of itself. The police give Popeye a two-thousand-dollar reward, and, of course, he uses it to buy Olive the fur stole. Indeed, an imaginative plotline.

Swee'pea Soup (1960)

Popeye, Olive Oyl, and Swee'pea visit King Blozo, whose kingdom is in revolt. They demand a new king and want "lovable Swee'pea." Blozo yells, "Popeye, since you brought Swee'pea here to visit, the people love him and can't stand me!" Blozo calls in the royal mad scientist to discover what makes Swee'pea so "sweet." To do so, the mad scientist captures the baby. He explains to King Blozo tomorrow for lunch he'll have Swee'pea soup, making him as sweet as Swee'pea. Swee'pea is the main ingredient in the soup, and Popeye comes to his rescue. However, the mad scientist holds Popeye at bay with a giant foot. Blozo's angry subjects toss food at him. One of which is a clump of spinach that makes it to Popeye's mouth. Popeye uses his pipe to launch Swee'pea into space, in which he has been cooking in a pot. The pot splits up in the air, and Swee'pea lands in King Blozo's arms in front of the angry mob. Upon seeing Blozo holding Swee'pea, one member of the group says, "Look Swee'pea's in King Blozo's arms. Any King who loves babies has a good heart! Long live King Blozo!" While it's fun to see King Blozo, the animation is very simplistic. In some scenes, Olive's white-collar is its usually flowered shape. In others, it's merely circular.

Hag-Way Robbery (1960)

Popeye, Olive Oyl, Wimpy, and Swee'pea are at sea searching for Eugene, the Jeep that The Sea Hag has captured. On board the ship are the crew's favorite foods, all in cans: hamburgers, olives, and baby food. Also on board is a lot of canned spinach. The Sea Hag's vacuum pulls the canned spinach out of Popeye's boat. With the same vacuum, the witch glues spinach labels on the other canned food. When Popeye's craft is in The Sea Hag's waters, he tells Wimpy, "Keeps a sharp eye out for an ugly dame." To which Olive replies, "Did you call me, Popeye?" The Sea Hag's vulture drops Popeye a note which says, "Dear Popeye, you are finished 'cause you have no spinach." The Sea Hag launches torpedoes at Popeye's vessel, and the sailor goes for his canned spinach. The sailor goes through can after can but finds nothing but hamburgers, olives, and baby food.

When he opens the last can, it contains an orchid, which is Jeep food. Suddenly Eugene the Jeep appears before Popeye! The Sea Hag realizes her submarine has run out of fuel. She burns the spinach, which billows out of her sub in smoke form. Popeye says, "Blow me's down I smell spinach, and smelling spinach is the next best thing to eatin' it." Popeye zooms towards The Sea Hag's submarine and leaves the witch on a beautiful island after the off-screen violence subsides. Popeye says to the hag, "You don't act like no lady, Sea Hag, but I cants socks ya anyway. But I'm leaving you on this island paradise where you cans learn ta be good." Olive, Wimpy and Swee'pea are sound asleep after eating so much canned food. Popeye sings, "I fights to the finich on one whiff of spinach, I'm Popeye the Sailor Man." A fun story diluted by simplistic animation. In one scene, Olive is holding on to an arm-less Swee'pea.

The Lost City of Bubble-Lon (1960)

Popeye is fishing on his boat when he hooks a man wearing a hat with a long mustache and beard. The mysterious man drops back into the ocean with Popeye in pursuit. Popeye finds the man who introduces himself as Professor Underwater. The pair go into the Professor's Sink Mobile. Popeye asks, "How do ya breath down here, huh?" The Professor replies, "Simple, I've invented my own air pills that last for hours." The Professor introduces his assistant, Brutus, to Popeye. The sailor remarks, "That's an assistant!" Popeye extends his hand to be shaken by Brutus. The bearded bully waves Popeye about and tosses him into a barrel.

The Professor takes control of the Sink Mobile and announces, "We're off! Next stop the lost city of Bubble-Lon." The Sink Mobile falls into a hole, discovering the lost city. Green sea creatures, speaking gibberish, take Popeye hostage and lock him in jail. The Professor and Brutus locate the creature's treasure. The seas creatures discover what Brutus and The Professor have found. The bearded bully busts open a wall and picks up the treasure. The Professor remarks, "Brutus, you're fired!" Brutus replies, "Okay, I'll just pick this up for unemployment insurance." The Professor is tossed in jail and explains to Popeye, "Without their treasure, the poor bubble-loians will really be lost." Popeye notices the air pills bottle on the floor, noting one of the ingredients is spinach. Popeye takes a good swallow of the pills and busts out of jail. He catches up to the escaping Brutus and sends him into orbit. Popeye returns the treasure to the creatures and goes back to his boat. A fun and colorful entry.

There's No Space Like Home (1960)

Popeye reads a newspaper headline that states, "Space ships sighted over town". "Wow! This gives me a swell idea for Olive's costume party tonight, huh? I'll calls the costume shop and dress up like a space man." Brutus sees Popeye put on his space man costume and calls the police. The police lock Popeye up, thinking he's a real space creature. Brutus encounters a real spaceman who he thinks is Popeye and attacks him. The space creatures take Brutus to their ship, and one declares "War!" The police explain to a jailed Popeye, "You're not under arrest; we just want to examine you, space man." Popeye replies, "Nots under arrest, huh? Then I donts have ta stay here if I don't wants ta. I'll take a li'l spinach appetizer." Popeye breaks down part of the jail with his charged muscles and takes off to Olive's party. Brutus escapes from the spaceship and arrives at Olive's costume party. The little space creatures are in pursuit and slam Popeye with a door. They pull out Olive's mail box and ram Brutus in his backside with it. Brutus revives and says, "This looks like a job for Popeye," and feeds the sailor his spinach. Popeye zooms off after the tiny creatures and punches each back into their spacecraft. He picks up the vessel and flings it onto a planet in the sky. Olive says to Brutus and Popeye, "Well, boys, you can unmask now, and we'll enjoy the party." Brutus says, "We're not wearing masks." Popeye follows with, "We've gots black eyes!" The trio then begins laughing. A fun cartoon with the interesting twist of Brutus feeding Popeye his spinach to save the day.

Potent Lotion (1960)

Popeye receives a package that turns out to be a bottle of after-shave lotion. Then he gets a note supposedly from Olive Oyl telling him to meet her at the corner of Elm Street and Oak Drive. Popeye says, "She musta sents me this lotion, now she wants ta see me." Popeye rubs the lotion on his face and heads off. Popeye encounters Wimpy, who sniffs the after-shave lotion and punches him. Swee'pea sees Popeye and sniffs his after-shave lotion, which makes the tyke bop him. A dog walks by Popeye, sniffs, and socks the sailor. Brutus and his henchman see Popeye coming and proceed to rob a bank. When the police arrive, they smell the lotion and pound Popeye instead of going after the criminals. Brutus says, "That punchy lotion we sent Popeye worked. While they're busy punching him it gives us time to get away." Popeye takes a sniff and socks himself, and figures out the criminals' plan. While trying to capture the crooks, he gets tied up while the criminals divide their loot. A bound Popeye looks at the cupboard and sees a can of spinach. He uses his teeth to open the can and breaks free of the ropes. Popeye pours some of the lotion on Brutus, causing his two henchmen to sock him. Brutus and Popeye brawl, but the sailor is victorious and carries the criminals to jail. An amusing cartoon with excellent animation by Halas and Batchelor.

Astro-Nut (1960)

A general says to Popeye, "Popeye, the future of our space effort depends upon your ability to stay inside this test capsule for sixty days." Popeye is locked up in the capsule, which contains a sixty-day supply of instant spinach. Also, a special recording of his friend's voices so he won't be lonesome. Wimpy's voice says, "If I had a hamburger, I'd gladly dedicate it to you before I ate it." Suddenly Brutus's voice comes on, saying, "While you dry up inside that nose cone I'm keeping company with poor lonesome Olive, ha! ha! ha!" An angry Popeye keeps pounding on the tape machine, which keeps repeating Brutus's message. Popeye says, "Oh no, Brutus has got sixty days alone with my sweetie." Brutus and Olive are seen going swimming, driving, at the race track, and on a roller-coaster. Popeye tries to keep his mind off the pair but instead shakes up the capsule, opening the lids of the instant spinach cans. The energy from the spinach causes the capsule to launch itself into orbit. It zooms with the speed of light making earth time go backward while capsule time goes forward and at sixty times normal speed. Brutus and Olive's activities are in a backward motion while the capsule lands. Popeye emerges, and a disgusted Brutus says, "Hey, what happened? I didn't get to spend a minute with Olive." Olive remarks, "Yes, that sixty days only seemed like sixty minutes." Popeye sings, "Through space in an hour on pure spinach power, I'm Popeye the Sailor Man."

Goon With The Wind (1960)

While on a sail boat with Popeye, Olive Oyl says, "I think there's something wrong, Popeye. The wind's blowing that way, but we're going backwards." It turns out a Goon from the moon is pushing their craft to a nearby island. The Goon makes off with Olive, and Popeye is trapped in a cage. A Goon says to Olive, "Shut up; we want you to be queen of Goon Island." Popeye tells Olive, "Makes a dash for the boat, Olive, and gets me spinach!" Olive likes the idea of being Queen until she learns this includes marrying the King. She dashes off to the boat but is captured and tied up. However, Olive has managed to hide a spinach can in her crown, which she gives to Popeye. Popeye breaks free of the cage and has a fierce battle with the whole tribe. Popeye releases a bound Olive by twirling her around while singing, "The Goon is defeated cause my spinach I eat-ed, I'm Popeye the Sailor Man."

Insultin' the Sultan (1960)

The cartoon begins with an argument between Popeye and Olive Oyl. The sailor yells, "Oh yeah, you wimmin' are as stubborn as a mule." Olive kicks Popeye out of her house, and he flies to Algiers. Popeye joins the Foreign Legion and ends up peeling onions. A nearby sultan is looking for his 75th wife and is shown a photo of Olive in a one-piece striped bathing suit. "Wowee, now she is different!" the Sultan exclaims. He orders for Olive to be brought to him via a magic carpet. While marching in the desert, Popeye sees Olive on the carpet and follows her to the Sultan's palace. Popeye is captured, and Olive begs the Sultan to let him go. He says to Olive, "If your boyfriend can defeat my champion wrestler, I shall set you both free." Popeye is getting beaten up by a huge monstrous brute. The fight is making the Sultan hungry. A bowl of spinach is brought out, and Olive says, "I'll take that spinach," and she feeds some to Popeye. The sailor defeats his opponent, and he and Olive sail off on a magic carpet. While flying home, Olive says to Popeye, "I'm sorry I quarreled with you.

I'll never do it again." Popeye replies, "I forgives ya, Olive." Olive comes back with, "Huh, whattya mean you forgive me…you started it!" The cartoon ends with the pair arguing once again.

Dog-Gone-Dog Catcher (1960)

Olive Oyl receives a package containing a brown and black dog who she names Zsa-Zsa. Olive lets the dog go out and play. Brutus, the dog catcher, is nearby singing, "Oh, it's such a lovely day, the air is full of smog. It's such a perfect day to catch myself a dog," Brutus snares Zsa-Zsa in a net with Popeye in pursuit. Popeye decides, "The best way to catch a dog napper is to be a dog!" The sailor puts on a dog costume, and Olive says, "Oh, Popeye, you look ten years younger." Popeye, the dog, is captured by Brutus and tossed in the pound with Zsa-Zsa. Popeye decides to bust out of the pound and pulls out "spinach-flavored dog biscuits." Popeye and Zsa-Zsa get away in Brutus's truck but are stopped by a policeman. Upon seeing a dog driving the car, the policeman zooms away on his cycle, crashing into Brutus! The policeman says to Brutus, "That dog couldn't have talked?" Brutus replies, "Of course not! Animals don't talk!" A rabbit pops up out of the ground and says, "I never heard of anything so preposterous!" Popeye sings, "I saved Olive's poodle because I used me noodle, I'm Popeye the Sailor Man." Although the animation is credited to Halas and Batchelor, it is different from their other films. It's not bad, just different.

Matinee Idol Popeye (1960)

Olive Oyl is playing Cleopatra and Popeye, Marc Antony in Brutus's movie. "Such acting, rotten! Popeye, you are a ham!" the disgusted director says to the one-eyed performer. Brutus wants to be Olive's leading man and tries to get Popeye killed. The director wants Popeye to prove his bravery by putting his head in a lion's mouth. As Popeye puts in his head, he mutters, "I feels like a Peeping Tom." The lion's jaws close tight, but Popeye frees himself by using smoke from his pipe. After a couple more failed attempts, Brutus says, "Now you will be Hercules at the temple. Popeye, make like you are pushing the temple apart." Popeye struggles to push while Brutus uses a hammer to make the temple fall on him. Under the debris, Popeye sees his spinach can, eats the contents, and punches himself out of the damaged temple. The pieces of the temple become a Sphinx, which looks like Popeye. Brutus says to Olive, "Now I'm your leading man." One punch from Popeye puts an end to the director's plans. A fun cartoon with excellent animation by Halas amd Batchelor.

Beaver or Not (1960)

Popeye is paddling in a canoe and says, "There just ain't nothing as relaxin' as a vacation in the wild north woods." Popeye decides to go swimming in the river only to find it blocked up by a beaver dam. After futile attempts to get rid of the barrier, Popeye says, "There ain't but one thing ta do, and I'm going to do it." He pulls out a can of spinach, and his muscles turn into buzz-saws. Popeye lifts the dam and says, "Ah, now I can enjoy me rushin' mountain stream again." The beavers, in awe over Popeye's sudden strength, see the empty can of spinach, and one says, "He ate some of this stuff, and wow!" The beavers discover another can of spinach and eat the vegetable themselves. They chow down on the legs of Popeye's cabin, causing it to break loose and collapse in the river. The beavers have created a new dam and dive into the river. One beaver says to Popeye, "C'mon in, mister; this is fun." Popeye replies, "If ya cants beats 'em, joins 'em." The sailor dives into the river and swims along with the beavers. The animation in this cartoon is not as simplistic as others from Gene Deitch's studio. The characters move more freely, although seeing Popeye's two opened eyes can be a bit distracting.

Partial Post (1960)

A spaceship arrives on earth, and a creature resembling a mailbox eats a fire hydrant. Popeye takes a walk to mail a birthday card to Olive Oyl. Unfortunately, he puts the card in the mailbox, which is the space creature. The creature spits out the card, and Popeye remarks, "It must have slipped out." Popeye puts the card back in the box, which keeps spitting it out. Popeye finally gets it in the mailbox and sees Olive, who shows him a rose she received. Olive explains, "An unknown admirer sent it to me for my birthday."

While Olive and Popeye discuss the rose, the mailbox settles near her house. Olive puts the plant on her windowsill, and the creature sucks it in. Then it really turns on the power, and Olive is nearly drawn inside. While Olive hangs on to a tree, the menace sucks Popeye inside of it. Olive exclaims, "Oh, Popeye! It got you!" She chases after the mailbox, but Popeye manages to get out of it and give Olive back her flower. The alien menace draws Popeye back inside and stops in front of a fruit and vegetable store. Popeye says, "*Hmm*...I smell spinach. Me favorite fruit!" Popeye bursts out of the creature and pounds him.

The alien falls back into its spacecraft. Before the creature takes off, it spits out Popeye's card to Olive, which she reads out loud, "Roses is red, violets is blue, sugar is sweet, like I am on you." Olive smooches Popeye saying, "Now this is from a known admirer." An exciting premise marred by some animation goofs. After Popeye and Olive are outside, she goes back to look at her rose on the windowsill. The outside backdrop suddenly becomes an indoor one. The card Popeye gives Olive goes through a few changes. At the beginning of the cartoon, it merely has the name "Olive" written on the front. Near the end of the film, when it's on the ground, it reads "Olive Oil." When Olive picks it up, a second later, the envelope reads "Olive Oyl".

Voice From the Deep or *See Here Sea Hag* (1961)

Popeye receives a phone call from King Knuckle-Bone of Phony Island. The King is in trouble, and Popeye takes a plane to his island. The crying King tells the sailor a volcano told his people to leave the island. Popeye laughs at the thought of this until he hears a menacing voice from the volcano. "You have until midnight to get off the island," the voice tells the King and Popeye. Inside the volcano, The Sea Hag sits near a radio saying, "My special volcano broadcasts have scared all the phony-islanders away. And by midnight, the whole island will be mine. I'll turn it into my Sea Hag resort. A vacation paradise for villains." Popeye finds himself inside the volcano using his parachute to float out with the aid of "natural hot-air." The sailor sees The Sea Hag, her vulture, and the King in a rowboat. She plans to deposit him in the middle of the ocean. Popeye eats some phony-island spinach and rescues the King. The Sea Hag and her vulture head back to the volcano with Popeye right behind her. Once Popeye enters the volcano, The Sea Hag is heard saying, "No! Please! Yow! No! No! No! We give up!" The witch is tied up by the radio, and she broadcasts, "This is your friendly volcano inviting all you phony islanders back, please." The King's people return to the island. A big feast is held while The Sea Hag and her vulture wash the dishes.

The Billionaire (1961)

Popeye is a multi-millionaire and, as the narrator says, "Every so often would call one of his friends and given him a million dollars." However, whoever gets the money has to spend it on a good cause. Olive Oyl buys a beauty salon to make herself, "The most beautiful woman in the world." Olive hopes this will get Popeye to marry her. Wimpy uses his money to buy lots of cows. The moocher says to Popeye, "I have purchased my own hamburger farm. Thanks to you, I will always have plenty of fresh hamburgers." But Wimpy can't bring himself to hurt the cows when he looks into their trusting brown eyes. Swee'pea offers Popeye one of his famous candy bars, but it has a bite in it. The lad explains he personally tests every candy bar which comes out of his factory. Brutus, decked out in a top hat and tuxedo, told Popeye his idea. Popeye thinks he's the only one to spend his money wisely until Brutus informs him he ordered all the spinach farms to be plowed under. The brute says to Popeye, "There ain't none left nowhere, but I still got plenty of your money left. Maybe you'd like some lettuce." He shoves the money into Popeye's mouth, who swallows it. Popeye's face glows, and he exclaims, "It's spinach! That money was printed with green spinach ink." Popeye punches Brutus, who becomes a stack of change!

Olive comes out of the beauty salon and shows off her new look to Popeye. She has a new face, blonde hair, and a bust. Popeye laughs so hard at Olive that she becomes angry, and her new look breaks off. The sailor comforts her by saying, "Don't be sads, Olive, I likes ya ugly." Wimpy, Olive, Brutus, and Swee'pea all ask for another million dollars from Popeye. However, after seeing what it did to all of them, he donates his remaining money to the "sailor's relief." Excellent animation by Halas and Batchelor highlights a witty story based upon *The Millionaire* television series.

Weight For Me (1961)

Popeye and Brutus have been at sea for six months and look forward to seeing Olive Oyl. An overweight Olive opens the door explaining, "I got so lonely while you boys were away, I just started eating like a horse." Popeye offers to buy a half a dozen reducing machines, but Brutus likes her new look. He says, "The nerve of that little runt criticizing your pretty figure that way." Popeye tries to get Olive to exercise, but Brutus upsets his weight-reducing efforts. At Olive's house, Popeye tries to get her to use the reducing equipment. A furious Brutus sticks Popeye's head between a machine, saying, "How about reducing your head a little, chum." The device squishes Popeye's cheeks while he moves up and down. This motion causes his spinach can to appear, and Popeye eats the contents. Popeye's muscles spin in rapid motion, and he turns Brutus paper-thin, who floats away from Olive. He then turns his muscles on Olive, which returns her slim figure. Popeye and Olive look over at Brutus on a reducing machine reading a book titled "How to Reduce." Brutus says to the audience, "If ya can't beat 'em join 'em." The trio burst out laughing at the cartoon's conclusion. A funny, imaginative premise with excellent animation by Halas and Batchelor.

Model Muddle (1961)

Olive Oyl says to Popeye, "I've got a surprise for you, Popeye. I'm taking you to an art museum. It's about time you got some culture." Inside the museum, Popeye wants to know what a bathtub is doing there. Olive corrects him and says it's a piece of modern sculpture. Two men carry out the piece, and one says, "C'mon Pete, let's get that bathtub outta here before someone thinks it's a piece of modern sculpture." The trip inspires Popeye to become an artist, and he begins creating a sculpture of Olive. Brutus tries to sabotage the project by making a mess of Popeye's piece, but Olive calls it "real modern art." Popeye and Brutus fight until the sailor reaches for a painting he finished. The image is a can of spinach which Popeye pulls out of the canvas and says, "Lucky I was out-a green paint when I painted this picture and had to use real spinach!" He picks up Brutus and uses him as a chisel to create a sculpture of Olive's head. Olive calls Popeye's sculpture, "the real me" while Brutus emerges from the rubble with two black eyes. A funny, satirical look at modern art featuring great animation by Halas and Batchelor.

Which is Witch (1961)

Popeye and Olive Oyl sail to The Sea Hag's island thinking they're going to surprise her, but she knows they're coming. The witch has created a robot Olive and says, "Popeye will follow Olive anywhere. Go get him." The Sea Hag's Goons capture the real Olive while the robot double takes her place. The robot leads Popeye into a trap, and the sailor is jailed. The Sea Hag says to Popeye, "Now that I've got you here, I can go out and do a little honest pirate work." The robot Olive walks past the jailed sailor, and he says, "Don't you remembers your ol' sweetie Popeye?" Those words cause the robot to fall in love with Popeye, and she uses her strength to break him out of jail. Unfortunately, The Sea Hag's Goon squad overcomes Popeye. Popeye and the real Olive end up in a cell. The robot Olive brings Popeye his spinach, and he trounces the Goons. The Sea Hag, a trio of Goons and vulture, are in a rowboat, but Popeye speeds in front of the craft. With his leg he pushes the boat back into The Sea Hag's mountain lair with a crash! In the process of defeating the witch, Popeye lost his pipe, which the robot Olive is smoking. The disgusted witch says, "Nah, foiled again and all on account of you and stop smoking that stupid pipe!" An amusing story highlighted by excellent animation by Halas and Batchelor.

Disguise the Limit (1961)

Olive Oyl is the secretary to both the Popeye and Brutus Detective agencies. She gets a call from the city zoo saying a gorilla has escaped. Brutus dons a gorilla disguise and says to Olive, "I'm gonna trap that gorilla with this gorilla disguise, and after I collect that big reward, you'll be working for me as my private secretary." Olive suggests to Popeye he wears a female gorilla disguise which includes perfume and a bonnet. They speed off to the zoo on a scooter. The real gorilla grabs Olive but takes a whiff of Popeye's scent and falls in love. The gorilla keeps smooching Popeye, and he remarks, "My gorsh he loves me." Popeye knocks out the beast and puts him back in his cage. Brutus sees Popeye and thinks he's the real gorilla. Brutus knocks Popeye's bonnet off, which ends up on the jailed gorilla's head. Olive thinks the gorilla wearing the bonnet is Popeye and frees him. Popeye and Brutus brawl until both their headpieces pop off. Popeye says, "This monkey looks familiar." Brutus decks Popeye, and he eats his spinach. Olive is held tight by the gorilla while Brutus slugs it out with the beast. Popeye knocks out both the gorilla and his rival. Brutus ends up in a reptile's cage. Popeye and Olive hurry away, and the sailor sings, "There's lots more surprises when I wear disguises, I'm Popeye the Sailor Man." Colorful animation highlights a fast-paced story.

Spoil Sport (1961)

Olive Oyl is reading the latest movie star magazine when she gets a phone call from Popeye. Popeye says, "Olive, how would you like to go for a ride with me on me new scooter?" Naturally, Olive thinks it's a sports car and says, "I've got to get dressed." We get a glimpse of the dresses in Olive's closet, and they're all the same outfit. When Olive discovers Popeye is driving a scooter, she tells him to "Get lost." Brutus shows up in his sports car, and Olive goes off with him. Brutus and Olive drive along a mountainside with a sign saying: Danger Curves Ahead! Brutus acts fearless while Olive becomes terrified. Olive covers Brutus's eyes, and his car ends up on a rock formation. Popeye uses a piece of fence to rescue the pair. Brutus knocks Popeye in the air and gets away on the sailor's scooter. Under Popeye's hat is his can of spinach, and he gobbles up the vegetable. Popeye lands in Brutus's sports car and catches up to the brute. He smacks Brutus into the sports car. He and Olive scoot along together, and the sailor sings, "There's nothing as cuter than you on me scooter, I'm Popeye the Sailor Man." A cute cartoon.

Have Time Will Travel (1961)

Olive Oyl sends Popeye to get some firewood, and he ends up with a do-it-yourself time machine. Popeye builds what's in the box, and Olive says, "Okay, genius, zip me to Florida." Popeye pulls a lever, and they end up in prehistoric times. They encounter a dinosaur with a thorn in its foot. Popeye pulls out the thorn and befriends the creature. Popeye calls him Oscar, and when Olive asks why he replies, "He reminds me of a guy I know in Brooklyn." Popeye and Olive are captured by King Rock Head and his tribe. The King wants Olive to be his queen. She agrees, but it's all a ruse to get close to a bound Popeye and show him what's growing nearby. Popeye takes a look and says, "Yahoo! Spinach, acres, and acres of 'em." Popeye asks for spinach as a last request, and the King says, "Oh dinosaur cabbage, cheap stuff, give you plenty." Popeye eats the spinach and flattens the King and his tribe by using the tree he's bound to as a weapon. Oscar, the dinosaur, picks up Popeye and Olive and leads them to the time machine. Popeye pulls the level and they're back home, but some of the tribe's spears accompany them. Olive uses the spears to create a fire, remarking, "Those prehistoric weapons certainly burn well." This exciting cartoon has a unique animation style that was well executed.

Intellectual Interlude (1962)

Popeye and Olive Oyl leave a movie theatre after watching the film "Sophisticated Lady". The film charmed Olive so much she and Popeye attend an adult education class. Popeye is given a dunce cap to wear by the teacher after failing to answer a simple math question. A scientist is concocting a formula using intellectual spinach, which he gives Popeye to drink. Popeye says, "Boy, that's some spinach!" The scientist asks him complex questions, which the sailor answers correctly. The *Daily Star* newspaper features Popeye's photo with the caption, "Scientist Discovers Mental Giant." Another paper reads, "Popeye Solves Problem of Interplanetary Travel while another state, "Popeye Controls Weather." Foreign agents lasso Popeye during a parade in his honor. They threaten Popeye to join up with them. If he doesn't, they will toss a bound Olive over a cliff. Popeye gets his spinach and pounds the agents into a wall. However, the criminals also have a hulking brute on their side. Popeye's fist to his face means nothing to the monstrous criminal. Popeye is punched towards the sky, heading for the ground. Olive screams in horror, but she finds herself in the adult education classroom along with a woken Popeye. They both had the same nightmare! Before leaving, Popeye says to his condescending teacher, "If a gang of foreign spies was about to throw you over a cliff, what would ya do?" The teacher replies, "Why, I don't know." Popeye quips while putting a dunce cap on her head, "Eats a can of a spinach." Like *Have Time Will Travel*, this cartoon has a unique animation style making the story more enjoyable.

Canine Caprice (1962)

Popeye is feeding squirrels in the park. A man sleeps next to him with a dog on his lap. The dog says to the sailor, "I see you have a deep affection for animals." Popeye believes the dog can talk and buys him from the man for twenty-five dollars. Once Popeye is out of sight, the man takes the money and says, "He sure fell for my ventriloquist act. Wait till he tries to make that dog talk." However, the dog can actually talk, calling himself Roger. Popeye shows Olive Oyl the dog, who won't speak to her. After Roger begins chomping on Olive's T-bone steak, she puts him in her yard. Roger spies Olive inviting a man into her home, and remarks, "How'd ya like that. No sooner than Popeye leaves, another guy shows up." Roger sees Olive and the man at a piano and calls Popeye. The angry sailor throws the man out of Olive's house. Olive screams, "That was my piano teacher!"

Roger is watching a prize fight on Popeye's television when the picture goes out. He drags Popeye to the actual battle in the arena. Roger hurls insults at the fighters who they think are coming from Popeye. The two fighters bop Popeye around the boxing ring, and the sailor says, "Hey Roger! Throws me a can of…spinach!" Roger throws the can at Popeye, who beats up the boxers. Popeye is then given a loving cup and declared, "The new amateur champion of the world." Popeye stuffs Roger in the loving cup and refuses to let him out until Roger explains what happened to Olive. Roger does just that and is thrown out of the house. The dog says to the audience, "You wanna know something. I'll let you in on a big secret. All dogs can talk, but they're smart. Look what happened to me when I opened my trap. From now on, I'm going to be a plain, dumb four-legged animal like the rest of them. Boy, I've had it — ARF! ARF! ARF! ARF!" A cute cartoon.

Roger (1962)

A knock is heard at the door, and when Popeye opens it, he sees Roger the Talking Dog. Roger says to Popeye and Olive Oyl, "If you'll take me back, I'll promise never to talk again except to you and Popeye." Popeye shakes his paw, and they agree. The sailor sends Roger to the store with a note for the proprietor. Along the way to the store, Roger overhears three criminals planning to rob Tiff's jewelry store. One of the crooks sees Roger and yells, "What are you lookin' at, ya little mutt...scram!" He kicks Roger, who goes running to Popeye. Roger and Popeye go to the Chief of Police, but the dog refuses to talk. The Chief tosses the pair out of his office. When Popeye asks Roger why he didn't speak up, the dog replies, "I promised I'd never talk to anyone else again, and when Roger makes a promise, it's a promise, so help me!" Popeye attempts to stop the criminals as they get away, but the police grab him thinking he's one of the crooks. Roger tells Olive what happened, and she confronts the criminals saying, "You! You! Aren't you ashamed of yourselves robbing a jewelry store and sending an innocent man to jail. Now you march right down to the police station and tell them exactly what happened." The crooks kidnap Olive and tie her up at the jewelry store. Turns out the owner, Mr. Tiff, is in on the scheme. Roger says, "He robbed his own store to collect the insurance money. This is a job for Popeye and his spinach!" Roger throws a can of spinach to Popeye, who is in jail. The sailor busts through the wall and beats up the gang. The police arrive, and the Chief says to Mr. Tiff, "Well, if it isn't Slippery Sam and his two cronies. The old insurance racket, eh Mr. Tiff? Hiring these crooks to rob your jewelry store." When the Police Chief asks Popeye how he knew about all of this, he explains Roger told him everything. Roger barks at the Chief. The Gene Deitch cartoons are known for their haunting musical scores, which in this case, enhances the cartoon.

Tooth Be Or Not Tooth Be (1962)

Popeye leaves a teething Swee'pea in Poopdeck Pappy's care. The tyke's teething becomes uncontrollable, so Pappy takes him to the dentist. The dentist says to Swee'pea, "Now, young fellow, open wide and let's see if that first tooth is about to come THROUGH!" Swee'pea chomps on the dentist's finger! The dentist tells Swee'pea when his tooth comes through to "brush your teeth twice daily and see your dentist twice yearly." At home, Pappy tells Swee'pea, who is teething on a tire, about the time he won a teeth contest. His picture was in the paper, which caught the attention of The Sea Hag. The witch says, "Bah, why should he have all those lovely teeth when I have none!" She orders her vulture to kidnap a sleeping Pappy. The ol' sailor wakes to find himself tied up with The Sea Hag brushing his teeth! Pappy asks her what she wants with him. The Sea Hag replies, "I don't want you, dearie, just those lovely teeth!" Pappy uses his choppers to eat through the ropes and dives into the ocean. The Sea Hag's vulture recaptures him, and he's chained to a wall. The Hag approaches Pappy with a big pair of pliers to yank out his teeth. Pappy chomps on the pliers and spits the parts back at The Sea Hag. He then beats up her vulture, who flies him home. His motto to Swee'pea is, "If you always takes care of yer teeth, yer teeth will always takes cares of you." Popeye comes home and finds a sleeping Pappy with Swee'pea brushing his first tooth. Popeye sings, "They'll last to the finich if he eats his spinach and brushes them twice a day." Despite Pappy's pipe appearing and quickly disappearing in a few scenes, this is a charming educational cartoon.

Cartoons Produced by Gerald Ray

PRODUCTION: Gerald Ray. DIRECTION: Bob Bemiller. LAYOUT: Henry Lee. BACKGROUND: Dave Weidman. EDITOR: Norm Vizents. ANIMATION: Izzy Ellis, Sam Kai, Casey Onaitus, Bill Higgins, John Garling, Ray Young, Barney Posner & Bud Partch.

Where There's A Will (1960)

Popeye receives a phone call from Clarence Marrow, the lawyer. He informs Popeye that both he and Brutus were mentioned in ol' Barnacle Bilges' will. The lawyer is reading the will at noon, and whoever is not present will be cut off without a cent. Brutus tries to prevent Popeye from being at the reading. The bully tosses dynamite in the hood of the sailor's car. The car develops a flat tire, and Popeye decides to take a taxi. When Brutus opens the hood of the car, it explodes! The brute says, "Just like I thought, a real good job." Brutus pretends to be the lawyer's butler to keep Popeye away. He slaps a "Closed for Business" sign on the front door. Popeye manages to make it in time for the reading, sitting next to an angry Brutus! The lawyer reads from the will, and the swabs learn they're left with "one can of spinach!" This infuriates Brutus, who grabs Popeye by the throat and tosses him into a large clock. As Popeye falls to the ground, Brutus throws the spinach can in his direction. As the bearded bully walks away, the spinach theme plays. Brutus looks at the viewers and says, "Whoops! I shouldn't have done that!" Popeye squashes Brutus into a ball and tosses him out of the room. Clarence Marrow then reveals the sailors were also left ten thousand dollars cash. Since Brutus isn't around, Popeye gets the money which he will "give to the poor little orphans." Brutus's head emerges from an outdoor clock Popeye tossed him into and mutters, "Coo-Coo, Coo-Coo." Simplistic animation style which doesn't detract from an entertaining story.

Take It Easel (1960)

Popeye and Brutus are painters who decide to compete for the best original flower painting. The cash prize is one thousand dollars. The two end up in the desert, searching for a flower to paint. Brutus tries a few tricks to stop Popeye, including using a car's motor to create a sand storm. Covered in sand, Popeye remarks, "Hey Brutus, where wuz you when the sand storm hit?" Brutus ends up painting train tracks, and he ties Popeye to them. The bound painter says to Brutus, "That ain't fair, how kin I paints wit' me hands tied!" Brutus removes Popeye's pipe, substituting it for a paint brush, yelling, "Use your big mouth." A real train comes zooming towards Popeye, who says, "If that's a train, then this is a can of spinach!" Popeye paints a can and eats the contents. He then lifts the train tracks, so the locomotive is after Brutus. Popeye picks up his blank canvas so the speeding train, along with a terrified Brutus, crashes into it. Popeye's painting of a dazed Brutus nibbling on a flower wins first prize. Popeye sings, "I winned at the finich 'cause I painted me spinach, I'm Popeye the Sailor Man."

I Bin Sculped (1960)

Olive Oyl is in her statue studio chiseling out a "model wanted sign". Popeye and Brutus see the sign and assume Olive wants a strong man. Olive informs them, "I don't want a strong man; I want a weak one. I'm doing a statue called "Pooped", and the model I want has to be run down and beat up." Popeye and Brutus attempt various ways to get beat up. Popeye tries to be flattened by a steam roller, Brutus dives off a building, Popeye paints himself red to get a bull to trounce him. Each time they fail until Brutus jumps out of an airplane. Popeye tries to catch Brutus, who lands right on top of him. This commotion happens in front of Olive's studio, and she sees the injured Brutus. Olive beams saying, "Oh Brutus, what a gorgeous mess! I want you to be my model." Suddenly Popeye's arm holding a can of spinach appears next to Brutus's mouth. The brute is fed the spinach, and he can't contain his strength. Brutus beats up Popeye while yelling, "I can't stop myself." Olive is seen chiseling out her "Pooped" statue using Popeye as the model. The injured sailor sings, "I was weak at the finich, I gave Brutus me spinach, I'm Poop-eye the Sailor Man." This cartoon is a remake of two theatrical films, *Hospitaliky* (1937) and *For Better or Nurse* (1945).

Fleas a Crowd (1960)

At the opening scene, a sign on a building reads, *Popeye in Thimble Theatre*. Inside, Popeye is entertaining the audience with his two wonder fleas. Brutus and Olive Oyl are in the audience. Olive thinks Popeye is so clever to have trained them. Brutus mutters, "Maybe I can fix it, so Popeye doesn't seem as clever as she thinks he is…eh, I think I understand what I mean." Brutus winds up a mechanical dog which Popeye's fleas hop on. "I've been flea napped!" the sailor yells, and he dashes after the dog. Popeye ends up in a dog catchers' truck and eventually at the zoo. Popeye sees the dog in a gorilla cage and bops the massive beast into three monkeys. The sailor then makes a fast get-a-away. Back on-stage, Popeye sees his two fleas all run down. He says, "Oh my gorsh! All that running around must have given them a bad case of pooped-i-t-is." Brutus is happy and says to Olive, "Good, now we can go home!" Popeye gives the insects some spinach which revives the pair. The bearded brute says, "Oh yeah, well, this time I'll take care of those fleas once and for all." Popeye starts to sing a song: "They were strong at the…" Brutus arrives on stage, and Popeye tells his fleas, "Sic 'im boys." The bully yells in pain while Popeye sings, "They were strong at the finich 'cause they ate the spinach of Popeye the Sailor Man."

Popeye's Junior Headache (1960)

Popeye is on the phone with Olive Oyl and says to her, "Aw have a heart, Olive. I've been working three days and night without sleep." Olive insists Popeye babysit her bratty pint-sized niece, Deezil, while she goes to the beauty parlor. Popeye goes to Olive's house, and when he opens the door, a water bucket, set up by Deezil, falls on his head. Popeye looks at the audience and says, "Oh, looks like it's gonna be one of those days." Deezil burns Popeye with a magnifying glass while he's reading a story to her. Then she uses Popeye as a horse to gallop around the house. Deezil ties Popeye up and brands his behind. Disgusted, Popeye says, "Things has gone far as they can go, Olive or no Olive." Popeye makes his way to the kitchen and eats what he thinks is a can of spinach. Deezil says, "That wasn't spinach, Uncle Popeye, 'cause I changed all the labels of the cans." When Popeye asks, "Where's me, spinach?" Deezil says, "I ate it… see!" The tyke's arm goes into a swinging motion! The scared Deezil asks Popeye what she should do. The sailor says, "You'll find out. I means, I'll find out!" She beats up Popeye and dresses him in woman's clothes. Deezil flops a mop on his head. Olive comes home from the beauty parlor with a new hair-do which looks precisely like the mop on Popeye's head.

Olive is insulted and clobbers Popeye with a flower pot. The injured sailor ends up in a hospital bed with his leg in an overhead cast. Popeye thinks he can finally get some shut-eye when Olive and Deezil visit. The pint-sized brat shoots an arrow causing a sandbag to hit Popeye on the head. Deezil sings, "Popeye is finched 'cause I ate the spinach for Popeye the Sailor Man." She then shoots two more arrows which land on Popeye's pipe. The pipe lets out two puffs of smoke. This cartoon is reminiscent of the theatrical films where an insect or animal gets the better of Popeye.

Egypt Us (1960)

Popeye, Olive Oyl, and Wimpy are traveling to Coney Island but end up in Egypt. Their little car overheats, and Olive decides to go swimming. Wimpy decides to cook up some hamburgers. Olive ends up missing, and Popeye says to Wimpy, "Now waits a second, ya gotta promises not ta eat until me and Olive gets back!" Wimpy responds, "Kind sir, that was the furriest thing from my mind." Popeye quips back, "Just so long it's the furriest thing from yer mouth." Popeye locates Olive, who has been chosen to be a high priestess of an Egyptian tribe. While trying to save Olive, Popeye keeps running back to Wimpy. Wimpy says, "Do not concern yourself, sir; I have a will of iron." Popeye runs back to Olive to see her suspended upside down with a fire underneath. When Popeye asks what's going on, one of the tribe members replies in gibberish. Popeye says to the audience, "What this show needs is some English subtitles." The nonsense in the tribe member's speech balloon is suddenly translated. Popeye reads what's in the balloon: "We are about to make a perfectly normal routine human sacrifice…nosy!" Popeye is dropped in an alligator pit and pulls out his spinach. He becomes a bowling ball and flattens the tribe. Popeye starts to sing, "I'm strong to the finich 'cause I eats me…oh my gorsh…Wimpy…c'mon, I just hopes we're not to…uh-oh!" Popeye and Olive arrive to see Wimpy has eaten the hamburgers, and he has an enormous stomach. Wimpy sings, "It's bad to be tardy to a hamburger party, says Wimpy the burger man." Two of his shirt buttons pop off! A delightful cartoon.

The Big Sneeze (1960)

Popeye, Olive Oyl, Swee'pea, and their dog, Bernie, are skiing in the French Alps. Olive is wearing a raccoon coat which suddenly gets torn off! She wails, "Oh! My coat! My brand-new beautiful raccoon coat is gone!" Olive follows a trail of footsteps and discovers a snow-covered shelter. She is captured by the man who stole her raccoon coat along with Popeye and

Swee'pea. Bernie waits outside for the trio while their kidnapper reveals himself as "Kasimoto, the half-back of Notre Dame." He refuses to give back Olive's coat explaining, "This is the first time I have been warm in years." Popeye asks him why he doesn't light a fire.

Kasimoto responds, "Every time I do, the fire melts the roof, which puts out the fire. Then, I catch cold and sneeze, which makes the avalanche, and I am buried until the spring thaw. As I'm the official echo, this is disaster!" Popeye asks him if he's the echo of the mountains? Kasimoto replies, "Always Yoo-Hoo and Hello! Today it was even I'm Popeye the Sailor Man, poop, poop. What a way to make a living." Popeye sneezes inside the snow-filled lair, which causes an avalanche. Bernie digs his way through the snow and sees everyone frozen solid. The dog feeds spinach to Popeye, who breaks free of the ice. The sailor rescues Olive, Swee'pea, and Kasimoto. Olive beats up the raccoon coat stealer who cries, "Now I will never get warm again!" Olive whispers in Bernie's ear, and the dog dashes off and brings back spinach. Kasimoto pours the vegetable down his throat. Popeye sings, "You'll be warm at the finich eatin' yer spinach, says Popeye the Sailor Man."

The Last Resort (1960)

At Creep Cod Inn, The Sea Hag and Toar are cranking out fake money. The Sea Hag explains to Toar, "These are the best three-dollar bills on the market!" Looking for a beach resort Popeye, Olive Oyl, and Wimpy stumble upon The Sea Hag's hideout. The ol' witch has to get rid of them before they discover what's going on. Popeye and Olive go to register at the Inn. The sailor says, "Looks like the kinda place where ya gets spooked before ya gets spooken to." The Sea Hag and Toar are unsuccessful in getting rid of the trio. Popeye and Olive end up in chains. The sailor says to the ol' witch, "Sea Hag! I might of known you wuz behind that funny money!" The Sea Hag explains she and Toar are ready to blow their hideout, placing a bomb on Popeye's head.

The witch lights the fuse and Olive yells if the bomb goes off, it will make hamburger out of them. The word hamburger reminds Popeye of Wimpy. Wimpy explains he's been in the kitchen preparing a small snack before dinner. The rotund cook says, "I have bagel burger, Spumoni burger, burger-burger, spinach burger, Ingrid burger..." Popeye yells, "Spinach burger, quick let me have it." Popeye eats the burger and busts out of his chains. He tosses the bomb outside, and it lands in the departing Toar's hands. While The Sea Hag counts down to the explosion, the bomb goes off. Olive says, "Now I'll direct us to Yucca Flats. You know I've always wanted to see the atomic proving grounds." Upon hearing this, Popeye asks Wimpy for another spinach burger and sings, "At home or vacation spinach is me salvation, says Popeye the Sailor Man." E.C. Segar's Toar is a welcome addition to this cartoon — although Toar is played more for laughs than the monstrous figure he was in the comic strip.

Jeopardy Sheriff (1960)

Poopdeck Pappy tells Swee'pea a story about how he stopped cattle rustlers as "Dead-eye Pappy." Pappy tells the lad, "They all knew I was a crack-pot, *er* — I mean, crack-shot." Popeye is angry at his Pappy for telling the lad "whoppers." The older man's feelings are hurt, and he leaves. Popeye watches television and hears his father is attempting to stop a bank hold-up. Pappy hitches a ride to the criminals' hideout and gets captured. One of the criminals asks, "Where'd this ol' goat come from?" Another criminal replies, "I don't know, chief; he'd come bustin' in saying we was all under arrest!" Popeye arrives, and the Chief says, "Rush him, boys, there's only one of him and thirty of us!" The sailor goes for his spinach but can't find it. The Chief says, "Pocket pick-it Peter took care of that." Popeye is tied up, but Pappy manages to pull out one of the criminals' guns. He shoots a bullet that goes wild but manages to pop open the can of spinach. The can's contents end up in Pappy's mouth. Fortified with strength, he captures the entire criminal gang. Popeye says to his father, "Pappy, that was the bravest thing I ever seen." The ol' man continues telling whoppers, but this time to both Swee'pea and Popeye. Pappy sings, "I may tell a whopper, but I am the popper of Popeye the Sailor Man." A good cartoon allowing the spotlight to shine on Poopdeck Pappy.

Baby Phase (1960)

Swee'pea gets a book in the mail titled "How to Juggle by Dexter Dexterity." The tyke juggles household objects on the roof, and Popeye punishes him. The sailor dreams Swee'pea is the world's greatest juggler. Popeye says, "He runned away and joined the circus 'cause I was so mean." Popeye rescues Swee'pea, juggling in a cage full of lions but learns he can't take the lad home. The sailor exclaims, "Holy smokes! Swee'pea, ya signed a ninety-nine-year contract." The ring announcer says to the crowd, "Swee'pea is gonna dive off of dat platform, juggling in the air all the way down and land in dis' here wet cloth." Swee'pea dives off the platform with Popeye right behind him. The sailor says, "Me spinach, it's our only chance." Popeye loses his grip on the can of spinach and wakes up from the dream. Popeye rushes in to see Swee'pea and sings, "He'll juggle his spinach and fights to the finich, says Popeye the Sailor Man." A fun cartoon.

Cartoons Produced and Directed by Jack Kinney

CHECKING: Christine Decker, Moley McColley, Evelyn Sherwood, Barbara Ruiz, Pat Helmuth, Paul Marron, Buf Nerbouig, Ruth Tompson, and Jane Philippi. FILM EDITORS: Joe Siracusa, Cliff Millsap, and Roger Donley. CAMERA: Jack Eckes, Bill Kotler and Jack Buehre. INK AND PAINT: Vera McKinney. SOUND: Ryder Sound Services and Marne Fallis. BACKGROUNDS: Raymond Jacobs, Boris Gorelick, Vern Jorgensen, Jules Engel, Connie Matthews, Peggy Morrow, Ervin L. Kaplan, and Rosemary O'Connor. MUSIC: Ken Lowman. Layouts: Raymond Jacobs, Noel Tucker, Ken Hultgren, Robert Givens, Jerry Nevius, and Bruce Bushman. STORIES: Dick Kinney, Joe Grant, Al Bertino, Raymond Jacobs, Jack Kinney, Jack Miller, Nick George, Ed Nofziger, Noel Tucker, Wesley Bennett, Warren Bennett, Walter Schmidt, Joe Siracusa, Ken Hultgren, Osmond Evans, Dennis Fraser, Rosemary O'Connor, Carol Beers, Tony Benedict, Jim Rivind, Milt Schaffer, Tom Hix, and Rudy Apodaca. ANIMATION DIRECTORS: Harvey Toombs, Hugh Fraser, Rudy Larriva, Ed Friedman, Eric Cleworth, Bill Keil, Volus Jones, Hal Ambro, Eddie Rehberg, Phil Duncan, Ken Hultgren, Murray McClellan, and Alan Zaslove.

Since the animation in the Jack Kinney Popeye cartoons varies in quality, I have indicated which ones are watchable and others not.

Barbecue for Two (1960)
Popeye sets up a backyard barbecue for himself and Olive Oyl. He notices the absence of flowers and says, "Oh, no flowers fer me sweety. I'll just borrow some from me good neighbor." The angry bearded neighbor growls, "My favorite pet petunias, why I'll…" He flattens Popeye with one blow, but the sailor pops up like an accordion. The neighbor wants to be invited, but Popeye yells back, "It's just for me and me sweetie!" When Popeye puts hamburgers on the grill, it attracts Wimpy. Swee'pea appears and wants to go on a swing. Frustrated, Popeye scoops up the neighbor, Wimpy, and Swee'pea! Olive sees everyone and says, "Oh, a party! I love big parties!"

Popeye gives Wimpy hamburgers and pushes Swee'pea on a swing. Olive says she loves rock and roll music, so the neighbor strums a guitar and sings, "Don't drop no mustard on my clean white shirt, baby, don't drop no mustard on my clean white shirt…" The bearded party-crasher slams Popeye with his guitar. A can of frozen spinach ends up on the sailor's pipe, which he thaws out. Wimpy and Swee'pea see an angry Popeye and quickly leave. The neighbor comes charging after Popeye, who punches him into orbit. Popeye and Olive are finally alone at last! This was one of two pilots for this series and is fast-moving, entertaining with fine animation. It is the only one featuring the comic strip designs of Popeye and Olive.

Battery Up (1960)

An announcer says, "Hello there, ladies and gentleman! Today's the big day of the big ball game for the championship of Meatball Meadows. On this side, we have the boil-maker boys from upper lower street versus Popeye and his pals representing the Spinach Street, A.C." Wimpy is the referee and says, "Play ball!" Popeye is the pitcher, and a baseball smashes right through a television set (which represents the audience watching this cartoon). Popeye appears and says, "Sorry folks, pardon the interruptions. Due to mechanical difficulties…" Wimpy calls Popeye back to the game. Frantically-moving baseballs are tossed towards Popeye, and one flings him into a building called "Sporting Goods and Spinach Store." Popeye eats some spinach and speeds back to the pitching mound. Olive Oyl, who has been cheering on Popeye in the stands, hands her boyfriend baseballs which he tosses at his opponents. Popeye's team is victorious. The sailor and Olive get clonked with a baseball at the cartoon's finish. A fast-paced story with excellent animation.

Deserted Desert (1960)

Popeye is looking for the Lost Dutchman Mine and walks through a hot desert to get there. As Popeye walks, he says, "Oh, them hot desert sands, they is makin' me dogs start ta barkin." The sailor's shoes start barking like a dog. Popeye deals with the residents of a ghost town and desert mirages. Unfortunately, Brutus has also been looking for the mine. The pair collide at the very top of a mountain filled with gold nuggets. Brutus says to Popeye, "Down is the way — out sailor pants," and punches Popeye, who falls to the ground with a thud! Popeye pulls out his spinach while Brutus lets out a victory cry. The energized sailor runs up the mountain and knocks his rival off of it. Popeye tosses the gold nuggets in the air and exclaims, "Eureka, I has found it!" Suddenly he is surrounded by Olive

Oyl, Wimpy, and a U.S. Treasury collector in a helicopter. Popeye says, "Friends, relatives, and taxes!" Fine animation.

Skinned Divers (1960)

Popeye is reading a book, "The Art of Skin Diving," and decides to search for sunken treasure. Brutus has the same idea and paddles his boat to where Popeye is searching. Underneath the water, Popeye reads further instructions which state, "Sixteen paces from the old wreck. Beware of giant clam and octopuses." An octopus grabs Popeye, but the two become friends. Brutus kicks the sea-creature and growls, "One side coo-coo puss, I'm lookin' for gold." Popeye finds the treasure chest, but Brutus knocks him out with an anchor. The brute walks off with Popeye's discovery. The injured treasure hunter is revived by a mermaid and says, "Ya looks jus' like me goil, Olive Oyl." Brutus goes after the mermaid, but Popeye eats some sea spinach. With the octopus's help, Popeye saves the mermaid. The cartoon concludes with the Olive look-a-like serenading Popeye. She plays a harp singing, "My Bonnie lies over the ocean. My Bonnie lies over the sea. Don't bring back! Don't bring back! Don't bring back my Bonnie to me!" Colorful undersea animation.

Popeye's Service Station (1960)

A narrator reads signs on display: "Popeye's Super Duper Service Station. Welcome, free air, free water, free information, free maps, free samples, plus service with a smile." Wimpy drives up on his bicycle, requesting free air. He explains, "For I'm tardy for a free dinner engagement." Popeye mutters, "Ah, he must be president of the freeloader's society." A whiskered man wearing a top hat arrives and says, "Fill her up, my good man, with free water." Popeye ends up giving the man's camel water. Olive Oyl arrives on her scooter requesting a little free service. Brutus drives up and wants a date with Olive. He grabs her and runs over Popeye, who pulls out his spinach. With one punch, he smashes Brutus's vehicle. The sailor propels Brutus and his automobile into the air stuck on a car lift. Popeye keeps sending Brutus, via the car lift, up and down. Olive says to her rescuer, "Oh, Popeye, my free hero! With a smile." She pulls down a sign which reads, "Kisses, $1.00 (Free)." An amusing cartoon with great animation.

Coffee House (1960)

Popeye visits Olive Oyl and discovers her dressed as a beatnik. She says to Popeye, "Enter my pad. Give me the hug, big-brain." Popeye is worried that Olive is sick! Suddenly Brutus drives through on his motorbike. Brutus hugs Olive and says, "Like I digs ya the most, baby." Olive responds with, "You're the coolest, daddy-oh." Brutus and Olive end up at a coffee house full of beatniks. Brutus reads Olive a poem: "Ode to an onion. Oh onion, onion, you are the gone-est. So green yet so honest. Onion, onion-like, I dig you the most-est. Oh, green and lovely hostess. Hip-hip-hip and crazy daisy. Like your breath just leaves me hazy." Popeye sneaks under the couple's table while Brutus recites more of his poem. Brutus bops Popeye, who says, "If ya cants' licks 'em, ya joins 'em." Popeye plays an accordion and dances in the coffee house, yelling, "Re-progressive!" After a few more nonsensical lyrics, Brutus picks Popeye up and throws him across the room. Popeye pulls out a can of cultured spinach, which causes him to dance faster. The coffee house crowd loves the bouncing sailor man and shout, "Cool, cool!" Popeye puts up a sign which reads, "Dance of the pugilist in the arena." Brutus charges at him like a bull, eventually being clobbered by Popeye's fist. Olive praises Popeye for being really cool, and he replies, "Like I am what I am!" This is a funny cartoon parodying beatnik culture at the time with fine animation.

Popeye's Pep-Up Emporium (1960)

This cartoon opens on a television set broadcasting a sign with an announcer saying, "Popeye's Pep-Up Emporium, we fix flats-slats-fats." Instructor Popeye is showing Olive Oyl and Wimpy the proper ways to exercise. Olive's muscles end tied up in knots. Wimpy's exercise is pulling a plate of hamburgers towards him. When Popeye questions his method of keeping in shape, Wimpy reads a sign which says, "Put it on, take it off at the same time." Popeye gives a live television commercial and lifts a weight. A butterfly lands on one side of the weight causing Popeye to drop it through the floor! Brutus emerges from the damaged floor and punches Popeye across the room. A case full of spinach cans falls near Popeye's face. The sailor opens one can, and he eats its contents. Popeye knocks Brutus upward but also sends Olive in a similar direction. The bearded brute falls back through the floor he emerged from. Olive's repeated pleas for help are ignored. With her feet dangling in the air, she says, "I guess I'll have to help myself." Olive pulls out a can of spinach and eats the vegetable. She then launches herself at Popeye. Olive stands on top of the sailor and lets out a Tarzan-like yell. Popeye says, "I guess I teaches 'em too good." It's nice to see Olive get herself out of trouble in this cartoon with a witty script and excellent animation.

Bird Watcher Popeye (1960)

Olive Oyl says to Popeye, "Well, we can learn lots of things from the birds." She orders Popeye to take up bird watching, and they go to the zoo. Popeye gets clobbered by an ostrich and looks at a penguin that resembles himself. The look-a-like penguin socks a mean-looking bigger bird. Upon seeing this, Olive says, "Oh dear, dear, dear, can't you ever change?" A parrot, wearing a sailor's hat, begins singing Popeye's song! Olive says, "How dare you teach that poor little parrot your dreadful song!" Sitting on a rooftop, Brutus spies Olive and sends his vulture to capture her. Popeye sees what's going on through his binoculars and says, "That bird just learned me he's got Olive Oyl, and I just learned that dere's Brutus waitin' ta get me goil!" Popeye plows through a spinach patch and uses his arms like propellers. Popeye socks Brutus and sends him flying in the air. The brute ends up in a bird's nest with an egg on his head. Popeye looks at him and says, "Here is a bird I understand." A cute cartoon with fine animation.

Time Marches Backwards (1960)

A narrator introduces the audience to Prof. O.G. WottaSnozzle, calling him "The World's Greatest Brain, there's no doubt, he's way out, so let's find out what he's all about." The Professor uses his giant time machine to send Popeye back to fifty thousand years B.C. Popeye sees prehistoric creatures and says, "I must be in a blasted zoo." The sailor comes upon Wimpy dressed like a caveman trying to club a prehistoric cow, saying, "Nice bossy! Nice bossy!" Olive Oyl is screaming for help while Brutus drags her on the ground by the hair. Brutus's club flattens Popeye! The cave-brute picks up a huge rock and smashes it onto Popeye. Fortunately, nearby is some "raw, primitive spinach," which Popeye gobbles up. He and Brutus bang each other with clubs until the brute falls to the ground. Olive kisses Popeye and the sailor is transported back to his own time period. Back watching television, Popeye discovers a raw spinach leaf and wonders where it came from. The animation is poor in this cartoon. Popeye's movements look as if he was animated on flip-cards. We're treated to the same animation of Brutus carrying off Olive Oyl. The conclusion where Popeye is smelling the spinach leaf and begins to laugh is too repetitive. This cartoon's most annoying aspect is Olive's constant yelling of "Help! Help! Help! OH...help...Popeye!" continually being re-looped. And how does a prehistoric Olive even know Popeye in the first place?

Popeye's Pet Store (1960)

Popeye is heard singing, "I'm Popeye the pet store man, I'm Popeye that's who I am. I gots pets for sale, I'll sells ya a whale, I'm Popeye the pet store man." Olive arrives and wants a French poodle. Wimpy comes into the store and says, "I will gladly pay you Tuesday for a hamburger-hound today." Swee'pea wants a pussy cat, but Popeye's sold out. The sailor reaches for a parrot and says, "I gots it. I'll give ya pretty pussy-cat bird." This makes Swee'pea very happy. Brutus is angry with Popeye's satisfied customers and decides to capture their pets. Popeye's once happy customers come into his store mad because of their stolen animals. Popeye aims to catch the thief and dresses up like a dog! Brutus grabs Popeye and throws him into his truck. The truck stops alongside a vehicle carrying spinach cans. Popeye consumes the contents of a can and busts open the back of Brutus's truck. This releases all of the captured animals. Popeye, still dressed as a dog, chases Brutus up a tree. Swee'pea exclaims, "We're satisfied customers now." Popeye says, "Of course I satisfies on accounts of I'm Popeye, the pet-store man!" Brutus, in the tree, concludes Popeye's song with an "Oo-ooh!" A fun cartoon with excellent animation.

Ballet de Spinach (1960)

Popeye visits Olive Oyl and finds her dressed as a ballerina with her hair pulled back (as in the comic strip). Olive explains, "Oh, Popeye, I'm a dancer, and tonight I'm going to be on the stage." Popeye tells Olive she looks ridiculous, which makes her cry! She wails, "You hate my dancing, so…you must hate me too!" Popeye apologizes, and Olive tells him she needs a dance partner. Olive gets Popeye to put on a ridiculous-looking costume. The angry sailor has a halo on his head and angel wings. She instructs Popeye on how to tip-toe towards a little rosebud and then sing, "Wake up, wake up li'l rose-bud." Popeye stomps over to the flower and yells, "Hey bud! Wake up!" Brutus is at Olive's window, observing what's going on. Brutus kicks Popeye from behind, and the sailor's head ends up in a fishbowl.

Popeye threatens to smack Brutus on his kisser, but Olive says angels don't do that. Popeye says to Olive, "Ya sez angels don't go around smackin' folks on their kissers. But do they smack them in their bread-baskets like this?" Popeye punches Brutus in the stomach and asks Olive if angels clonk their conks. The sailor wallops Brutus on the head with his fist. He then picks up Brutus and swings him around the room. Olive demands Popeye let go of Brutus, and the brute goes crashing to the ground. Popeye says, "My act was a knockout." Nice to see Popeye get the better of Brutus without eating spinach. The annoying aspect of the animation is the repetitive use of Olive bouncing up and down. Other than that, it's an enjoyable cartoon to watch.

Sea Hagracy (1960)

A collector from the Internal Revenue arrives at The Sea Hag's door. He explains, "You forgot to send in your ill-gotten gains tax this year." The collector proceeds to take The Sea Hag's stolen jewels for the payments she owes. The Sea Hag needs wealth but knows Popeye won't let her go back to piracy. She decides to make him a partner, saying, "Popeye dear friend be my partner and we'll be as rich as Kings! Will rob every ship at sea." Naturally, Popeye refuses, so The Sea Hag asks Wimpy to help her. The witch offers Wimpy two hamburgers if he'll clonk Popeye with a mallet and tie him up. The Sea Hag mutters, "Soon, I'll be back in the piracy business." Wimpy can't do it, and Popeye puts The Sea Hag over his knee, spanking her. The angry hag sends a lightning bolt to Popeye's house, which blows it up. A second bolt strikes Popeye, and he pulls out his spinach. The Sea Hag blasts Popeye with lightning, which turns him into a human lightning bolt. The sailor speeds towards The Sea Hag and charges right into her. The defeated witch says, "Ah, what's the use." An imaginative story marred by some sloppy animated sequences. When The Sea Hag talks to Wimpy, the top part of her face is dark green while her chin is in a lighter shade. When Popeye asks Wimpy what he's doing with a mallet, the sailor's mouth doesn't move. When Popeye flies in the air, filled with electricity, he's wearing a nightgown. After defeating The Sea Hag, he suddenly has on his sailor's uniform.

Spinach Shortage (1960)

A narrator says, "For the first time in history, someone has cornered the world spinach market. World health experts are gravely concerned. The United Nations is calling a special spinach session as quotations from Wall Street report ever-increasing prices on this vital product." Brutus is behind the problem and says they'll have to pay his prices if people want spinach to eat. Popeye visits several stores to purchase spinach, but none have any left. The weakened sailor attempts to break into Brutus's warehouse but fails. Finally, Popeye ends up inside the warehouse, but he's too weak to open up the crates of spinach. Brutus says, "Poor little guy, if he wants spinach that bad, maybe I can help him out." Brutus's machine grabs a crate of spinach and drops it on Popeye. Popeye is now covered in spinach and gobbles it up. He socks Brutus into a sign which reads, "Eat More Spinach." The strengthened sailor says, "He oughta practice what he preaches." A creative story with satisfactory animation.

Popeye and The Dragon (1960)

A dragon has carried off Princess Olive Oyl, and Popeye says, "I Sir Popeye will save thee." Popeye goes to Wimpy's Armour Shoppe and is fashioned into protective gear. Popeye uses credit cards to buy a horse, and he speeds forth to rescue Olive. The Princess pleads, "Please have mercy. Oh, spare me, Sir Dragon. Help-eth me, save-eth me." Popeye's horse is frightened by the dragon's fire! The dragon bops Popeye about until he lands into "Ye Olde Spinach Patch." The dragon shoots fire at Popeye with no effect. In turn, Popeye blasts the dragon with fire from his pipe. The sailor beats up the beast and gets him to say, "Uncle." In return for rescuing her, Princess Olive gives Popeye his own Spinach Shoppe. The dragon is the chef at the eatery, cooking food with his fire. A colorful, action-filled cartoon with excellent animation.

Popeye the Fireman (1960)

Olive Oyl is yelling for help in a very tall building. Wimpy hears her screams and alerts the fire department. Hotel Star is on fire, and Popeye wakes up to realize that's where Olive is staying. Popeye darts out of bed, saying, "Gotta saves me sweetie." Popeye uses a ladder to reach Olive to discover the smoke is coming from Brutus's cigar. Popeye says, "Why dat dirty cigar puffin-ruffian." Brutus keeps creating havoc while Popeye tries to save Olive. Popeye finally says, "Where's me spinach at?" and charges up the ladder! He punches Brutus and flings him in the air. The brute ends up stuck in a sign which reads "Help Prevent Fires." Wimpy climbs the ladder and sees Popeye and Olive. He asks the romantic pair, "I'll gladly pay you Tuesday for a hamburger today. With onions, pickle, and tomato both." Movement, in several scenes, appears as if they were created by flip-cards rather than animation. The running sequence where Popeye is chasing after a fire truck was pulled from *Popeye and The Phantom*. A fireman's helmet was drawn on Popeye's head to create continuity. It's quite noticeable as Popeye's facial design differs from how he appears in the rest of the cartoon. When Wimpy, watching Popeye get lifted by a ladder, mutters, "Oh, oh mercy goodness gracious," it's in a different voice from what's heard in the rest of the cartoon. A truly poorly animated film.

Popeye's Pizza Palace (1960)

At the meatball manor, chef Popeye is making pizzas when Wimpy walks in. Wimpy says, "I would gladly repay you Tuesday if I could have two hamburger pizzas today? Maybe just one pizza? Two half pizzas? One eighth? Sixteen? Maybe just a tiny, weensy piece of pizza?" Popeye yells back, "No! not even a teensy. No money, no pizza! Cash on the line!" Brutus sits next to Wimpy and offers to pay for the pizzas. Popeye has to determine what kind of pizza Brutus wants. He provides different selections, including doughnut pizza, sunbonnet pizza, parasol pizza, and the leaning tower of pizza. Brutus wants an authentic tamale pizza, but Popeye explains he doesn't make that. Brutus punches Popeye and rolls him in pizza dough, calling his creation "The Sailor Tamale." Popeye makes a spinach pizza, eats it, throws pizzas at Brutus, and kicks him out of meatball manor.

Meanwhile Wimpy has eaten his pizzas and pays Popeye for them. Popeye sings, "I'm Popeye the Pizzaman, I'm Popeye the Pizzaman, I beats 'em and rolls 'em as fast as I can 'cause I'm Popeye the Sailor Man... pizza!" After Popeye says "Cash on the line," his mouth remains open. You hear Brutus's "uhhh" come out of the sailor's mouth (the brute just sat in a chair). Choppy animation though tolerable.

Down the Hatch (1960)

Popeye shows Swee'pea his family album. He tells the lad about one of his Popeye'd ancestors who was on a ship. The vessel was commanded by Captain Wimpy when Brutus, the Pirate, invaded it. The brute says to a tied-up Wimpy, "I'm in command here!" Brutus pounds Popeye, in various means, across the ship until the sailor eats his spinach. Wimpy says to Popeye, "Give him the ol' what for!" Popeye and Brutus have a sword fight until the brute loses his pants. Brutus falls in the water and swims away with sharks after him. Swee'pea says, "He was brave," and Popeye replies, "Yeah, 'cause he was great, great grand-Popeye the Sailorman." A good animated cartoon tainted by one sequence. To create the grunting noise between both sword fighters, the audio was slowed down. Unfortunately, one of Wimpy's "Bravo Popeye" was also heard slowly.

Lighthouse Keeping (1960)

Olive Oyl and Brutus visit Popeye's lighthouse. When Popeye asks Brutus, who invited him, the bully replies, "This is a public place, ain't it, and you're a public servant, ain't ya? Well, then start serving!" Popeye goes on to tell historical information about the lighthouse to Olive and Brutus. Popeye and Brutus brawl, and the sailor knocks the bully on his boat. The boat's rope gets tied to Olive's leg, and she unintentionally goes off with Brutus. Brutus sees a shark and says, "Uh-oh, I ain't gonna be tied to no woman's apron strings no how! Especially with sharks around." A huge shark menaces Olive, but Popeye eats his spinach and knocks the beast onto Brutus's boat. Brutus ends up stuck on a buoy as Popeye and Olive sail past him. Popeye shouts, "No riders." A cute cartoon with respectable animation.

Popeye and The Phantom (1960)

On a stormy night, a television announcer says, "Attention! Attention everybody! The Phantom strikes again. Lock your windows, close your doors. Beware this is a public service announcement." Olive Oyl is hiding while a ghost appears in Popeye's house, causing objects to float in the air. Popeye remarks, "That flying chair must be looking for a flying saucer." The ghost performs various tricks, and Popeye says to Olive, "I needs ta take me spinach. This will settle me imagination." However, the ghost swipes the can of spinach. Popeye keeps taking flying leaps in the air to grab his spinach but fails each time. The sailor ends up poking his head out of a chimney only to have the ghost strike him with a mallet four times. A defeated Popeye waves a white flag and says, "Alright! Alright! You wins! I believes you're a real ghost. Let's sit down like gentlemen, and I'll shares me spinach wit' ya." Popeye explains to Olive they're friendly ghosts. After playing bridge, using ghostly money, the spirit departs. Olive chuckles, "Oh, Popeye, you don't think they were really ghosts? That's ridiculous." Suddenly a blood-curdling sound fills the room. Popeye and Olive hide underneath a table. The ghost appears wearing a sailor's hat, an anchor on one arm, and a pipe in its mouth. The animation is good, and Popeye admits once again, "If ya cants lick 'em, ya joins 'em."

Popeye's Picnic (1960)

Olive Oyl is thrilled she and Popeye are going on a picnic. However, she feels the sailor's mind is always on food and asks what he knows about butterflies. On the way to the picnic, Popeye says, "Uh, oh, I thinks I caught a flat." Olive is complaining Popeye has to take time to change a flat tire. She's anxious to go butterfly hunting. While Popeye changes the tire, he mutters, "Women, ya cants gets along wit' em, and ya cants get along wit'out 'em." Popeye struggles with the tire, and Olive goes off with her butterfly net. While attempting to snare a butterfly, Olive runs afoul of a bull. Eventually, the bull butts Popeye into a spinach patch. The bull and sailor charge after each other. The butterfly Olive wanted to catch floats just above the beast and sailor. Now everyone is calm, and they all enjoy the picnic. Pleasant story and acceptable animation.

Out of This World (1960)

The opening scene utilizes stock footage from *Time Marches Backwards* with Prof. O.G. WottaSnozzle snatching Popeye from his living room to the time machine. The sailor man is transported to Twenty-five hundred years, A.D. Once in the future, the cartoon begins with new footage. An announcer says, "This is the age of tomorrow. The avenues of tomorrow's city are airwaves. The atomic age has reached perfection." Swee'pea is splitting atoms while Popeye asks what's for dinner. Olive Oyl replies, "Spinach tablets, roast beef pills, soup, and salad crystals." Popeye, Olive, and Swee'pea go aboard the Spaceliner rocket ship. The rocket takes a five-minute stop, and Swee'pea gets stuck to a meteor. Popeye gobbles some spinach crystals and saves the lad. The ship lands on the moon and encounters earth-style houses, which Olive calls "prehistoric." Popeye is delighted to see the old hamburger stand where Wimpy asks the chef, "I will gladly pay you next Tuesday for two hamburgers today with onion, relish, and pickle." A fun cartoon with fine animation once you get past the opening consisting of stock footage.

Madam Salami (1960)

Popeye and Olive Oyl are walking around at a carnival. Olive wants her fortune told by Madam Salami. The fortune-teller is Brutus in disguise, and he says to the audience, "This is my chance to get even with that no-good sailor shrimp." Brutus informs Olive Popeye must complete tasks to prove his love. The first task has Popeye fighting lions in their den. For the second task, Popeye jumps off a tall building. When Olive asks Madam Salami if he's done enough yet to prove his love, the phony fortune teller growls, "Enough, no! He's still alive!" The third task has Popeye launching himself in a rocket ship. Madam Salami tells Olive since Popeye left her, she should marry Brutus. However, the rocket returns, and Popeye discovers Brutus's scheme. After being flattened by Brutus, Popeye eats his spinach and knocks him out of the carnival. Olive smooches Popeye, who is now wearing a space helmet, and says, "How could I have ever doubted you?" A fun cartoon with good animation.

Timber Toppers (1960)

Popeye is a lumberjack walking through the woods with Olive Oyl. After cutting down several trees, Popeye notices they and Olive have vanished. The one-eyed logger says, "Where's all me trees? I don't see none of them! I've been robbed! Hijacked! Tree-jacked! And I has lost-ed' me sweetie." It turns out Brutus is the thief who stole Popeye's logs and has tied Olive

Oyl to a tree. Popeye and Brutus brawl until the one-eyed lumberjack is tied to a tree heading for a buzz saw. Fortunately, there is a can of spinach nearby.

Popeye uses the buzz saw to open the can. He quickly eats the contents and socks Brutus into a big barrel. Popeye says, "Ya makes a perfect nose cone," and lights the barrel with his pipe. Brutus zooms off into the air, landing in the water. Still tied to a tree, Olive is headed for a the blades of the buzz saw, but Popeye stops it just in time. In this cartoon, we're treated again to a seemingly endless loop of Olive crying for help. Sloppy animated scenes are visible in this cartoon. When Brutus is first smacked with a tree, his yellow shirt suddenly becomes blue. Then it's back to yellow. Popeye's red attire switches to all white when he grabs onto the spinach can. Then it's red again. There are no fisticuffs between Popeye and Brutus once the sailor is fortified on spinach; only a scene of Popeye calmly walking towards a charging Brutus. Then an explosion effect with Brutus landing in a barrel. When Popeye turns off the buzz saw which threatens Olive, his pipe vanishes. The two hairs on Popeye's head appear and disappear as he speaks at the cartoon's close.

Skyscraper Capers (1960)

Popeye reads a sign that says, "High position available for the right man. We start you with a raise. The sky's the limit." Popeye begins working on a construction site with Wimpy as his supervisor. Brutus is the boss of the operation. The sailor keeps bungling his tasks which include dropping bricks on Brutus. The brute ends up punching Popeye until the lunch horn goes off. The sailor is holding a can of spinach, muttering, "Doggone it, I cants seem to open this blasted can." The working horn goes on, and Brutus yells, "Lunchtimes over, get back to work." Brutus and Popeye resume fighting. However, the sailor's spinach can is open now! Popeye consumes the vegetable and goes after his boss. Brutus screams at Popeye, "You're fired!" Popeye says, "Oh yeah, I quit!" Brutus replies, "Me too!" Good animation.

Private Eye Popeye (1960)

A police chief explains to Popeye there's been another wave of diamond smuggling. Popeye says, "Sure, I'll gets me private eye right on it." The only clue is the Captain of a pickle boat. Popeye tells Olive Oyl, "We may needs the Jeep on this job. Bring your private eye nose along to sniff out them smugglers." The Sea Hag and Brutus are the diamond smugglers. The Jeep drops a pickle box on Popeye which busts open.

The diamonds are being encased in each pickle. Popeye says, "And the smugglers figured they could ship loads of diamonds through customs without being noticed." Olive and The Jeep are tied up while Popeye goes after Brutus. The bearded smuggler attempts to escape in a helicopter with a pickle jar. Popeye and Brutus brawl in the sky, but the sailor eats his spinach. Brutus ends up eaten by sharks, and Popeye remarks, "Boy, are those sharks gonna have a bellyache." Popeye lands on the Captain's ship, but The Sea Hag holds him at gunpoint. Olive grabs the witch's gun, which goes off in a skyward direction. The bullet hits a pickle jar which crashes on the hag's head. When Olive praises Popeye for saving her life, he remarks it was nothing. An angry Olive replies, "Nothing, is it! I'll show you what's nothing!" She punches Popeye in the eye, who remarks, "Olive Oyl yas' blackened me private eye. But I can see things clearer now. Oh, she loves me." An exciting story with excellent animation.

Little Olive Riding Hood (1960)

Popeye says, "Swee'pea, I'm about ta tells ya a real true fairy story." The story is about Little Olive Riding Hood taking hamburgers to her sick friend Wimpy. The Sea Hag smells the hamburgers and is about to snatch them when Popeye comes along asking for directions. Olive agrees to show Popeye the way out of the woods if he carries her picnic basket. The Sea Hag arrives at Wimpy's house and throws him out. Olive arrives and sees The Sea Hag wearing Wimpy's hat. Little Olive Riding Hood comments on her big nose. The disguised witch replies, "The better to sniff hamburgers with, my dear." Olive remarks on the hag's giant teeth, and she replies, "The better to bite hamburgers with." The Sea Hag launches herself at Olive and her picnic basket. Popeye runs to Olive's aid, and the picnic basket bounces out of the house. Popeye picks it up and says, "These hamburgers ain't for free, and they ain't for no stealin' witch." Wimpy and The Sea Hag head off to Rough Houses' Hamburger Stand. Popeye and Olive enjoy a hamburger lunch. When Popeye finishes the story, Swee'pea cries and says, "I want a hamburger." The story goes off course. At first, the hamburgers were for a sick Wimpy, but then they have to be paid for. A pleasant cartoon with fine animation.

Popeye's Hypnotic Glance (1960)

Brutus begins reading a book titled "How to Hypnotize," which states, "Make the girls love only you." He says, "Well, that's what I'm going to do." Brutus visits Olive Oyl and begins wiggling his fingers at her. Suddenly

Olive goes into a trance, saying, "I love Brutus." Popeye arrives, noticing Brutus's book, and yells, "Ya swab! You hypnotized me sweetie!" The sailor gives Brutus a punch demanding he undoes his spell over Olive. Instead, Brutus hypnotizes Alice the Goon to fall in love with Popeye. Brutus says, "I hypnotized her, and now she loves you." Olive sits on her couch saying, "I love Brutus," over and over again. Popeye asks Alice if she can cook, saying, "The girl I loves has gotta cook me favorite dish, spinach, and cook it fast." Alice whips up some spinach and feeds it to Popeye. Popeye clobbers Brutus, and the sailor hypnotizes Olive to fall in love with him again. Popeye snaps Brutus into a trance to love Alice the Goon and vice/versa. Everyone confesses their love to one another, and Popeye says, "And I love this little double dating 'cause I'm Popeye the Sailor Man." A witty script with excellent animation.

Popeye's Trojan Horse (1960)

Popeye tells Swee'pea a story about the Trojan Horse. A bad Prince from the city of Troy kidnaps Princess Olive Oyl and takes her to his castle. Prince Popeye sails off to rescue her. Prince Brutus sends a vulture carrying dynamite after Prince Popeye. Swee'pea looks at the audience and says, "They didn't have dynamite in those days." Popeye's ship explodes, but he hops on a friendly dolphin. The evil prince keeps pounding Popeye with a draw bridge, and Swee'pea says, "History was never like this!" Popeye keeps trying to get into the castle but fails each time. He decides to build a Trojan horse and manages to defeat the evil Prince and rescue the Princess. Popeye concludes his story by saying, "So The Prince and Princess sailed for home where they set up a shop to make Trojan rocking horses for Spartan kiddies." Swee'pea, again looking at the audience, says, "Like ya history teacher's gonna flip when you tell her this one." A cute cartoon with fine animation.

Frozen Feuds (1960)

The announcer says, "Somewhere in the bleak waste of the Alaskan Klondike, there wanders alone, a monster. Feared by all and friendless. It is the truly incredible Alice the Goon. No one has been able to capture her, and confidentially I don't think anyone ever will." The narrator goes on to explain that people who see the Goon turn all white. Saloon singer, Olive Oyl, asks Popeye to go after Alice because she wants one of her hats. Alice is pining for Popeye and hurls a rock at him. Attached to the stone is a note from Alice which states, "The best way to catch the Goon is to toot on your pipe, signed Alice." Popeye toots on his pipe, and Alice appears. The two chase after each other, and the sailor eventually falls into the monster's arms. Alice begins communicating with Popeye, who can understand her. Popeye says, "Okay, Alice, get me a hat like yours, and I'll get you me picture." Olive gets her hat while Popeye gives Alice a television set with the sailor on screen. A cute script, but the animation suffers from abrupt scene changes.

Popeye's Corn-Certo (1960)

Tonight is the Battle of Music between Popeye and Brutus as Olive Oyl announces, "And now ladies and gentlemen, the main event of the evening!" She continues, "In the black corner at three hundred and fifty pounds, Brutus, the box of the backwoods." Olive introduces Popeye saying, "And in the white corner at one hundred and twenty pounds, Professor Popeye, the popular pro-Vader of papillating pleasant pop music." Brutus slams Popeye's piano lid on his fingers. The prize is a loving cup and kiss from Olive. Brutus sabotages Popeye's musical attempts, and the sailor ends up wrapped in a tuba. Olive discovers Brutus using a player piano and disqualifies him. Angry, he takes off with the loving cup and Olive. Popeye says, "It's time for me spinach serenade." Popeye explodes out of the tuba and socks Brutus. The sailor contorts Brutus's body as if he was playing musical instruments. Olive declares Popeye the winner. A fun story with adequate animation.

Westward Ho-Ho (1960)

Popeye tells Swee'pea the story of when his great grandpappy, Poopdeck, was the Captain of a Prairie Schooner. Pappy's shipping orders were to get to California. While his schooners were traveling, they encountered trouble from the Cleveland Indians. Emerging from the rocks, these Brutus-looking Indians carried baseballs and bats shouting, "Murder the bums. Belt 'em! Spike 'em! Batter-um up! "The Indians pelted the schooners with baseballs, so they hot-footed it out of Ohio! The schooners took off, leaving Poopdeck stranded. More Indians carrying baseballs and bats appeared. Poopdeck was facing the Milwaukee Braves, and the bulls transporting his schooner got scared.

Popeye said to Swee'pea, "— and ran to the bullpen." Pappy hoisted his sail, and the wind blew him safe. Pappy got caught up in hay fever meadows and managed to sneeze his way to California. Pappy sneezed his way to China from California, encountering a Chinese-looking Wimpy who said, "Honorable Sailor come from home of hamburger?" Chinese Wimpy offered to buy Pappy's schooner saying, "I will gladly pay you

Tuesday for that old junk today." Popeye said to Swee'pea, Pappy went into the Chinese junk business, adding, "Only the first junk had wheels, and it was great grandpappy's United States prairie schooner."

Interestingly when Pappy speaks, it's in Popeye's voice. That's probably because Popeye is telling Swee'pea the story. A fun cartoon filled with baseball puns featuring great animation.

Popeye's Cool Pool (1960)

Olive Oyl, sweating, says, "Oh Popeye, if you were a gentleman, you'd build a swimming pool." Swee'pea cries, "I wanna swimming pool!" Popeye says it's too hot! Neighbor Brutus growls, "Why don't ya dig the kid a swimming pool, cheapskate!" Popeye says he's not a cheapskate and offers to dig it. The sailor reads the instructions from his Popeye Mechanics Book. While Popeye digs, Brutus says, "Hurry up, slowpoke, I wanna dive in!" Popeye replies, "You ain't invited!" Brutus plots to steal Popeye's pool once it's finished.

After going through Summer, Winter, Spring, and Fall, the pool is finally completed. Brutus pushes the fence so that most of the pool is on his property. When Olive and Swee'pea attempt to dive into the pool, they slam into the fence instead. Olive remarks, "Oh, Popeye, you built the pool too close to the fence." Swee'pea cries, "This is just a bathtub." Popeye eats his spinach and drags the pool back onto his property. He smacks the fence, which wraps around Brutus. Popeye says, "Like the Popeye Mechanics says, if the weather makes you drool, builds yourself a nice cool pool." When Olive and Swee'pea call Popeye a "cheapskate," Swee'pea's voice comes out of Olive's mouth, and Olive has Swee'pea's voice. However, Mae Questel's voice for both characters sounds similar; it's not a noticeable error. A humorous plot with fine animation.

Jeep Jeep (1960)

Swee'pea went out to play but can't find his way home. He runs across a Jeep who gives him a piggy-back ride back to his house. Swee'pea asks Popeye if he can keep the Jeep. Popeye says, "Can he makes himself useful?" The Jeep barks like a dog, but Popeye explains he doesn't need a watchdog. The Jeep turns his nose, and music comes out, but Popeye says he has a radio. After the Jeep shows off his mathematical skills, Popeye decides he can help Swee'pea with his homework. The Sea Hag and Brutus are at Popeye's window, eavesdropping. Brutus says, "If we had that know-it-all Jeep, we could get rich!" The Sea Hag replies, "An' I got a plan to swipe him…listen." Brutus, disguised as a "daddy Jeep," kidnaps Swee'pea. The

Sea Hag chuckles, "Will make that Jeep fill me up with chests of gold!" The Sea Hag has a note delivered to Popeye, stating, "Give us da know-it-all Jeep an we'll give ya Swee'pea back, signed Sea Hag, Brutus." Popeye delivers the Jeep, and Swee'pea is returned to him. The Jeep draws The Sea Hag a map where she and Brutus can find ten tons of gold. The Jeep leads the villainous pair on a treasure hunt. When they finally start digging, Brutus realizes they've dug into jail. Popeye explains to the criminal duo, "Dat the Jeep don't play ball wit' no dishonest people!" A fun story with good animation.

Popeye's Museum Piece (1960)

At the City Museum, Prof. WottaSnozzle admires a painting and says, "After fifty years as museum manager, our first great masterpiece." The Professor tells Popeye, who is the museum's janitor, to guard the painting with his life! Brutus sneaks into the museum, and despite a warning from Eugene, the Jeep steals the valuable picture. After a frantic chase, Brutus punches Popeye and says, "I'll put you away for good this time, sailor boy." Popeye ends up tied to a guillotine, but Eugene appears next to his head and feeds him spinach. The sharp blade comes zooming towards Popeye's head, but he deflects it with his fist. The edge becomes a whirling buzz saw headed for Brutus. The bearded criminal yells, "That thing will cut me to shreds! Yow, it'll chop me head off! Ruin me curly locks!" As Brutus dives out the window to escape the blade, he tosses the stolen painting back to Popeye. The Professor comes out of his office and collides with Eugene the Jeep. A giant dinosaur skeleton head falls on the Professor, and when he asks Popeye for help, the sailor replies, "I'm sorry, but I don't talk ta dinosaurs." A colorful cartoon with fine animation.

Golf Brawl (1960)

At Meatball Meadows, the champion golf tournament is starting. Competing are Popeye, Olive Oyl, Wimpy, and Brutus. While Popeye attempts to swing, Brutus keeps coughing. Naturally, when Popeye hits the ball, it lands near a tree. Olive hits her ball backward, but it ends up on the green. She just can't manage to get the ball in the hole. Wimpy keeps missing his ball. The main competitors are Popeye and Brutus, and the brute says, "Play the ball where it lies, eh." Popeye replies, "Ya gotta have rules." Brutus's ball ends up in a bird's nest. He hits what he thinks is a golf ball, but it turns out to be a bird's egg. The egg hatches in mid-air and the bird attacks Brutus. Popeye remarks, "Oh, it looks like ya gotta birdie on this hole, Brutus." While Popeye and Brutus continue to compete, Olive finally manages to sink her ball in the hole. After one hundred and twenty-four strokes, Wimpy hits his golf ball, which lands on Popeye's pipe. Popeye remarks, "A hole in one!" A unique premise without the usual physical brawling with good animation.

Wimpy's Lunch Wagon (1960)

Wimpy asks Popeye to watch the diner, and while there, he makes himself a submarine sandwich. The sailor uses pastrami, spinach, salami, olives, onions, and tomatoes. Popeye reads the newspaper, which says, "Merchants is being terrorized by jukebox hoodlums," while eating the sandwich. Popeye isn't worried because he doesn't have a jukebox until Brutus brings one in the diner. Brutus remarks, "I'll be back, bud, when that machine gets filled with dimes." Olive Oyl, who is in the kitchen, shouts, "Turn off that noise." Popeye finally gets the jukebox out of the store, only for Brutus to smash it over Popeye's head. Brutus ejects Popeye from the music menace and grabs Olive. Unfortunately, while Brutus keeps laughing at Popeye, he slams his hand on the sailor's spinach-filled submarine sandwich. Popeye says, "That's spinach, me favorite muscle-building kind!" Popeye eats the green vegetable and wallops Brutus. He tosses the brute and jukebox out of the diner. A fast-paced cartoon with excellent animation.

Weather Watchers (1960)

Olive Oyl is in charge of the weather bureau where Brutus wants to work. Brutus complains about the incorrect weather forecasts. Olive explains to weatherman Popeye, "We've had complaints, Popeye, and you'll have to be more exacting in your reports or else!" Brutus says, "A couple of more phony weather predictions like this, and I may get his job yet." Popeye prepares for his next weather report, which goes by his back, bunions, and corns, which don't ache. Then Popeye spins his weather wheel and tells Olive it will be fair and sunny. Wimpy Weatherbee, the local weathercaster reports on television, "We have rain today, folks, but tomorrow promises to be fair and sunny." Brutus, in a helicopter, flies over the clouds and pours in red pepper and mothballs. The clouds sneeze, causing rain which ruins Popeye's weather prediction. The weatherman loses his job, and Olive hires Brutus to take his place. A depressed Popeye walks the streets and discovers the mothballs. Brutus predicts sunshine, but Popeye fills up a water tank with king-size spinach. Using his lungs, Popeye blows up the tank and creates artificial rain. Soon green rain is pouring down! Olive tells Brutus she fell for his mothball gag. Brutus grabs Olive, but

Popeye flattens him, telling the brute he's all washed up! A creative story with excellent animation.

Popeye and the Magic Hat (1960)

Brutus performs on stage and presents his magic hat. The hat produces petunias which he gives to Olive Oyl. Popeye mutters, "Who'd give ya those petunias, Olive?" Brutus asks for a volunteer, and Olive says, "Go on, Popeye! Help the dear sweet man!" Brutus uses his magic wand to embarrass Popeye. The sailor suddenly wears a diaper and bib. That's followed by a caveman's outfit, clown's attire, a ballet dancer's outfit, and a woman's dress. Suddenly the Jeep pops on Popeye's head. Brutus begins humiliating both Olive and Popeye on stage. When the sailor is turned into a giraffe, he uses his long neck to grab Brutus's magic wand with his teeth. He produces a colossal can of spinach and eats it. Popeye changes back to himself and says, "All I needed was me spinach." Popeye, Olive, and Brutus all dive in the magic hat and fight each other. The hat becomes larger, and the brawling trio emerges from it. Brutus says, "A beautiful performance if I do say so myself." Olive says, "Oh, you were both adorable!" A fun cartoon with good animation.

Popeye and the Giant (1960)

The cartoon opens with Wimpy by Brutus's house, then switches to footage of Popeye waking from *Ballet de Spinach*. Wimpy says, "I'll gladly pay you Tuesday for a hamburger today." Whether Wimpy is talking to Popeye or Brutus is made unclear by the use of stock footage. Brutus reads the newspaper, saying, "Wanted, wanted world's biggest giant for carnival act." Brutus wonders if his garden giant grow pills would work on Wimpy. The bearded brute puts the grow pills on hamburgers which he gives to Wimpy. Wimpy grows to an enormous size, busting through Brutus's roof. Brutus offers him a contract to sign, offering Wimpy all the medium-rare hamburgers he can eat. Wimpy agrees, and Brutus ends up exhausted cooking hamburgers. The bearded brute is seen on a hamburger assembly line and says, "I can't supply the demand." When Brutus tries to sell Wimpy to the circus owner, he fails. The owner says, "He's too big. He wouldn't fit in the big top, and it would cost over a million dollars to feed him." Brutus consults The Sea Hag, Shyster at Law, who leaves a crying Wimpy in a massive crib on Popeye's doorstep. Popeye feeds Wimpy essence of spinach to reduce him, but that makes him bigger. Next, he tries the essence of hamburger which shrinks him back to normal. Wimpy says to Popeye, "Thanks, ol' pal, but all those reducing exercises have made me hungry. I will gladly pay you

Tuesday for a hamburger today." Popeye looks at the audience and says, "Big or small, Wimpy always keeps his appetite." A totally sloppily animated cartoon from start to finish. As previously mentioned, the cartoon begins with stock footage of Popeye walking down the street pulled from *Ballet de Spinach*. While Wimpy is eating all of the hamburgers, Brutus is at his right-hand side. When Wimpy begins to snore, Brutus is suddenly outside looking through an open window, laughing. The laughing footage, at the open window, is pulled from *Ballet de Spinach*. When Popeye reads the note attached to Wimpy's crib, he's wearing his nightgown. In the next scene, Popeye is on top of Wimpy but suddenly in his white sailor's uniform. The two scenes where Popeye feeds Wimpy essence of spinach and hamburger via a baby's bottle are used twice. To differentiate what Popeye is providing Wimpy, we're shown a brief close-up of a hamburger. Wimpy is thanking Popeye while the sailor's mouth is opening and closing *sans* dialogue in the last scene. To cover this obvious mistake, Popeye begins mumbling incoherently. Then the sailor is laughing for no particular reason. A dreadful cartoon.

Hill Billy Dilly (1960)

Olive Oyl and Popeye take a ride in the country for a picnic. Olive tells Popeye she doesn't want him fighting. She says, "Isn't it fun to get away from it all in the peace of the country?" Suddenly bullets go flying, and two clans of Brutus-looking hillbillies emerge from the woods. It's a feud between the Hictfields and the Magoos with Popeye caught in the middle. Olive stops the gunfire, and one of the hillbillies asks her, "What'cha doing up here in our mountains, gorgeous?" Olive explains she wanted a quiet place in the country to visit. Both hillbilly clans argue over who is going to protect her. Popeye intervenes and begins fighting the hillbillies. Olive says to Popeye, "Well, Popeye, I hope you're satisfied, you always find rowdies to play with." One of the hillbillies takes off with Olive, who screams for Popeye to save her. Popeye comes to her aid and fights off one hillbilly clan. He eats his spinach and rescues Olive from the other group. Popeye sings, "The rowdies was rude, so I stopped the feud, I'm Popeye the Sailor Man." In the final scene where Popeye is singing, his mouth movements diminish while he's saying, "I'm Popeye the Sailor Man." The animation is good, and the plot mildly entertaining.

Pest of the Pecos (1960)

The cartoon starts with Brutus the Kid's wanted poster. Brutus holds up a train and says, "You conductor, collect me ten gallons of loot." Then the criminal rides off and encounters a cactus with another one of his wanted posters. This poster reads, "Wanted Brutus the Kid for train robbery, nag nabbin', cattle rustlin', schoolmarm pinchin', tiltin' pinball machines and income tax evasion, etc., etc., etc.,,, see other side." Brutus rides into Gravestone Flats, where Popeye is the Marshal. Brutus shoots up the town, and Popeye has to listen to the townspeople's complaints. Olive Oyl says, "Marshal Popeye, I wish to complain about Swee'pea's lollipop." Popeye says, "That does it! Shootin' a lollipop out from under a baby!" Brutus drives Marshal Popeye away with a pitchfork. The Marshal pulls out his spinach and lassoes Brutus and hurls him into jail. Popeye gives Swee'pea a new lollipop, but he wants to be a Marshal like Popeye. The tyke grabs his gun and shoots two holes in Popeye's sailor hat. Popeye says, "So I have another desperate desperado on me hands." The brief scene of Wimpy as an undertaker is stock footage from *Bottom Gun*, which also has a western theme. This is an exciting cartoon with fine animation.

The Blubbering Whaler (1960)

Olive Oyl is having trouble getting Swee'pea to sleep. Popeye says to the lad, "Most everything that lives is asleep but you." The sailor tells Swee'pea if he promises to go to bed, he'll recount the story of how he sang baby whales to sleep. Swee'pea agrees, and Popeye explains, "We was homeward bound after a long whaling hunting voyage." Captain Brutus spots two whales playing in the water. Popeye says, "If it ain't a mother whale and her baby child whale. I just hasn't the heart to separates them." Brutus growls, "C'mon, harpooner will take both them spouters!" Popeye tells Brutus he can't shoot a mother and child. The sailor destroys the harpoon gun and brawls with Brutus. Popeye, on the losing end of the battle, pulls out his can of spinach. Unfortunately, he holds on to the can too long without eating the contents. A wave splashes, taking his spinach can, which the colossal mother whale then swallows. The whale batters the ship with its tail. Popeye and Brutus end up in the ocean. Brutus ends up in a barrel labeled "Whale Oil," attacked by a shark. The baby whale lets Popeye hang on to its fin. The pair swim toward an island. Every night, while marooned on the island, Popeye sang baby whales to sleep. When Swee'pea asks Popeye how he got off the island, the sailor pretends he's asleep. A cute cartoon with good animation.

Popeye and the Spinach Stalk (1960)

The narrator says, "Once upon a time there was a poor girl named Olive. And one day, Olive, who could bake better pies than anyone, decided that she should go into business." Popeye, driving a jalopy filled with pies, came across The Sea Hag and asked if she would like to buy a pie. The witch had no money but gave Popeye a magic can of spinach for the pie. Olive was furious, yelling, "Magic my eye! You're fired!" She tosses the can out of the window. The can opens up, and out came a spinach stalk which Popeye climbs up. At the top is a castle where a giant lives. The Brutus-looking giant has captured Olive and wants her to bake him one thousand pies every day. He also wants her to sing to him, but after hearing Olive wail says, "Tell ya what, we forget the music. What ya say? Just bake pies and keep the place tidy." Brutus, the giant, asks Eugene the Jeep where Popeye is hiding.

Popeye appears when the Jeep is threatened. The sailor is asked by the giant what makes him so tough and Popeye replies, "Spinach!" Brutus feeds Popeye several spoonfuls of spinach and asks him, "Now do you feel tough, runt?" Popeye socks the giant, and he, the Jeep, and Olive head for the beanstalk. When the giant follows, Popeye shakes the beanstalk causing Brutus to smash into the ground. Olive gives Popeye a spinach pie, and the sailor sings, "I'm strong to the finich 'cause I eats me spinach, I'm Popeye the Sailor Man." Creative variation on the classic fairy tale with good animation.

Shoot the Chutes (1960)

An announcer blares, "Take your seats, everybody, the contest is about to begin." The event is the world's parachute jump where Popeye is competing with Brutus. Brutus puts an anvil in Popeye's parachute. Olive Oyl says, "I want that trophy, Popeye." Popeye replies, "Okay! I'll wins it for you, Olive." Popeye and Brutus take off in a plane for their parachute jumps. Brutus dives off, saying, "Here goes the winner." Popeye jumps off, but the anvil replaced his parachute. The anvil heads downward and strikes Brutus on the head. Popeye lands on top of his competitor's parachute. Brutus growls, "I don't allow no hitchhikers!" Brutus manages to shake Popeye off, and the sailor heads towards the ground. Popeye eats spinach, and his pipe begins to twirl. The twirling pipe causes him to land safely right into the loving cup. Brutus ends up stuck in a rooftop and grouses, "Nah, I didn't want the ol' trophy anyways." A fun cartoon with good animation.

Tiger Burger (1960)

In darkest "Inja," Popeye and Wimpy are tiger hunting. They enter Puka-Puka, the fastest-growing slums in Kasha County. Needing information, Popeye taps natives, from behind, who all run in fright. Popeye asks a native policeman why everyone runs away. The policeman asks the sailor how he is approaching them. Popeye taps the policeman from the back and gets clobbered by his club. The policeman says, "Oh, beg your pardon, sir. I forgot myself. I thought it was Gonga." He goes on to explain, "Gonga is the most vicious, cruel, meanest, lowdown, ferocious, good for nothing, lowdown, fiendish, man-eating tiger in all of Inja. Gonga approaches all his victims from the rear."

Using a giant turtle for transportation, Wimpy and Popeye set out looking for the tiger. The tiger snatches Wimpy and takes him to his lair. Popeye tosses a hamburger towards the tiger hoping the beast will grab it, giving Wimpy a chance to escape. Naturally, Wimpy eats the hamburger, but he still manages to escape. Popeye sets bear traps all around the tiger's lair. Then the sailor throws in a stick of dynamite. The tiger tosses the stick in the air, which lands near Popeye and Wimpy. The hunters try to run away but both get caught in bear traps. Popeye yells to the turtle, "Hey turtle! Run to the village and get help!" The turtle strolls while Popeye yells, "Hurry!" The dynamite explodes, and Popeye asks the turtle, "What's the matter wit' you! Why didn't ya run faster!" The turtle replies, "If you're gonna yell at me I'm not gonna go and get help." It's nice to see a cartoon focusing on Popeye and Wimpy without relying on the typical spinach ending. Fine animation.

Bottom Gun (1960)

Popeye is inspecting his eggs while bandit Brutus harasses Olive Oyl at the general store. Brutus says to Olive, "I did want to buy a skillet, but first maybe youse-a sell me a kiss, huh sugar?" Olive replies, "Sugar, yes, sir. One lump or two!" She bops Brutus over the head with a massive sack of sugar. Popeye goes over to Olive's store and learns she is being bothered by Brutus the Kid. Popeye fills Brutus's gun holster with molasses and challenges him to a duel with pistols. Popeye fires wildly at Brutus. The bearded bandit can't pull his gun out of his holster, thanks to the molasses. Brutus says to Popeye, "Humiliate me in public," and he punches the sailor. Popeye lands in a pile of spinach cans and says, "My, what a coincidence; me favorite brand of spinach!" Popeye smashes Brutus over the head with a skillet. Then he dumps molasses on him, followed by chicken feed. The chickens poke at Brutus's belly, causing him to laugh uncontrollably. An action-filled cartoon with excellent animation.

Olive Drab and the Seven Sweapeas (1960)

Popeye says, "Once upon a time there lived a beautiful Princess named Olive Drab. One day while a royal ship was transporting a chest of gold to the kingdom and it was never seen or heard from since." Olive's father tells her she has to go out in the world and find Price Popeye. He explains Popeye is the only one to get the gold back, and the seven Sweapeas can tell her where to find him. Olive finds the seven little fellows who set out to find the Prince for her. Before leaving, one of the Sweapeas warns her to lock the door as The Sea Hag is anchored nearby. Prince Popeye arrives at the Sweapeas' home and tells Princess Olive, "And as soon as I finds The Sea Hag, I'll returns your gold to ya." The Sea Hag overhears Popeye's plan and mixes up a sleeping potion that she puts into a spinach can. The witch gives the can to Princess Olive, who tastes it. She promptly falls asleep while Popeye and the seven Sweapeas locate The Sea Hag's boat. The witch grumbles, "It's the whole cotton-pickin' Navy!" The Sea Hag rams the Sweapea's craft, and Popeye's head gets stuck in the witch's ship. Fortunately, the sailor's head is right next to a box of spinach leaves. He pulls apart The Sea Hag's boat and grabs the treasure before it sinks. Sadly, Popeye sees the sleeping Princess Olive without a way to wake her. The Sea Hag's vulture whispers in Popeye's ear, and he says, "Well, okay if youse says so." Popeye kisses Olive, and she wakes up. The sailor says, "And so Princess Olive Drab and Prince Popeye lived happily ever after." A fun variation on the classic fairy tale with good animation.

Blinkin Beacon (1960)

Popeye, the lighthouse keeper, receives a note in a bottle. The note says, "Dear Popeye, I has kidnapped Swee'pea. Now, unless you douse that light this very night, the worst might happen. Don't answer; just turn out thet ("That" is spelled this way in the note) light! Affectionately, Haggie." Once Popeye puts out the light, the witch intends to wreck a ship carrying gold. Popeye replies to The Sea Hag's note, saying, "No, No A Thousand Times, No!" The concerned sailor says, "Gosh, I cants turns out the light, and I cants lets Swee'pea down!" Popeye heads towards the witch's lair by a submarine which is detected by her radar.

Swee'pea pleads to The Sea Hag, "Oh, no, do what you want with me but spare good ol' honest Popeye the Sailor." The Sea Hag's vulture says to the viewing audience, "How corny can you get." The Sea Hag's vultures drop depth bombs near Popeye's submarine. The witch says to Popeye via radio, "Now, Popeye, I wouldn't destroy that nice child. Come on up. He's in an inflated raft right above you." Popeye suspects a trap but agrees to get Swee'pea. First, however, he takes his spinach pills. One of The Sea Hag's vultures is also on the raft. The bird is instructed to let Popeye have it once the sailor opens the hatch. Popeye wallops the bird with one punch and sends torpedoes towards The Sea Hag's lair, which explode on contact. A fun story, but the animation suffers due to several abrupt scene changes.

Azteck Wreck (1960)

Popeye and Olive Oyl are looking at the Azteck ruins. Popeye says, "Them teenage dancers did kind of shake things up." Olive explains the ruins look that way from being old. She also tells Popeye the people hid their gold among the ruins. Eugene the Jeep is sniffing among the wreckage. The Jeep agrees to lead Popeye and Olive to the gold if he is fed orchids. Suddenly, Brutus, the Mexican Bandit, appears and says, "Ah, I look for this gold all my life. Nobody gets her but me! What kind of dog is this? Eating orchids, reading? There's only one thing to do! Steal this dog that reads."

Eventually, Brutus captures Popeye and Olive. Popeye is tied up while Olive will be sacrificed to the Corn God by having a colossal wheel run over her. Popeye asks Eugene for spinach, but Brutus has a firm grip on the creature. The villain says, "The little one will pull no more tricks, senior, I have him" The Jeep vanishes while in Brutus's hands and feeds Popeye his spinach. The sailor belts Brutus and rescues the damsel in distress. Olive says, "Well, I didn't get the treasure, but I got something much better, my sailor man." Popeye sings, "Me spinach is pleasure its better than treasure, I'm Popeye the Sailor Man." Popeye's two opened eyes are a bit more annoying in this cartoon. There are brief scenes where his pipe appears and disappears. A cute story with adequate animation.

The Green Dancin' Shoes (1960)

Popeye tells Swee'pea a story about the green dancing shoes. He says, "Once there was a beautiful girl who lived in the woods, and she loved dancing." Olive Oyl is the girl who sings about dancing. Popeye brings her the last can of rare Tasmanian spinach. The Sea Hag not only wants the can of spinach but also to make Popeye a pirate. The witch gives Olive green dancing shoes in exchange for the spinach. The Sea Hag commands, "Start dancing green shoes fast as you can; keeps on dancing 'till I gets that sailor man." Olive can't control her dancing and bumps into The Sea Hag. The witch drops the can of rare Tasmanian spinach. She and Popeye have a furious fight over it. Olive's dancing causes her to dig a hole to China.

Popeye eats the spinach and leaps into the hole to save the helpless dancer. Olive, now in China, comes across a Chinese Wimpy who says, "Crazy girl make funny dance. Chop! Chop!" Popeye pulls off the green shoes, but The Sea Hag fills the hole they traveled through with boulders. She chuckles, "They'll never come back." Popeye, holding onto Olive, plows through the huge rocks which strike The Sea Hag. The Green Dancing shoes end up on The Sea Hag's feet which launch her into orbit. Although Popeye has previously said he can't strike a woman, even The Sea Hag, he gives the witch some socks on the chin. A fun story with good animation.

Spare Dat Tree (1960)

Popeye is telling Swee'pea a nature story about two trees wearing crowns. They wore crowns because each was a five-thousand-year-old forest monarch. The trees were guarded by Popeye the Ranger Man. Brutus arrives yelling, "Wowee! What a tree, I'll chop it up fer toothpicks." Popeye punches Brutus to get him to stop chopping and says, "Nobody can cut this tree on account of it's a monument tree for the people of the United States." Brutus digs under the tree, cutting it down from its roots. Popeye stops him, and the endangered male-tree says, "That ranger's a good scout." The female-tree adds, "Oh, he's real cute." Brutus uses dynamite, blasting the male-monument tree skyward. When the tree lands, it's stuck, midway, into the ground. Brutus begins cutting down the female monument tree, but Popeye chomps down some wood-spinach. Popeye lifts the male-monument tree and puts him back where he belongs. Popeye bops Brutus in the direction of the male-monument's fist. The tree's punch sends Brutus crashing into the office of the U.S. Forest Department. Attached to the bearded brute is a note attached stating, "Dis Brutus is choppin' monument trees, signed Popeye the Ranger Man." A cute cartoon with fine animation.

The Glad Gladiator (1960)

Popeye is in Rome 800 B.C. He must fight Brutus, the Mightiest Gladiator of all! Before the fight, a Roman announcer informs the crowd, "Ladies and Gentlemen, her royal majesty, the Empress, Olive Oyl." He then calls the fighters into the ring; "That popular favorite at two hundred seventy pounds, Brutus! And in this corner a completely unknown, puny, one hundred twenty-pound weakling in his first and last fight, ha, ha, ha… Popeye the Sailor." Olive rings a bell, and the two fighters battle each other. Brutus has the upper hand until Popeye eats his spinach. Popeye burns off Brutus's protective armor with his pipe and socks him out of the arena. Popeye jumps over to where Olive is sitting and rings her bell. An action-packed story, but the animation suffers from abrupt scene changes.

The Golden Touch (1960)

Swee'pea tells Popeye he has a brand-new penny, leading into a Popeye "Phairie" story. King Popeye's people are happy, but he wanted to make them more comfortable. The King wishes everything he touched to turn into gold. Suddenly a magic Jeep appears and grants the wish. King Popeye remarks, "What's this! Me tin crown turned to gold! And me pipe's gold! And so's the smoke! That Jeep wasn't kidding!" After turning Princess Olive Oyl into gold, the King tries to eat his spinach because it's better than magic. However, once he touches the spinach can, it turns to gold. The King wants the Jeep to take back his wish. The Sea Hag has captured the creature. King Popeye locates the Jeep, but the witch tosses kitchen objects to keep him away. King Popeye says, "I jus' gotta eats dis solid gold spinach!" He charges at The Sea Hag, who cries, "No, don't touch me! I'll release the Jeep! Don't make me a gold hag!" The Jeep takes back the wish, and everyone in the kingdom remains happy. A pleasant story marred by a couple of distracting animated scenes. While Swee'pea is on Popeye's lap, the sailor's right eye is colored white when he's looking at the book. It should be closed without the white coloring. A member of the happy kingdom is Alice the Goon. While her left arm is its usual muscular shape, her right arm, which is waving at the King, is uncharacteristically skinny.

Hamburger Fishing (1960)

Swee'pea is telling Popeye, "I wish, I wish, I wish I had a wish." This leads to the sailor telling the lad about Wimpy, the hamburger fisherman. Wimpy was fishing for cows, but they always outwitted him. He does manage to hook a Princess who was turned into a cow by The Sea Hag. The enchanted cow pleads with Wimpy, "If you will only let me go, I will give you three wishes." Wimpy lets the Princess go, but The Sea Hag wants the three wishes for herself. The witch captures Wimpy and says, "Use your wishes and wish for gold, gold, gold!" Wimpy replies, "I cannot eat gold. I wish I had a hamburger." A burger pops in Wimpy's mouth, but The Sea Hag knocks it away. A mouse ends up with the hamburger, and the ol' hag demands Wimpy wish for gold. Instead, he wishes for his hamburger back and ends up sitting on it. The mouse bites Wimpy's behind and reclaims the hamburger. Wimpy wishes for a whole room full of hamburgers. Thousands of hamburgers appear, and both Wimpy and the burgers burst out of the witch's lair. Without explanation, all of the hamburgers are gone, with only one remaining. The Sea Hag tells Wimpy the lone burger is his if he gets her another three wishes. Wimpy catches the enchanted cow, but she doesn't have any wishes left. Popeye comes along and rescues her. The cow kisses Popeye, and she turns back into Olive Oyl. Wimpy gets a can of spinach from Popeye so he can make spinach-burgers. Wimpy says to the audience, "I could learn to like spinach-burgers if I were a cow." It's a pleasant script, but Swee'pea's lip movements are sometimes out of sync when he speaks to Popeye.

Popeye the Popular Mechanic (1960)

Olive Oyl complains Popeye is an awful housekeeper. The sailor decides to build a robot housekeeper. Popeye wonders, "Nows what do I calls ya?" From the robot's mouth comes a strip of paper that reads "Call Me Mac." Mac cleans the house and prepares Popeye a stack of flapjacks. While Popeye sleeps, Brutus grabs the robot and rewires him. Popeye ends up grappling with Mac and straightens out his wiring. Brutus gives Mac a bomb and says, "*Psst*, your boss will get a bang out of this!" Popeye gets the bomb in Mac's mouth, who, in turn, spits it out in Brutus's direction. As Mac dumps the tattered Brutus in a trash can, Popeye says, "That'll teaches the big lummox ta stays away from me servant." Popeye goes back to sleep and dreams of Olive Oyl, who says to him, "I just love a man who keeps his house clean." A fun story, but the animation is generally sloppy. While Popeye hungrily anticipates eating the flapjacks, his pipe appears and disappears. Popeye's wearing a short-sleeved pajama top in bed. It suddenly becomes long-sleeved when he's under the bed. Brutus laughing at the window is stock footage pulled from *Ballet de Spinach*.

Popeye's Folly (1960)

Popeye is reading a book about ships to Swee'pea. The sailor tells Swee'pea about his great, great grandpappy's first experiment in building steamboats. The Sea Hag, with Captain Brutus, is in a ship called "Blackhawk." The witch says, "Look, it's that fool Popeye and his grandpappy tinkering with that silly steamboat engine." Brutus replies, "Imagine building a ship to use legs when we already got wings." The Sea Hag's vulture drops dynamite in the partially-built steamboat, and it explodes. Pappy decides to build another boat. Brutus wails, "Steamboats, bah! How ya gonna make 'em sail if ya can't make 'em float!" Popeye and his Pappy build a new steamboat, and Brutus is concerned they will start competing for his river business. The two competitors compete in a boat-race billed as "Steam Vs Sail." The Sea Hag attempts to use her vulture to blow up Popeye's steamboat, but fails this time. Brutus is gaining in the race, but Popeye pulls out his spinach. He feeds half to himself and tosses the rest of the can's contents in his steamboat. The steamboat's power increases, and it blows Brutus and The Sea Hag's ship right out of the race. Popeye is happy they won the race. Pappy says, "Yep, you tell 'em son, steamboats is here ta stay." A charming cartoon with good animation.

Popeye's Used Car (1960)

Popeye asks Olive Oyl if she's ready for their walk in the park. Olive replies, "Sorry, Popeye, but I've given up walking since Brutus got his new car." Popeye is in the market for a vehicle and goes to Honest Wimpy's Used Car Lot. Popeye buys a car, but Wimpy learns he doesn't have a driver's license. Wimpy shows Popeye how to drive but leaps out of the car when they reach the highway. A helicopter notices Popeye's driving and says, "Some idiot down there is tying traffic in knots." Frustrated drivers use their cars to bounce Popeye off the highway, and he crashes into Olive's house. Popeye says to Olive, who is applying "Beauty Mud" to her face, "Olive, it's me new car! Ain't it a beauty? Hurry up an' get dressed and we'll go ridin'." Olive demands he gets his car out of her bedroom. Popeye backs up and smashes into Brutus's car. Brutus picks Popeye up and says, "There ain't no easier way of committin' suicide than banging bumpers with Brutus!" Brutus punches Popeye, but the sailor gets on his feet and fights the brute. The cartoon concludes with Wimpy towing the sailor's car with Popeye and Olive in the front seat. Wimpy says, "Be careful when you're driving. The guy in the other car might be Popeye." It's unusual to see Popeye defeat Brutus in a fight without eating spinach beforehand. A fun story with satisfactory animation.

Spinachonara (1960)

Popeye tells Swee'pea the story of a beautiful Princess whose name is Butter Oyl. She was wooed by an evil, wealthy bandit against her wishes. Her Uncle, Wimpy, promised the bandit the Princess's hand in marriage if he was constantly supplied with hamburgers. The Princess sings out her window, "Oh pure and placid moon! Please hear my plaintiff tune. Send my true love soon to save me from that fool." A brave samurai, Popeye, heard the Princess's sad song of woe. The bandit brings out a plate full of hamburgers for the Uncle but taints them with "Hamburger Off, Appetite Exterminator." The bandit says, "Eat well, Papa-Son, while you can." The bandit grabs the Princess and beats up the Samurai. However, the defeated warrior finds a "Royal Spinach Garden." He eats spinach with chopsticks and throws the bandit in water. The cartoon ends with the Princess singing to the Samurai while he eats spinach with her Uncle chomping on hamburgers. This cartoon pays homage to Oriental culture and features the singing voices of Jack Mercer and Mae Questel. Interesting story and fine animation.

Popeye and the Polite Dragon (1960)

Swee'pea wants to hear a story about dragons from Popeye. The sailor tells the story of how a poor mother dragon left her baby on a doorstep during his great granpappy's day. The mother dragon burns a message on Popeye's door, saying, "Please take care of Percy — He's a good dragon, signed Darlene Dragon." Popeye tickles the baby dragon, who spits fire in his face. He discovers the baby dragon speaks proper English. The narrator says, "And so the years passed and Percy grew, and he grew." When the dragon grew too big for Popeye's house, the sailor sent him out into the world. Popeye gave him some spinach in case he got hungry. Percy comes across a sign which states, "Welcome to the Elite Dragon Inn, good food." The sign is just a lure for Black Brutus, the exterminator, to capture Percy. Brutus says, "Now I'm the champion exterminator of them all." Popeye comes across a jailed Percy, and Brutus hits him with a club. The brute tosses Popeye in the cell with Percy. An injured Popeye says, "This is yer poor ol' daddy talking son. While I'll borrow a li'l of your spinach muscle builder." Popeye twists Percy's tail, and a stream of fire hits Brutus, who charges off. Swee'pea wants to buy a dragon, but Popeye explains they're an imaginary creature. Suddenly Percy is in the room next to them and says, "I beg to differ with you, sir." A fun cartoon with fine animation.

Popeye the Ugly Ducklin' (1960)

Swee'pea asks Popeye if he was strong and handsome while a little boy. Popeye replied, "No, I was ugly! They called me the ugly ducklin' Popeye." Popeye shows a photo of himself as a little boy to Swee'pea. The tyke looks at the picture and remarks, "Ooh, you wuz ugly!" Little Olive Oyl and Brutus are playing school, and Popeye asks if he can join them. Olive says, "Oh no, you're too ugly." Brutus punches Popeye, and the sailor runs away. Traveling in a little boat, Popeye is swept out to sea, finally landing on Goon Island. The Goons pick up the lad, and Popeye says, "You don't think I'm ugly? Ya thinks I'm handsome? Hooray me Goon friends likes me!" Popeye explains he was happy with the Goons. They taught him their culture, and he read their books titled "The Wizard of Goon" and "Alice in Goon Der Land." Popeye explained, "But best of all, they fed me spinach and I grow-ed and I grow-ed and I grow-ed. One day they said I was a man, and they gave me a song, Oh, I'm Popeye the Sailor Man. And they gives me a pipe." Popeye waved goodbye to the Goons and headed back to a now-adult Olive and Brutus. Olive squeals, "Oh, Popeye, you're big and handsome now, and you're not an ugly duckling anymore." Brutus smacks Popeye, and the sailor eats his spinach. He punches Brutus, and the brute lands on Goon Island. Popeye said, "To see if the Goons could teach him a lesson." A delightful cartoon with excellent animation.

Popeye's Tea Party (1960)

The opening scene is stock footage of Popeye being transported to Professor O.G. WottaSnozzle's time machine from *Time Marches Backwards*. Popeye arrives in colonial days to witness Brutus hanging up a sign for the townspeople to read. The sign states, "Proclamation Tea Tax. The usual tax plus fifty percent for tax collector, Brutus." The townspeople decide to throw the tea overboard in retaliation. Popeye, Olive Oyl, Wimpy, and Swee'pea stow away on the ship carrying the tea. The foursome tangle with Brutus, and eventually Popeye ends up stuck in a cannon. During the chaos, Wimpy brews himself a cup of Spinach tea. Popeye says to Wimpy, "Give me a whiff of that spinach tea!" Wimpy replies, "Two schillings for tea." Popeye says, "I'll gladly pay you Tuesday for tea today." The tea is poured into the sailor's pipe. Popeye bursts out of the cannon and lands in Brutus's belly. Swee'pea shoots an arrow which hits Brutus's rear sending him flying into the air. The bearded tax collector lands in the ocean. We're treated, again, to a re-looping of Olive Oyl screaming. The animation is only fair, and the story weak. Another question is how Olive, Wimpy, Swee'pea, and Brutus ended up back in time. Did the Professor send each of them before Popeye?

The Troll Wot Got Gruff (1960)

Swee'pea asks Popeye to tell him a fairy story. Popeye says, "Once there was a little bridge what led to a little town. And under the bridge, there lived a troll." The troll (Brutus) decides to have people pay him to cross the bridge. He stops Swee'pea and Olive Oyl from crossing. Popeye arrives and says, "That ain't no toll bridge! I'll fixes that troll." The troll keeps Popeye from crossing, and the brute says to the viewing audience, "Imagine that, jus' cause I swiped this bridge they won't pay toll." After a few more failed attempts to cross the bridge, Popeye lands in a spinach patch. Popeye says, "What's this, Spinach?" Swee'pea replies, "Ha, ha, ha, what did you expect: horseradish?" Popeye gobbles down some spinach and beats up the troll. Swee'pea and Olive can cross the bridge. The opening scene has Popeye, not wearing his sailor's hat, seated in a chair holding a storybook. Swee'pea is at Popeye's right-hand side. When Popeye begins telling the story, we see a close-up of his face, and suddenly he's wearing a sailor's hat. Swee'pea is now in his arms. After the troll is defeated, we see this same sloppy animated sequence, only this time Swee'pea's "Um-hum" comes out of Popeye's mouth. The fairy story is cute, and only the scenes with Popeye telling Swee'pea the story are animated sloppily.

Popeye the Lifeguard (1960)

The cartoon opens at the beach, with pretty girls surrounding Popeye the Lifeguard. One girl says, "Isn't he handsome?" Another gushes, "I think he's cute." Still, another offers, "And you're so strong, Popeye." Popeye, loving all of the attention, responds with, "The lifeguard has got to keeps himself in shape, ya know." Olive Oyl is angry at all of the female attention Popeye is getting. To make Popeye look at her, she jumps off a pier and cries for help. Popeye rescues Olive but then goes back to the admiring girls. Olive goes into the ocean on an inflatable toy but loses control of it. Popeye saves her but returns to the pretty girls. Brutus appears and suggests "The Buddy System" to Olive. Brutus explains, "We looks out for each other." Olive agrees until the bearded beachcomber gets too aggressive. Brutus puckers up and says, "Now Olive, how about a li'l kiss!" Olive screams for help, and Popeye runs to her aid only to be punched by Brutus. Popeye eats his spinach and wallops Brutus into a bunch of garbage cans. Popeye says to Olive, "No more pretty girls for me, only you, Olive." When Olive turns around, Popeye is back with the pretty girls who continue to admire him. A fun story with excellent animation.

Popeye in the Woods (1960)

Popeye and Wimpy travel to the woods for peace and quiet. Relaxing in the woods, Popeye says, "Ain't this great, Wimpy. Listen to that silence. Smells that fresh air." Wimpy responds with, "I would rather cook a hamburger." Popeye informs Wimpy he can't cook a hamburger in the forest. Popeye tries to fall asleep, but the animals and insects keep him awake. While Popeye is being bothered, Wimpy is sound asleep, dreaming of hamburgers. Finally, Popeye yells, "Quiet!" and he's able to fall asleep. Suddenly the quiet wakes up Wimpy. Wimpy sees tiny mushrooms and decides to cook them over a fire. A firebug fills the forest with smoke. Popeye coughs and screams, "Oh my gorsh! Smoke! Smoke! I gots ta stop it! This calls for spinach!" While Popeye deals with the blaze, a little firebug hits Wimpy. Wimpy runs into the river to put out the fire, but his mushroom burgers turn to mush. An angry Popeye says to Wimpy, "Picture these beautiful trees all burned up. Imagine the forest folks burned out of their homes. And then comes the rains and chokes the rivers and fish with mud." Wimpy says he's learned his lesson, and Popeye cooks him a hamburger in a camping area where fires are permitted. A funny, educational cartoon with good animation.

After The Ball Went Over (1960)

Olive Oyl is watching a ping pong game between Popeye and Brutus. She promises the winner a kiss and an extra portion of lunch. Popeye and Brutus try various tricks against each other. Popeye whispers to Olive, "Fat boy doesn't have a chance. If I gets in trouble, I can always uses me spinach gimmick." After some more ping pong antics, Popeye says to Olive, "Ya knows I always win in these stories." Popeye fills the ping pong ball with an explosive and throws it at Brutus. Brutus serves it to Popeye, and the sailor wonders why it didn't explode. Suddenly the ball does explode, and Popeye falls to the ground. Brutus says, "C'mon chum, try some soup." Olive asks Popeye, "Is there something special you'd like, Popeye?" The defeated sailor says to the audience, "Ya, a new writer ta writes me spinach back in the script." When Popeye says, "No kisses on account of…oop…I'm going to win." The "oop" was not backed up by animation of the ping pong ball stuffed in Popeye's mouth. When Brutus says to Olive, "I got brains, I have, Olive," the animators did not provide Olive with a mouth. After Popeye says to Olive, "Why waits?" we see a close shot of Olive's face. She mutters, "Oh…mmm," while Brutus, off-camera, says, "That's good." This brief scene makes no sense. When Brutus says to Olive, "That sailor shrimp can be irritating," his audio is pulled from the cartoon *Skyscraper Capers*. Unfortunately, the sloppy animation does not do justice to an imaginative story.

Popeye and Buddy Brutus (1960)

Brutus suggests to Popeye they be skin-diving buddies. The pair dive into the ocean. Brutus says, "There's a handsome fish," as he admires one who has his face. Popeye laughs and says, "A dog-fish." Brutus sees a fish with Popeye's kisser. The divers end up in the Lost City of Atlantis, which is an ancient western town. Popeye finds a chest of gold which he splits with Brutus. The bearded skin-diver decides to take it all, muttering, "I like this buddy system." Popeye fights Brutus with a water pistol, and the brute retaliates with a spear gun. They chase each other when suddenly Brutus's body becomes bent out of shape! Brutus yells, "Help ol' buddy!" Popeye exclaims, "Me buddy's got the bends!" Suddenly a fish hook appears, and Popeye attaches Brutus to it. It's Wimpy's fish line, and he brings Brutus to the surface. Wimpy asks Popeye what he should do with Brutus, and the skin diver replies, "Throws him back or takes his picture." Popeye admires the photo and says, "You caughts a prized catch, Wimpy." Colorful story with excellent animation.

Popeye's Car Wash (1960)

Popeye says, "I am disgusted Brutus has took all me business!" Popeye decides to cut his price, and Brutus follows suit. When Popeye offers car washes for free, he's mobbed with customers. Olive Oyl drives up in her new car. Brutus says, "That dirty little sailor shrimp is washing Olive's new car." The brute causes Popeye to wash Olive's car with super-hot water. Suddenly Olive's car shrinks, and she yells, "Oh Popeye, you-you brute, you've ruined my new car!" Brutus offers to fix her car, and Olive brings it to his car wash. Once there, Brutus says to Olive, "But first, sweetie, how's about a li'l kiss?" Olive replies, "But you said you were going to fix my car?" Brutus laughs and chases Olive around his car wash. Popeye gets flattened, trying to rescue Olive. He pulls out his spinach and punches Brutus into a water fountain. Popeye uses his muscles to restore Olive's car to normal. A cute cartoon with fine animation.

Camel Aires (1960)

Popeye reads a newspaper headline which states, "Rare Stone Discovered in Egypt. Five thousand offered by Museum for Possession." Popeye decides he's going to Egypt. Brutus is also reading a newspaper (stock footage from *Popeye and the Giant*). After seeing the same headline, he decides to go to Egypt. Popeye and Brutus both travel to Egypt, both on a Camel. But Popeye's female, Camille, falls in love with Brutus's male, Sampson. The rivals end up traveling together and arrive at a golden palace. Inside the palace is Princess Olive wearing a gem in her hat. The Princess is guarded by Wimpy holding a weapon. Wimpy says, "Death to anyone who comes near the Princess." Brutus whispers to Wimpy, "Listen, buddy! You help me kidnap the Princess, and I'll give you real money, see." Wimpy refuses the money but offers to help Brutus if he gets two hamburgers. After being led to Princess Olive, Brutus punches Wimpy twice and ties up Popeye's body like a mummy. Brutus places Popeye over a fire and takes off with the Princess. Wimpy feeds Popeye spinach and the sailor speeds off to rescue Princess Olive.

During the chase, Brutus's camel stops short, sending him flying in the air. The brute lands headfirst in the sand. When Wimpy feeds Popeye his spinach, he asks for a hamburger in return, but the sailor takes off instead. Yet, Wimpy says to Popeye, "Oh thank you, sir, mankind is indeed kind." Thank you for what? Was the scene of Popeye giving Wimpy a hamburger not animated? While Wimpy is thanking Popeye, his nose whiskers appear and disappear. An exciting cartoon marred by sloppy animation.

Plumbers Pipe Dream (1960)

Olive Oyl's dripping faucet drives her crazy, and Swee'pea suggests she call the plumber. Popeye the Plumber is sleeping when Olive calls him. He dashes over to her apartment. Popeye says, "Madam, I'll stop your drippy-drip before ya can flip a quip." Popeye realizes the faucet needs a new washer but, before putting it on, fails to turn off the water. After asking Olive where her water meter is, Popeye heads towards the basement. But Popeye breaks her water meter, which turns the streets into rivers. The plumber yells, "I gots ta shut off the water main leading into the apartment." Popeye's mishaps cause more water to flood into the streets. The sailor heads for the city's waterworks, looking for the shut-off valve. The Statue of Liberty's light is in danger of being extinguished. Popeye says, "I must keep the torch of liberty burning above all else." He pulls out a spinach can from the water, eats the contents, but discovers his muscles have sprung leaks. With increased speed, Popeye locates the flood control valve and begins turning it. Suddenly he's being sucked down the drain! It turns out Popeye was dreaming and is awakened by Olive's telephone call. Popeye tries to fix her leaking faucet but, again, fails to turn off the water. A frantic-paced cartoon with adequate animation.

Popeye and the Herring Snatcher (1960)

The narrator says, "It was after midnight in Finnan Haddies Herring Cannery." Wimpy says, "My feet are killing me! I wish Popeye would show up." Popeye arrives to relieve the tired watchman. Wimpy warns, "Watch out for the herring snatcher; he's real sneaky." The herring snatcher sneaks in the cannery and brawls with Popeye the Watchman. Olive Oyl arrives to surprise Popeye with a little midnight snack. The weary watchman ends up in a can of herring. Olive uses a key to free the sailor and says, "This spinach sandwich will pep you up, Popeye." The sailor's muscles turn into bongo drums, and he zooms off towards the herring snatcher. The criminal says, "Uh, oh, a flying herring!" The two have a furious fight, and the herring snatcher is canned! He ends up crammed alongside other herring who say in unison, "They're not particular what they pack in herring cans these days." A fun cartoon with fine animation.

Invisible Popeye (1960)

Olive Oyl is dusting Professor O.G. WottaSnozzle's time machine when she's suddenly transported to another planet. The Professor calls Popeye, who gets in the machine to go after Olive. Popeye says, "A sealed city, huh! I'll bust this bubble-head wide open." The sailor's pounding fails to burst the bubble. Popeye asks The Professor, "Hasn't ya got some solution?" The Professor gives pills to Popeye which turns him invisible. The sailor arrives in the city to see one of its inhabits putting up a sign which reads, "The earth specimen will be on exhibition at the Palace Circle." Popeye finds Olive, and they frantically try to elude their pursuers. The Professor sees their plight and says, "Poor Popeye! He needs help! I'll get him back." Back home, Olive accidentally inhales the pills, turns invisible, and kisses Popeye. When the Professor wonders if someone has been tinkering with his time machine, he excitingly says, "Wow, they've got Olive!" Who has Olive? Apparently, he knows Olive was captured before the audience does. Was a scene not animated? In one scene two aliens guarding Olive suddenly disappear without explanation. Overall, the animation has a sloppy feel to it which distracts from any creativity in the story.

The Square Egg (1960)

Swee'pea is all excited as The Wiffle Hen has laid a square egg. Olive Oyl says, "Let's call the Professor." He arrives and, after being told the news exclaims, "That's magnificent! A genuine square egg! It's a very valuable discovery for science!" Brutus, hiding in the bushes, hears the Professor's words. Popeye leads the Professor to the egg but in its place finds a note. The note reads, "If ya wants yer egg back bring all da money ya gots in da sugar bowl. This is no yolk. Masked Man." Swee'pea tells The Wiffle Hen to find the crook. A frantic chase ensues to catch Brutus, who is clutching onto the square egg. During the frenzy, the egg breaks, and a baby hen hatches from it. The Professor says, "Dat is the greatest phenomenon of them all!" The hen suddenly grows in size, and the egg-snatcher says to him, "Can't you just see your name up there in lights. Why you'll be a star!" The Professor wants him for science. Swee'pea tells everybody to let the hen decide for himself. The baby's mother calls for her offspring. The baby and mother lie on a nest together, and Popeye says, "Ya cants beat it. A boy's best friend is his mother." Delightful script based upon a *Thimble Theatre* comic strip storyline from 1951 by Tom Sims (writer) and Bela Zaboly (artist). Excellent animation.

Old Salt Tale (1960)

Popeye, Olive Oyl, and Swee'pea are at the beach. Olive proclaims how she loves the salty water. Swee'pea asks Popeye how water gets salty. Popeye says, "Once a shipwrecked sailor was floating on the unsalted seas with his last can of spinach." He managed to land on Goon Island. The Sea Hag was whipping the Goons! The ol' witch cackled, "Tote that barge, lift that brick, build me a castle and make it quick!" Popeye eats his last can of spinach and tosses The Sea Hag in the ocean. To thank the sailor, the Goons give him a salt grinder.

The grinder says to Popeye, "Ask me politely, man, and I will grind you all I can. Ask impolitely and ask for bad, and I'll grind you something to make you sad." Popeye sails home, but The Sea Hag follows him. The old witch says, "I'll swipe that grinder, and I'll make it grind all the gold in the world for me!" In her lair, the witch asks the grinder for gold impolitely and gets a wooden nickel in return. An angry Sea Hag asks for gold dust, but the grinder gives her salt instead. Salt fills her lair, and she tosses the grinder in the ocean. The Sea Hag yells for the grinder to stop, screeching: "You're salting the water!" The grinder says, "If you ask politely, I'd gladly stop, but you're impolite, so the sea is salt." The grinder hurls a considerable stream of salt at The Sea Hag. Popeye explains to Swee'pea that's why the sea is salty. The tyke replies with a scientific reason for saltwater due to mineral and animal deposits of sodium chloride in solution. When The Sea Hag first asks the grinder for gold, she's wearing her typical short-sleeved black outfit. However, this attire suddenly is long-sleeved when she starts pounding on the grinder. Then it goes back to being short-sleeved. Near the conclusion of the cartoon, after Olive says, "Anybody knows that Popeye," an eyeball appears, briefly, under her nose. Popeye is a quick-change artist. Near the end of the cartoon, he suddenly switches from wearing a bathing suit to his sailor's uniform. A unique story muddled with sloppy animation.

Jeep Tale (1960)

Swee'pea asks Popeye how Eugene the Jeep learned to do so many tricks. Popeye tells Swee'pea the story of Eugene and his family, who lived in a Jeep house. On one side of the house lived Popeye, the good farmer. However, on the other side, there was farmer Brutus. The bearded brute growled, "Jeeps is pests, that's why I raises thistles to keep out Jeep pests." Mama Jeep taught her children how to do tricks, but Eugene wouldn't listen. Instead, he went into Brutus's yard. Brutus chased Eugene into an ammo dump with "Danger" and "Keep Out" signs all around it. Eugene hides among the dynamite, which Brutus kicks and they both get blown sky-high. Brutus manages to grab Eugene and lock him in a cage. The brute begins chopping the Jeep tree down. Mama Jeep stops him, and Popeye says, "The Mama hypnotized the bad farmer." Brutus says, "I feel funny! I think I am a Jeep!" The bully begins bouncing around in the direction of Eugene, still locked in a cage. Popeye says, "Eugene seen him comin', and he disappeared for the first time in his life." Brutus smashes into the cage and becomes trapped inside it. A cute story with excellent animation.

The Super-Duper Market (1960)

Brutus says over a loudspeaker, "Welcome, welcome, welcome everybody to Brutus's Super Duper Market. Bigger and better bargains." Popeye, Olive Oyl, and Wimpy head to the supermarket. Popeye encounters an old man with a long white beard who says, "Please, sir, where is the exit? I've been trying to find it for fifteen years." Before Popeye can answer, the older man is lost in the crowd of shoppers. Brutus, at the controls, says, "Hah! I'll decoy that spinach-eater into a trap and swipe his girl." Popeye and Wimpy get wrapped up like pieces of meat and tossed into a deep freeze area. Brutus says to Olive, "Hello baby, lets you and me wrap up a few kisses in the candy department." The old man who Popeye encountered before finds the sailor and Wimpy. Popeye tells the old man, "Quick, Grandpa, slip me that frozen spinach!" Popeye punches Brutus and rescues his girlfriend. The cartoon concludes with the older man pushing Wimpy, who is frozen in a block of ice. The elderly shopper asks, "Can you direct us to the nearest exit." A fun cartoon with excellent animation.

Golden Type Fleece (1960)

Popeye explains to Swee'pea the Golden Fleece came from Greece. An angry queen says to her plump husband, who is Wimpy: "Nah, I'm sick of this wooly fleece. I want golden fleece. All you do is eat hamburgers!" The King fetches Jason the Popeyed Argonaut, who sails away in search of the Golden Fleece. Jason's singing angers The God of Thunder, who sends down lightning bolts. Jason punches each bolt back towards the Thunder God. A God from Neptune is also angered by his singing and forces Jason's craft into the ocean. Jason eats his spinach and punches

Neptune straight into the cloud where his brother, the God of Thunder, resides. Jason says, "Huh, it's the Lorelei loons, cousins of the Goons!" The creatures sing, "Rock, rock, rock, rock-a-bye sailor and a rock, rock, rock." The creatures try luring Jason to the rocks, but he eats two cans of spinach. Jason placed the empty cans over his ears and sailed over the loons. Instead of finding the Golden Fleece, he discovers Golden Fleas! After defeating a half-man and half-horse, Jason takes the Golden Fleas. King Wimpy says to Jason, "I am very happy, Jason. All-day, the Queen plays with the Golden Fleas leaving me in peace with my hamburgers." The Queen is seen scratching herself. A fun take-off on Greek Mythology with good animation.

Popeye the White Collar Man (1960)

Olive Oyl just loves a white-collar man and wants Popeye to become one. Wimpy offers Popeye a job selling insurance, and the sailor attempts to sell it to an actor working at Flim-Flam Studios. Popeye approaches the actor, Brutus, and says, "You're in a risky business and needs insurance!" Brutus is a stunt man and takes Popeye along while he's performing. Brutus drops Popeye out of a plane and gets him to engineer a train which causes a collision. Popeye then becomes "Zoomo the Human Cannonball". The sailor causes an explosion which lands Brutus into a lion's cage. Brutus yells, "I'll sign anything if you get me out of here!" Brutus lands in the beast's mouth, and Popeye says, "Okay, lion, this has gone far enough!" The one-eyed insurance salesman eats his spinach and says, "Nobody can do that to my client," and begins pounding on the lion. It turns out the beast is a man wearing a lion's costume. The man, who resembles Mr. Magoo, says to Popeye, "Give me one of those indigestion policies, bub; this job is more than I can swallow." Popeye replies, "Me too! I Yam What I Yam and that's a sailor man, not a white collared man!" An amusing story with fine animation.

Sweapea Thru the Looking Glass (1960)

Popeye is going golfing and Olive Oyl to a card party. Popeye explains to the lad, "Eugene will takes care of ya." After the pair leave, Swee'pea says, "Oh, I wonder what's through the looking glass, Eugene?" Suddenly a bird emerges from a Coo-Coo clock and encourages Swee'pea and Eugene to walk through the looking glass. The pair head to the Queen's golf and card game but become separated. Swee'pea discovers Eugene tied up with a pair of talking card-swinging vultures over him. Swee'pea says to the Queen, "That's my Jeep!" The lad drags Eugene away, and the Queen says,

"Come back! It's not your turn! Call out the guards!" Swee'pea defeats the cards by sneezing at them. His sneezes cause each card to fly far away. Eugene and Swee'pea go back home just as both Popeye and Olive arrive. Olive asks Swee'pea what he's been doing. The lad replies, "Well, we went to a golf and card game through the looking glass." Naturally, the adults don't believe him. Olive walks through the looking glass, and Popeye says, "Hey Olive! That's impossible!" When Popeye tries to follow Olive into the looking glass, he crashes against it. Olive pops her head out and sees the fallen Popeye. Swee'pea looks at the audience and says, "Shucks! Nobody ever believes nothing!" A creative reworking of the *Alice in Wonderland* story with excellent animation.

The Black Knight (1960)

Professor O.G. WottaSnozzle is reading about King Arthur and The Round Table. He mentions Popeye happens to be in his time machine. The Professor sends the sailor back to Camelot, England, A.D. 528. Popeye ends up a prisoner of The Black Knight and is brought to King Wimpy. When smoke comes out of Popeye's pipe, the King believes it's witchcraft. Popeye laughs and says, "These characters is afraid-eth of me pipe." Popeye is led to a door to escape, but it leads to a jail cell. His jailer says, "Prisoner of Merlin the Magician, Ethel Merlin. Tomorrow thou die-est on the jousting field." The next day Popeye faces the Black Knight. During the match, King Wimpy keeps requesting a mid-evil hamburger be tossed to him. He can't seem to be able to catch one. The sailor says, "Me only weapon is it, me spinach!" The Black Knight fails to best Popeye, and loaded with weapons, he gallops towards his one-eyed opponent. The sailor turns the Black Knight's armor into a small black automobile that speeds out of the Kingdom. The Professor sends Popeye back home but out drops a mid-evil hamburger. After chewing a bit of it, The Professor says, "I save it for Wimpy." A fun story with good animation.

Jingle Jangle Jungle (1960)

Popeye, Olive Oyl, and Brutus are in the jungle. Brutus says, "Olive, I'm gonna get ya the biggest tiger skin in the world." Popeye responds with, "And I'm going to get ya the prettiest tiger skin in the world." Popeye and Brutus grab their rifles and head off in search of a tiger. Brutus says, "Dat li'l pest ain't gonna beat me to the tiger! I'll get the tiger and get his girl, too." However, Brutus is grabbed by a huge lovesick cannibal plant. The plant keeps kissing Brutus over and over again.

Meanwhile, the tiger has found Olive and is licking her. Olive tickles the tiger's stomach and calls him a great big pussycat. Popeye is captured by unseen natives and tied up. The tiger bounces Olive in the air while Brutus manages to tie up the cannibal plant. With natives rumbling in the bushes, Popeye is being cooked in a giant pot. He discovers they're making him into a spinach stew! Popeye bursts free, and his fists clobber the unseen natives. Olive decides she hates tigers, and Brutus adds, "And I hate flowers, and I hate this jungle!" The scenes with Brutus getting kissed and then trying to escape from the flower are repetitious. Otherwise, it's a cute story with good animation.

The Day Silky Went Blozo (1960)

King Blozo is complaining his kingdom has gone completely crazy. It's due to a dragon who tells his subjects only what they want to hear. Blozo sends Captain Wimpy to capture him. The dragon wins Wimpy over with his philosophical talk. King Blozo says, "Now I need the strongest, most honest, and ugliest man in my kingdom to get rid of that monster." He summons knight Popeye into action against the creature with the gift of gab. The dragon says to Popeye, "When I saw you, I said to myself there's a unique chap, a different sort, with a beautiful soul." Popeye demands the dragon chooses weapons to duel with. The creature selects yo-yos which he has mastered, but that Popeye has a lot of trouble with. A yo-yo rolls towards King Blozo, who becomes delighted playing with it. Popeye eats his spinach and is about to destroy the dragon, but King Blozo intervenes. The cartoon ends with Popeye, the dragon, and King Blozo all playing with yo-yos. The story is unique, and the animation adequate.

Rip Van Popeye (1960)

Swee'pea is very afraid of thunder and lighting. The lad asks Popeye what makes the banging and booming. Popeye says, "It tells all about it in this book here about my ancestors Rip Van Popeye. He was a fren' of the guy whats makin' all the ruckus." Rip Van Popeye and his dog were always wasting time. Rip's wife, Olive Oyl, wanted him to hunt for something to eat. Instead of locating food, the pair find a higher spot to rest out of the sight of Rip's wife. Suddenly a cloud covers Rip and his dog. It's Brutus throwing a bowling ball and striking pins. When the pins are struck, lighting and thunder are created. Rips says, "Well, blow me down, so that's how they makes thunderstorms." Olive spots her husband and demands he comes down. Brutus says to Rip, "Ah, ya sissy! I wouldn't let no woman talk to me like that! I got a special antidote, spinach squeezins!" Rips drinks some and bounces in the air and bowls. The bowling causes lighting to strike Olive. In trying to escape, she runs into a door and is knocked out. Brutus drinks some spinach squeezins and lifts the barrel containing the liquid. He throws it in the air. The barrel hurls from the sky and lands near the unconscious wife. The spinach squeezins fall into Olive's mouth, and she throws rocks at her lazy husband. Using lightning bolts as stairs, Olive travels to the cloud where her husband is. She says, "Why Rip, it's beautiful up here. Let's just stay up here and play nine pins forever." Popeye says, "So ya see, Swee'pea thunder ain't nothing but a game of bowling." When Brutus says, "I got a special antidote," we see a close-up of Popeye's face, and his mouth is moving, but you can't make out what he's saying. He's also muttering over Brutus's dialogue. Rip is given spinach squeezins oozing out from the top of a green mug. The spinach squeezins pinch Rip's nose then suddenly disappear from the top of the mug. A second later, the green liquid is again on the top of the mug. A creative storyline that is hard to focus on due to the sloppy animation.

Mississippi Sissy (1960)
Popeye is sailing aboard the riverboat called The Bella Queen. Olive Oyl, wearing a red bonnet, comes screaming towards him. Popeye asks her, "Is somethin' wrong wit ya?" Olive explains people are after her and asks Popeye to take a letter to New Orleans. She gives Popeye the letter and zooms off. Popeye comments, "Wait, there ain't no stamp on it!" The sailor keeps the note under his hat. Popeye is approached by a Brutus-looking bandit, called Gene Batista Le Brute, who asks if he took a letter. Popeye says, "I ain't no secretary." Brutus replies, "That's obvious. You're too ugly." Brutus picks up Olive and tosses her overboard for not giving him the letter. Popeye rescues her, and Olive takes the note back. Popeye, curious about what's in the letter, follows Olive and meets her father, Wimpy the Indian Scout. Wimpy explains the letter is from a secret agency. Brutus barges in and takes the note. A fight on deck with Popeye ensues, but the sailor ends up walking the plank. Popeye asks, "Could I have a bit of spinach?" Brutus says, "I never refuse the last request. Spinach coming up!" Popeye eats the spinach and causes Brutus to bounce on the plank. This shakes the letter loose, and Popeye grabs it. He delivers it to Four-Four-Four Bagel Street, New Orleans. Brutus opens the door, and the letter says, "You owe for one scout knife, signed Wimpy the Indian Scout." Popeye asks if he has an answer. Brutus says, "Here is your answer!" The sailor is then socked in the face and comments, "That's what I gets for interfering

with the mail delivery." After Popeye says, "Wait, there ain't no stamp on it," his mouth and pipe momentarily vanish. When Popeye opens the door to see where Olive went, there is no one in the room. Suddenly both Olive and Wimpy appear out of nowhere. Sloppy animation in this action-oriented cartoon.

Double Cross Country Feet Race (1960)

Wimpy, the announcer says, "Ladies and Gentleman! You are about to witness the start of the greatest endurance foot race of all time. From here to Los Angeles and return. The contestants are Brutus at two hundred and forty-five pounds and Popeye the Sailor Man." The winner of the race gets a date with Olive Oyl. Brutus cheats right away, tying Popeye in knots. The bearded brute diverts a road sign leading to Los Angeles, but his trick fails. Both Popeye and Brutus burn up the highway. They enter a corn belt, and the heat from their running causes it to pop! After a few more mishaps, they see a sign which states, "Los Angeles City Limits, Fastest Growing City on Earth." The narrator says as houses and streets pop up out of nowhere, "Los Angeles is the fastest growing city in the far west growing by leaps and bounds and bounds and leaps." Once in Los Angeles, the pair race each other back to the starting point. Popeye eats his spinach to increase his speed at the finish while Brutus throws tacks on the road. Popeye's feet pick up the tacks, and he is stopped. Brutus runs right into fresh cement, and Popeye races right by him to win. Olive and Popeye go dancing, but the sailor's feet are in a bucket. Although Wimpy is the announcer, his voice is not the usual one supplied by Jack Mercer. It's as though the animators weren't supposed to use Wimpy but someone else. When Popeye is hanging on to a snow bank, his white shirt becomes flesh-colored. Then it's back to white. Some of the dialogue between Popeye and Brutus is out of sync with their mouth movements. Nice visual puns can't make up for the sloppy animation.

Fashion Photography (1960)

Olive Oyl has a camera tied to her toes. She plans on taking her picture for a fashion magazine. Instead, the camera falls on Olive's foot, and she hollers, "Oh!" Popeye approaches Olive's house (stock footage from *Popeye's Used Car*) and offers to take her picture. Olive lies on the floor, holding a bunch of grapes toward her mouth. Popeye accidentally smashes the grapes on her face, and the sailor remarks, "That's funny! Ya, look like a bug on the rug." Olive says, "Oh! What a picture taker, you amateur! Get out!" She kicks Popeye and the camera out of the house.

Popeye bumps into the approaching Brutus. Olive demands Popeye give back the camera, and Brutus punches it in her direction. The camera smacks Olive right in the face. When she cries, won't anyone take her picture, both Popeye and Brutus offer. The men brawl and break the camera. Both men buy new cameras with stands. Brutus and Popeye clobber each other with their cameras in front of Olive's door. Olive opens her front door to inquire about the noise and gets clobbered by both cameras! Popeye and Brutus set up their cameras with flashbulbs, ready to take Olive's picture inside the house. The flashbulbs go off, blinding Olive, and she yells, "Oooh, I hate cameras, I hate Brutus, I hate Popeye." The fighting photographers are thrown out of Olive's house along with their equipment.

As they fight outside of Olive's house, they see Alice the Goon carrying paint supplies going inside. Olive looks at Alice's painting and remarks, "Oooh, it's lovely. Better than Popeye or Brutus's pictures. Now I can be in the fashion magazine." Popeye and Brutus see the modern-looking painting and laugh at it. Olive smashes the painting over their heads, calling both men "Uncouth." Popeye and Brutus say they're "couth' and sing, "Cause we're real couth fighting men!" A funny story where Olive gets a lot of physical punishment. Aside from the stock footage at the beginning of the cartoon, the animation is entirely satisfactory.

I Yam Wot Yammesia (1960)

Popeye, Swee'pea, and Wimpy are at Olive Oyl's house on a quiet Sunday afternoon. Popeye is playing with Swee'pea, but in the process, they're both bonked on the head and switch personalities! Wimpy tells a panicked Olive, "Calm yourself, dear lady. As a referee in the prize ring, I have observed this phenomenon many times." Wimpy explains they both now suffer from amnesia. When he offers to bonk their heads to restore each to normal, Olive intervenes. Instead, Olive and Wimpy's heads get bonked, and they trade personalities. Confusion reigns, and Brutus knocks at the door. The bearded visitor says, "First invite I ever got from Olive, hope she doesn't notice my five o'clock shadow." Brutus kisses Olive, but Wimpy's voice comes out of her mouth. Brutus is totally confused by the switched personalities. Swee'pea, with Popeye's personality, punches Brutus, and the blow causes objects to fly across the house. Olive, Wimpy, and Swee'pea are restored to normal. Popeye and Brutus now have the personalities of babies. Wimpy offers to restore them to normal with a blow on the head, but Olive says, "No, no a thousand times no. T'is far better thus." A delightful cartoon with good animation.

Paper Pasting Pandemonium (1960)

Olive Oyl feels her house looks terrible and wants it re-papered for her guests to see that evening. She calls Popeye and says, "I want new wallpaper, Popeye. I want my whole house repapered by five o'clock.' Popeye agrees and heads toward Olive's house with supplies to do the job. Popeye creates chaos, and Brutus arrives to see what's going on. Olive explains to him, "Oh, Popeye's just wrecking my house!" Brutus says he can do a better job than Popeye. Olive growls, "Oh, stop bickering, boys! Times a wasting. Start pasting both of you, or I'll paste both of you." Brutus uses nails and a hammer to put the paper on the wall. He clonks Popeye on the head when the sailor objects. In retaliation, Popeye splashes paste on the brute's face with his brush. Brutus puts up actual Popeye comic strips, illustrated by Bela Zaboly, on the walls and says, "Hey, this is funny wallpaper." Popeye tears it off, explaining that's for the playroom. With only five minutes until company arrives, Popeye eats his spinach and bops Brutus, who flies out of the house. Brutus says, "I didn't know this was flypaper." With super speed, Popeye throws various kinds of wallpaper on the walls. Olive's company arrives and say, "Man, it's crazy!" "Way Out!" "It's the Endsville!" Olive goes to kiss Popeye, but his face is covered in wallpaper paste. Olive says, "I'm stuck on you, Popeye." Popeye sings, "'Cause I'm Popeye, the paper hanging man." A fun, colorful cartoon with excellent animation.

Coach Popeye (1960)

Popeye is reading the newspaper when a baseball crashes through his window bonking him on the head. This is followed by a football, basketball, horseshoe, and arrows, which pin him to the wall. Swee'pea and Deezil are playing in the yard. Popeye comes out and says to both of them, "Now listen, you kids, I am gonna shows ya how to play the game the right way without bustin' things all up." Brutus appears over the fence and tells Popeye to let the kids have some fun. Popeye pulls out the rule book, and Brutus says, "I make up my own!" Popeye and Brutus engage in a game of catch with a baseball.

Brutus gets rough, so Popeye decides to pull out a can of spinach. The sailor says to the children, "Kids, this is the wrong way, but I gotta teach him a lesson." As Popeye eats his spinach, Brutus looks at the viewers and says, "Gee, I didn't count on this!" Popeye kicks a football which gets wedged in Brutus's mouth. The brute picks up a heavy ball and throws it, which bops Popeye on the head. Both men charge at each other and create a lot of clouds. Within the clouds, tennis rackets, balls, bats, and footballs go flying through the air. Once the dust settles, Brutus is skipping rope, and Popeye is playing jacks.

Brutus says, "Wheee, I get the message being a good sport is fun!" A fun cartoon with excellent animation. Mae Questel gives a nasal twang to Deezil's voice which was not heard previously in *Popeye's Junior Headache*.

Popeyed Columbus (1960)

Professor O.G. WottaSozzle uses his time machine (via stock footage from *Time Marches Backwards)* to send Popeye back to the days of Columbus. Popeye assumes the role of Columbus. He announces to his crew, "Before we sails on upon this most perilous voyage of our lives, I wishes to propose a toast. A toast to one who has hocked her jewels to make this voyage possible. To none other than her majesty, the Queen." Columbus's crew keeps clanking their containers full of alcohol. Each time this is done, some of the alcohol falls on Columbus, which causes him to get hiccups. The Queen tries to cure the hiccups by salting Columbus's tongue, but he ends up swallowing the container. She suggests making funny faces and he hold his breath.

Meanwhile, Brutus, the ship's Captain, warns the crew, declaring, "I tells you swabs this voyage is senseless! Columbus is sending us all into certain danger. Our ships will be crushed like eggshells by giant squid. And will all be swallowed alive by the monstrous sea serpents." The Queen tells Columbus about a mutiny brewing, and he pulls out some Spinacho. Columbus punches the crew back onto the ship. Then the Queen eats some Spinacho and joins the fight. The team is back on board, and Columbus sails while still having the hiccups. The Professor remarks, "And the hiccups is maybe why Columbus smashed into American instead of finding a quick way to the West Indies." A fun story with adequate animation.

Popeye Revere (1960)

Swee'pea asks, "Popeye, did Paul Revere really ride like it says in the poem you just read to me?" Popeye replies, it was really great, great granpappy Poopdeck who made the ride. As the sailor tells Poopdeck's story, Swee'pea holds up a sign called "Real Corn." Popeye explains, "But there was a tore named a Brutus who was skulking in the shadows watching Poopdeck." Brutus wonders where Poopdeck could be riding this time of night? The ride's signal appears, but Brutus attempts to stop Poopdeck by throwing him in a barrel of molasses. Popeye says, "And it looked like the fate of the nation was all gummed up when Poopdeck remembered his spinach stuff with a pinch of snuff." Poopdeck sneezed himself out of the barrel and managed to shove Brutus in it. Poopdeck was off on his horse, spreading the alarm. Swee'pea asks Popeye if Poopdeck was really beat from the ride. The sailor explained he could make the ride because he was stuck to his saddle by molasses. Swee'pea says to the viewers, "Huh, that's a pretty sticky story if you ask me." Popeye replies, "Yeah, but you're stuck with it!" A cute history lesson with good animation.

Popeye in Haweye (1960)

Olive Oyl is in Hawaii needing a guide. Popeye and Brutus compete for her business. Olive says, "I'll take both your tours on one condition. I only pay off to the one I think is the best." Brutus takes her on a frantically-paced tour. When her tour with Brutus is finished, Popeye says, "Oh you poor thing, ya looks a little beat. Maybe ya better rests a bit." Olive doesn't want to rest and goes on a calm, relaxing tour with Popeye. When Popeye and Olive return, Brutus, remarks, "Better give me my dough, sugar." The check is made out to Popeye, and Brutus punches the sailor. Then the brute slams a guitar over Popeye's head. Olive leans over to the injured tour guide and asks if he's hurt. Popeye looks at the leis she's wearing around her neck and says, "Spinach!" Popeye consumes the leis and knocks Brutus so hard he lands in the middle of a luau. Popeye then takes Olive on another tour in the moonlight. A humorous cartoon with adequate animation.

Forever Ambergris (1960)

Olive Oyl puts on a perfume called "Man-Slaughter by Mac Fracture." The aroma puts Popeye in a trance, and he agrees to babysit Swee'pea. The tyke screams the sailor's name, and he snaps out of his spell. Swee'pea says to Popeye, "If you don't tell me a sea story, I'm gonna yell and cry!" Popeye tells the story about ambergris which comes from big whales and is worth thousands of dollars. Swee'pea wants to know if Popeye ever found any. The sailor tells the story about the time he, Wimpy, and Brutus went looking for ambergris. Popeye sees a big whale and ambergris in the ocean. Popeye, Wimpy, and Brutus work in unison to get the ambergris out of the sea and lock it in a treasure chest. Popeye says, "I'll build an orphan's home with my share." However, Brutus has other ideas and steals the treasure chest.

Brutus, in Paris, mutters, "There oughta be a perfumery factory around here somewhere." Popeye catches up to Brutus, and they climb a tower. Popeye knocks the treasure chest out of the criminal's hands, and it lands inside a cement mixer. Popeye concludes his story to Swee'pea and says, "And ever since that street in Paris has been forever ambergris." The ending makes Swee'pea cry, which infuriates Olive. She smashes a vase over Popeye's head, and the sailor sings, "That perfume's me 'finich' it smells just like spinach, I'm Popeye the Sailor Man." A creative story with adequate animation.

Popeye de Leon (1960)

Popeye tells Swee'pea to wake up as he has bought him a present. The excited lad pops out of bed and says, "Oh, candy, pop, cookies, ice cream, fire engines, or money?" The gift is a brand-new history book. Upon seeing the book, Swee'pea goes back to bed. Popeye convinces Swee'pea to listen to his version of how the Fountain of Youth was discovered by his gran-ancestor. Popeye, Wimpy, Brutus, and Swee'pea are sailing and land in Florida. Suddenly they are attacked by bows and arrows. Popeye says, "I'm going to shore to make friends with the natives." Popeye meets an Indian Princess who calls herself Olive-Ha! Ha!

The Princess shows Popeye and Brutus where the Fountain of Youth is located. Olive explains, "It's guarded by little ol' evil spirits." The spirit is a crocodile who tangles with Popeye. Brutus and Princess Olive are sitting in a tree, witnessing Swee'pea approaching the crocodile. Popeye grabs the beast by the tail and says, "Gets away from Swee'pea ya blast'id handbag." The sailor tosses the crocodile into the Fountain, and it turns into an egg. The branch Brutus and the Princess are sitting on snaps. Olive manages to grab onto another branch, but Brutus falls into the Fountain, turning into a baby. Popeye drains the Fountain and discovers the bottom is full of green weeds. The Princess says, "We little ol' natives call that stuff Spinach." Popeye concludes his story to Swee'pea by showing him a can of "Fountain of Youth" Spinach. Popeye failed to mention the ancestors of Swee'pea, Brutus and Wimpy were included in his story. A nonsensical history lesson with choppy animation.

Popeyed Fisherman (1960)

Olive Oyl and Swee'pea knock on Popeye's door. Olive asks the sailor, "Popeye would you teach Swee'pea and I how to fish." Swee'pea wants to catch a whale. Popeye agrees and grabs his fishing pole. Popeye explains to Olive and Swee'pea they must be patient while trying to catch fish. While he goes on and on, both Olive and Swee'pea catch a lot of fish. All Popeye manages to catch is a giant tire. Olive holds up their fish and says, "Did we catch these right, Popeye, did we, huh?" Popeye takes the pair boat fishing, and Swee'pea asks, "Popeye, what's the biggest fishy in the whole, whole world?"

Popeye tells the lad it would be a whale and goes on to describe fictional ones. As he describes these fantastic whales, they go past their boat. Popeye says, "Well, the gray ones is the most common type. Then there's the purple ones. And *err-uh, uh* blue ones. Pink ones too, but the pink ones is kind of sissy lookin'." Popeye says the meanest whale is white and the kind no one has ever really seen. A giant white whale approaches the boat and swallows it. Popeye pops out of the whale's spout and holds on to its tale. Olive Oyl takes out a mop and cleans the inside of the whale. The whale swims towards Fishland, where it belongs. Swee'pea is given a reward for bringing back the whale. The cartoon concludes with Popeye fishing in a goldfish bowl, muttering, "Inexperience is the best teacher." A fun cartoon with good animation.

Popeye in the Grand Steeplechase (1960)

Popeye and Olive Oyl read a sign which states, "Big Steeple Chase Today for Gentleman Jockeys." Olive wants Popeye to enter the race, and he goes off to buy a horse. Brutus, who owns a Glue Factory, overhears the pair and disguises himself as Colonial Brumus. The phony Colonial tells Popeye, "I has a horse, sir, that not only jumps, sir, but he'll fly, sir." Popeye buys him but, after removing the horse's blanket, discovers he's been gypped. The sailor says, "You ain't no jumper. I don't think yer even a horse even." Popeye still enters the race, but Brutus puts springs on his horse's hoofs to give him an edge. Popeye feeds his horse organic spinach alfa. This provides the animal with the energy to win the race. Popeye's horse knocks Brutus and his nag into a water hole. The sailor wins the race, and Olive shouts, "Oh, Popeye, my hero! My gentleman jockey!" Brutus's horse keeps pushing the bully into the water hole meant for Popeye. An amusing story with excellent animation.

Uncivil War (1960)

Swee'pea says, "Popeye tell about some scary things, huh. What's the most dangerous things in the whole world? Popeye shows him pictures in an album. The sailor says, "Long ago dragons were considered pretty scary, but then they discovered there ain't no such things. Goons is really scary at first, but nots when ya gets to know them. Sea Hag and vultures aren't very nice to meet in the dark. But now we comes to a real scary thing, the bad driver." Popeye explains how this driver has an uncontrollable urge to show off in front of people. Popeye, seen driving a car, explains how it's important to read traffic signs while on the road. He halts his vehicle to read a sign which says "No Stopping". This causes three cars behind him to collide with each other. Popeye explains how speeders always try to beat a traffic signal. Brutus, behind the wheel, keeps racing his car only to be stopped three times by a red light. Wimpy, driving past him, comments, "Say, do you know something? You're not very smart!" Brutus looks at the audience and remarks, "You know, I think he's right." Popeye explains about how tail riders hate to see a safe distance between them and the guy in front. After more harrowing driving tales, Popeye asks Swee'pea if he's learned anything. Swee'pea says, "Ho! Ho! Ho! You bet; I'm never, never going to drive my bike over two hundred miles an hour." The lad zooms off, and Popeye remarks, "Well, you can't learn 'em too young." A humorous cartoon with excellent animation.

Popeye the Piano Mover (1960)

Popeye and Brutus are in the piano moving business. Olive calls Popeye and tells him she needs her piano moved. It turns out to be a giant piano, and Brutus asks, "But how we gonna move it, Popeye? It won't go through the door." Popeye replies, "We ties a rope on it and pushes it out the window." Popeye's plan works, and the piano is tied to their automobile. Popeye pushes the piano up a flight of long stairs, but Brutus hits it by accident. The piano ends up zooming into the street with Popeye right behind it. The musical instrument smashes into Wimpy, the policeman who shouts, "Arrest that piano!" Popeye plows into Wimpy, who yells, "Arrest that piano chaser!" After a hectic chase, Popeye ends up on top of the piano, which, again, crashes into Wimpy. With Popeye on top of it, the piano smashes in and out of stores but makes its way back to Olive's house. Popeye grabs a light fixture on the ceiling, and the piano bumps into Brutus. Brutus lands on top of the piano, and Wimpy shouts, "I arrest you for reckless piano driving." A fast-paced cartoon with excellent animation.

Popeye's Testimonial Dinner (1960)

A handsomely dressed and top-hatted Popeye says, "Gee Olive, I feels foolish in these sissy clothes." Olive Oyl replies, "Oh, but Popeye, you just look darling. Hurry up now, or we'll be late for a surprise party." Olive blindfolds Popeye, and we see a parade of colorful characters enter a building. They include The Sea Hag, King Blozo, Professor O.G. WottaSnozzle, and Eugene the Jeep. Popeye is having a dinner in his honor which makes

Brutus jealous. Olive removes Popeye's blindfold, and he sees Wimpy, Alice the Goon, Eugene the Jeep, The Sea Hag, and Swee'pea singing a song.

The group sings, "Popeye, you've done it again! Popeye and spinach did it again. You went through that spinach patch, scooped it up and down the hatch, Popeye, you've done it again." King Blozo recalled Popeye's mighty deeds from *Popeye and the Dragon*. Then he remembered the time Popeye and Brutus played golf in *Golf Brawl*. Brutus shows up and says to the audience, "They're making out like I was the villain. I oughta be the hero." Olive brings up the time she was minding the store when a bully came along, and Popeye helped her. Brutus replies, "Now hold on, that ain't the way I seen it. Now listen to my side of it." Popeye says, "Go ahead, lets him talk." Brutus continues, "Naturally, I had to protect myself, so what was I to do? I asks ya. So outnumbered, I asked for help from a kindly ol' witch who agreed to help. And who got blamed for it me!" Brutus then recounts his fight with Popeye from *Coffee House*. Brutus begins bawling, and Popeye's guests feel sorry for him. Popeye says to Brutus, "I cants stands seeing a strong man cry. Be my guest." The guest of honor gives Brutus his spinach. After the brute eats it, he socks Popeye in the air. The sailor's guests sing how Popeye again saved the day. When Popeye hands Brutus his spinach can, it slightly changes color. An interesting premise allowing both Brutus and Popeye to be victorious. Fine animation.

Around the World in Eighty Ways (1960)

Popeye and Brutus read a sign which reads, "Win a Barrel of Money on the Easy Come, Easy Go Show." They both enter a race running around the world. Wimpy, the show's host, announces that the winner receives a barrel of money. The pair begin racing around the globe, and Brutus ends up in a hot air balloon while Popeye travels on the back of a turtle. After some hazardous encounters, they both land in Siberia. Popeye asks, "Hey Brutus, you hungry?" Brutus replies, "Yeah." Popeye offers him his can of spinach. Brutus thanks him while Popeye winks at the viewer. Popeye asks the spinach-fortified brute, "How'd ya like to sock me on the kisser."

Brutus wallops the sailor who travels all around the world. Brutus realizes he'd been had. Popeye wins the race and is anxious to get his prize. Wimpy says, "Here is your barrel of money containing a cool one million, five hundred and seventy-five thousand, nine hundred and twenty-eight lead pazookas. Worth a cool two U.S. Bucks!" The angry sailor slams the barrel over Wimpy's head. When Popeye picks up the barrels, you hear him say "Lead," followed by "Pazookas" in Brutus' voice. The script called for Brutus to be in the final scene, which was not conveyed to the animators. A fun cartoon with excellent animation.

Popeye's Fixit Shop (1960)

Popeye and Brutus both have Fixit shops next to each other. Olive Oyl brings her phone in to be repaired at Popeye's store. She walks into Brutus's establishment by accident and asks the brute, "Oh Brutus, are you one of Popeye's employees?" Brutus replies, "A silent partner, c'mon in." Olive asks Brutus if he can fix her telephone. The bearded Fixit man goes over to Popeye's shop and asks to borrow his telephone. He takes the sailor's phone and leaves Olive's broken one in its place. Popeye receives a phone call about four clocks needing repair. He will be paid five hundred dollars cash and heads over to the fourth floor, main, upstairs City Hall. Brutus overhears the call and rushes over to fix the clocks. Olive asks Popeye, "Oh, how exciting Popeye, can I come along?" He agrees, but Olive gets dizzy, and Popeye says to her when they get to the top floor: "You just stands here an' tells me when I gets the hands on the clock fixed the right time." Popeye enters the room where the clocks are, and shouts, "Brutus, What are you doing here?" Brutus replies, "Beat it. I'm gonna fix these clocks." The two brawl, which affects how the clock hands move. This causes complex problems for Olive. When things settle down, she observes Popeye and Brutus shouting at each other.

Popeye says, "I tells ya I'm gonna fix this clock!" Brutus yells back, "No, you're not!" Olive pulls out a can of spinach from Popeye's lunch pail and declares, "I'm going to fix both their clocks!" She eats the spinach and bops the boys' heads together. Olive orders both of them to fix the clocks, even if it takes forever. Popeye and Brutus repair the clocks by using their own arms as hands. When Popeye enters a room called "Head Clock Watcher," he discovers a drowsy Wimpy. The animation of Popeye entering the Head Clock Watcher room is reused when he enters the Clock Room. It's the same scene because, after being told it's the Clock Room, the sign says Head Clock Watcher. A fun cartoon with adequate animation.

Bell Hop Popeye (1960)

At the hotel Waldorf Hysteria, Brutus, the manager, calls for Popeye, the bellhop. He shows Popeye a newspaper that states, "The Maharanee Olive Oyl Arrives Today. To Stop at The Waldorf Hysteria." When she arrives, Popeye is there to greet her, and he bows. Suddenly Brutus steps on him, saying, "Out of my way, runt! I'll handle this." However, it's Popeye who brings up her luggage. The Maharanee kisses him in return. Brutus asks,

"Where'd you get the kiss?" Popeye, in a lovesick daze, says, "It's a tip from the Maharanee." When the Maharanee calls and wants sixty pounds of raw meat delivered to her room, Brutus takes Popeye's bellhop job. Brutus is greeted by a ferocious tiger who wants the meat. The growling beast chases Brutus around the hotel. Popeye remarks, "So ya wanted to takes me job, huh?" Brutus ends up tossing the meat and himself in a safe. The Maharanee goes looking for "Tootsy," her tiger, while Brutus shouts from inside the safe, "Popeye, get me outta here!" The cartoon concludes with the tiger trying different combinations to open the safe. A fun story with excellent animation.

Cartoons Produced by Paramount Cartoon Studios

STORY: Seymour Kneitel, Carl Meyer, and Jack Mercer. SCENICS: Anton Loeb and Robert Owen. MUSIC: Winston Sharples. ANIMATORS: WM B. Pattengill, I. Klein, Jim Logan, George Germanetti, Morey Reden, Dante Barbetta, John Gentilella, Dick Hall, Gerry Dorvak, Jack Ehret, Irving Dressler, Nick Tafuri, Sam Stimson, and Al Pross. DIRECTOR: Seymour Kneitel

The animation in these cartoons is generally excellent; however, I will note errors that occurred.

Hits and Missiles (1960)
Popeye, Olive Oyl, and Wimpy visit Cape Canaveral and shown a rocket ship called Luna No. 1. The trio is informed it will be the first rocket to land on the moon to see if there are inhabitants. Wimpy uses a small frying pan under his hat to cook eggs. When Olive goes searching for him, she looks at his head and says, "For heaven's sake, what's cooking?" Two fried eggs cover Olive's eyes, and she stumbles onto the blast-off lever. The ship roars off into space and lands on the moon. The planet is ruled by a King made of cheese who imprisons Popeye and Olive. The King shouts, "Send in the taxpayers." A little cheese person stumbles and crushes his payment which consists of crackers. The King roars, "Just a worthless pile of crumbs! Take him to the torture chamber!" The little cheese man is dipped in hot mustard, and this angers Popeye. The sailor uses his pipe to bust out of prison but is flattened by the cheese King. Popeye eats his spinach and smacks the King into little pieces of cheese!

All the little cheese people cheer Popeye as he prepares to take off in the rocket ship. Popeye sings, "Cheese is strong to the finich when mixed with some spinach, says Popeye the Sailor Man!" One of two pilots produced for the series. *Hits and Missiles* featured Olive in the style of dress she wore in the color Popeye theatrical cartoons by Famous Studios.

The Ghost Host (1960)

Popeye and Olive Oyl are driving when suddenly the car gets a flat tire. Olive thinks they should turn back because it looks like it's going to storm. Popeye says, "Olive, sailors have a seventh sense about the weather from sailing the seventh seas, and me sea-faring eyes tells me it's gonna be clear sailing." Suddenly a thunderstorm hits, and Olive asks Popeye, "Well, Mr. Weatherman, what does your sea-faring eyes tell you now!" As she speaks, Popeye's sailor's hat turns into a dunce cap. The pair find shelter in a haunted house inhabited by three ghosts. The spooks scare the couple with various tricks, including having a table full of food appear. When Popeye says he's hungry enough to eat a horse, the animal appears on the dining table. While Popeye and Olive rub their eyes, the horse vanishes. Popeye says, "Olive, did you saw what I seeded?" A frightened Olive replies, "I did if what you seeded was a horse!" Then the table cloth scoops up the food and smacks Popeye against a wall.

An angry Popeye declares, "Tha's all I can stands I can't stands no more!" Popeye eats his spinach and lifts the house. The three ghosts plop out! One of the spirits says, "He's a real kook!" Another spook says, "Like way-off, like berserk." The trio of ghosts runs away, and Popeye sings, "When ya visits a ghost, he should be a nice host like Popeye the Sailor Man." When you see Popeye singing in the car, he has his pipe with Olive by his side. However, Popeye's pipe is missing in his close-up.

Strikes, Spares An' Spinach (1960)

Brutus arrives at Popeye's home and wants to go bowling with him. The sailor says, "Sorry Brutus but I has a date with Olive ta teaches her how to bowl." At the alley, the treacherous Brutus secretly pours glue into the holes of Popeye's bowling ball. The sticky substance causes Popeye to slam into the pins. Olive Oyl says, "But Popeye I thought you were supposed to let go of the ball when you throw it?" Brutus puts rubber cement into the holes of Olive's ball. She goes crashing down the alley! Olive Oyl says, "Popeye, that's the end! I'm through this game is to rough!" Brutus' hearty laugh reveals his presence. Popeye spots both the glue and rubber cement. He eats his spinach and tackles the departing jokester. Brutus is formed into a ball and hurled at several trash cans. Popeye sings, "I strikes and I spares when any culprit just dares to fool Popeye the Sailor Man!" A fun cartoon!

Jeep is Jeep (1960)

Olive Oyl leaves Swee'pea with Popeye while she goes shopping. Olive advises the sailor not to let Swee'pea out of his sight. Popeye receives a package in the mail from an old friend from India. A funny animal appears out of the box and hands Popeye a note which states, "Dear Popeye, Happy Birthday! This is your birthday present. His name is Eugene the Jeep, and he has magical powers." The Jeep vanishes in front of the sailor, proving he can perform magic. While this is going on, Swee'pea crawls out of the house. Popeye asks the Jeep to help locate Swee'pea. Popeye follows the Jeep, who walks through a stone wall. Popeye bonks his head, trying to do the same. The sailor winds up his fist and says, "I ain't got no magical powers, but I got this!" Popeye's fist smashes through the stone wall. Swee'pea is on a railroad track picking a flower. A speeding train is headed right for the baby. Popeye shouts, "Swee'pea, get off those tracks!" The sailor eats his spinach and wallops the train before it reaches Swee'pea. The Jeep carries the lad back to Popeye's house. Olive returns and sees Swee'pea all alone and yells at Popeye. The flustered babysitter says, "I can explains it all, Olive. It all started with Eugene the magical Jeep!" Olive doesn't believe a word of what he's saying, and as she continues to yell, the Jeep pops up on her behind. This cartoon is a reworking of Fleischer Studios *The Jeep* (1938).

The Spinach Scholar (1960)

Olive Oyl informs Popeye she won't see him again until he gets an education. Popeye explains, "But, but, but Olive! I've been to sea since I was a kid and I ain't never had a chance to get edjumcated." Olive insists it's never too late to start and says she won't see Popeye again until he decides to go to school. Popeye visits the Principal at the local school and asks him, "Is this the place ya enrolls ta gets an edjumication?" The Principal replies, "*Hmmm*...you look like a smart young fellow. I think you can start in our highest grade!" Although Popeye begins as a student in the eighth-grade class, he ends up in kindergarten due to his mistakes. The dejected sailor enters the kindergarten class and sadly says, "This is my last chance on encounter their ain't no lower grade."

The teacher asks her small students who can spell 'cat'. They all raise their hands except Popeye. The teacher says, "I'm sure Mr. Popeye can spell 'cat', can't you, come, come." Popeye pulls out his spinach and eats it. His brain grows in size, and he exclaims, "C-a-t, Cat!" Popeye visits Olive, and she asks him how school was? The confident sailor replies, "Why there was nothing to it, Olive! I went through the whole school in one day!" Popeye sings, "Your edjumication must start if you wants to be smart like Popeye the Sailor Man!" A delightful cartoon.

Psychiatricks (1960)

Brutus tells Olive Oyl that Popeye is slug happy and going off his rocker. Olive says, "Oh Brutus, you're his best friend. What can we do to help him?" Brutus gives Olive a business card and wants Popeye to see a particular psychiatrist. Popeye visits Olive, but she grabs him and shouts, "Popeye, it's about time someone did something about all your unnecessary fighting!" Popeye is lying on the couch in the office of Professor Ed Shrinker. The Professor asks Popeye to recall the first time he was engaged in a battle. Popeye recalls, "It was a long, long, time ago when I was a little baby kid about two years old."

Baby Brutus came along and flipped over the carriage Popeye was lying in. The one-eyed baby took a good swig of his spinach juice and socked the bully. Professor Shrinker asks Popeye when he was older, did he still have occasion to fight? Popeye recalls that Brutus flipped the pair up in the air when he was riding Olive to school on his bicycle. The young sailor boy pulled out his spinach and socked Brutus. Upon hearing this second story, Professor Shrinker shouts, "Ah-ha! That's it! It was the spinach which was the cause of all your troubles!" Popeye tosses his spinach can out the window, realizing it was eating the vegetable which gave him strength for his fighting. The can lands on Olive's head, and she says. "That's funny; it's Popeye's special brand." Suddenly Professor Shrinker reveals himself as Brutus, who growls, "Now runt, I'll take the fight out of you without that spinach crimping my style." Popeye is socked near an open window, and Olive witnesses the fight. She feeds Popeye his spinach, and he bops Brutus! Popeye sings, "Spinach ain't the diagnosis, Brutus was the neurosis of Popeye the Sailor Man." A fun cartoon! It's interesting to learn Brutus is Popeye's best friend!?!

Rags to Riches to Rags (1960)

Popeye, Olive Oyl, and Wimpy are listening to a lawyer who says, "And to my only living heir, J. Wellington Wimpy, I bequeath my entire estate, signed Lord Percival Wimpy." Popeye congratulates Wimpy on being a millionaire. Wimpy is soon living in a grand estate with a butler. While eating his hamburger breakfast, Wimpy listens to the morning news program. The announcer says, "For the latest on the fight of the century, we switch you to the training quarters of Popeye the Sailor. And now to the training quarters of his opponent, Kid Nitro!" Kid Nitro is seen socking fighter after fighter! Wimpy decides to bet his entire fortune on Kid Nitro. Wimpy's butler says, "I've been thinking, sir, suppose Popeye wins the fight?" Wimpy explains to ensure his investment he will be referring the bout. In the ring, Wimpy and his butler use dirty tricks to give Kid Nitro the advantage. Popeye is down, and Wimpy starts the count. Suddenly he begins shedding tears and cries, "I can't do it…my good friend, Popeye." Wimpy pulls out a can of spinach from Popeye's bucket. The fortified fighter gives Kid Nitro his twister punch and wins the bout. Wimpy is poor once again and asks the sailor, "Popeye, my good friend, would you please buy me a hamburger for which I will gladly pay you Tuesday." Popeye agrees and sings, "Even down to the end, you're still the best friend of Popeye the Sailor Man!" A charming cartoon.

Hair Cut-Ups (1960)

Popeye brings Swee'pea to the barbershop for his first hair cut, but the tyke won't remove his hat. Popeye tells him the story about another fellow who didn't like to get his hair cut. The sailor explains. "There was a young fella named Sampson who was the strongest man in the whole wide world. He never had his hair cut 'cause he believed his strength came from his long hair." Another fellow thought he was stronger than Sampson and challenged him to feats of strength. He always lost until realizing where Sampson's power came from. Disguising himself as Delilah, he lures Sampson into a barbershop. Sampson is put to sleep, and his hair is cut off! The bald ex-strong man shouts, "Yikes me hair is gone-est, and so is me strength!" Sampson is socked into a spinach garden where he chews the vegetable and shouts, "Me strength is return-ith." Sampson socks his rival, who ends up spinning around the world. Popeye explains to Swee'pea that Sampson was stronger after he had his haircut. The lad takes off his head to reveal one lone hair which shocks the barber. An entertaining cartoon.

Poppa Popeye (1960)

A man visits Popeye and says, "I am the real father of the orphan Swee'pea, and I've come to claim him." The man gives Popeye a fake birth certificate to prove his claim and takes off with Swee'pea. It turns out he's a circus performer and needs the lad for his act. Under the billing "Sando and Son," Swee'pea is subjected to a dangerous high wire act. Popeye is so sad that he turns into a baby! Olive Oyl calls the doctor who examines

Popeye and discovers he has Melakonkas. The doctor explains, "Which means he has lost someone he loves very much." The doctor and Olive find it is Swee'pea who Popeye is missing. Swee'pea leaves the circus and heads home. Unfortunately, the father returns to reclaim him, but Popeye says, "If he comes to you when you calls him instead of staying wit' me ya can has him for good."

The phony father briefly leaves but comes back and says, "Come to me, Swee'pea, see the nice toys!" Swee'pea clings to Popeye's leg, and the faker leaves. Olive says to Popeye, "Oh Popeye, it was wonderful how Swee'pea resisted temptation to stay with you…why Swee'pea's clothes were nailed to the floor!" Popeye explains, "Oh the nail, huh. That was just an ace in the hole. Just a sort of 'in case'." This episode was based on a 1937 *Thimble Theatre* comic strip story from the Sunday page, where Swee'pea's mother came back to claim him. As in this cartoon, Swee'pea's clothes were also nailed to the floor when the mother tempted him with toys. During the scene where the doctor takes Popeye's temperature, the lower half of his baby bonnet briefly disappears while the sailor chews the thermometer.

Quick Change Ollie (1960)

Wimpy says to Popeye, "Ah, if we only could go back to ye olden days when men ate real meals. Roast venison, wild roast boar, and whole roasted oxen!" Popeye tells Wimpy all he thinks about is food. If the sailor were living in ye olden days, he'd be a fighting hero. The Wiffle Bird strolls by, and Wimpy grabs the creature. The bird pleads not to be eaten and says, "If you just rub my head feathers, your wishes will all come true." Wimpy rubs the feathers and wishes they were all living in ye olden days. Popeye encounters a crying King who says, "Ollie the wicked magician has captured my castle and holds my daughter, the Princess, a prisoner. Popeye meets the magician who bests him with various tricks. When the magician grabs the sailor, he becomes a giant. He asks Popeye, "Now what magic has ye got to top-est this, ya runt?" Popeye says, "Me spinach magic!" Popeye eats the vegetable, and his arm turns into a drill. He drills the magician back down to the ground defeating him. The King offers The Princess's hand in marriage to Popeye! She is very ugly, and the sailor rubs the Wiffle Bird's head feathers to wish himself and Wimpy back home. An exciting cartoon.

Valley of the Goons (1960)

Popeye is eating a spinach burger at Rough House's cafe. Another sailor sits next to Popeye. This shifty-looking swab pours knock-out powder in

Popeye's milk. Quickly Popeye falls asleep, and the sailor, who drugged him, carries him out of the cafe. When Popeye wakes up, he finds himself aboard a ship headed to the Valley of the Goons. The ship's Captain says, "We're headed for the Valley of the Goons to take on a cargo of Goon skin." Popeye rushes towards the Captain, hollering, "Waits a minute! Ya cants hunts fer Goons, that's inhuman. An I won't let ya do it!" The Captain orders Popeye thrown in the brig. The Captain's men invade Goon Valley, which is called "The Backwards Country." Everything the Goons do is done backward. For example, a Goon tosses away his sandwich and eats the plates instead. The Captain's men end up capturing all of the Goons using carrots as bait. Popeye, in prison, sees what's happening and says, "They've got them nice Goon people as prisoners." He pulls out his spinach and busts out of jail. Popeye heads to the island and feeds spinach to the captured Goons. The sailor says to the Goons, "Just eat this spinach, and you'll be able to takes care of them water rats!" The men approach the Goons, but full of spinach, they use their chins to sock their attackers. Each man goes flying back onto their ship, and Popeye socks the last of them. Popeye plants spinach seeds so the Goons will always be able to protect themselves. A baby Goon eats spinach and, with his newfound super-breath, blows Popeye, on a raft, to sea. Popeye sings, "They'll be strong to the finich 'cause they learned to eat spinach from Popeye the Sailor Man." An excellent cartoon based on a *Thimble Theatre* comic strip storyline from 1938 by E.C. Segar.

Me Quest for Poopdeck Pappy (1960)

Popeye, Olive Oyl, and Swee'pea are sailing in the ocean. Olive asks, "Popeye, what makes you think your Pappy is alive after all these years?" The sailor replies, "Olive, for a long time, I thought I was an orphan just like Swee'pea. But one day, I runs into a sailor what told me he saw a swab that looks just like me but in an old-ish way on the island of Goona. And that's where we're sailing for now." Popeye leaves Olive and Swee'pea on his boat while he searches for his Pappy. Pappy sees him and says, "I don't want no strangers on me island!" The ol' man sends an octopus and gorilla to stop Popeye, but both fail in their attempts. Finally, Popeye confronts his father and says, "I am yer offspring!" Pappy counters with, "I hates relatives." While Popeye continues to plead with his father, the monster of the sea emerges from the ocean. The beast grabs Popeye, and Pappy says, "Gorsh! I almost feel sorry for the stranger." The creature squeezes Popeye so tight his spinach can pops out and rolls towards Pappy. The excited old man says, "Shivers me timbers, spinach! I ain't seen none of that in years!" He eats the spinach and punches the monster back into the ocean. Pappy explains he knew Popeye was his son because he carried a can of spinach with him. Poopdeck sings, "Now I am happy, I found I'm the Pappy." Popeye continues with, "...of Popeye the Sailor Man." An exciting cartoon based on a *Thimble Theatre* comic strip storyline from 1936 by E.C. Segar.

Mobey Hick (1960)

The Sea Hag says to her vulture, "My wicked plans are going to make me filthy rich or me name ain't The Sea Hag! All I need is a scurvy crew for my ship, dear vulture, and The Seaman's Orphanage Treasury that Mobey Hick swallowed is mine!" The Sea Hag goes to the Crow's Nest Saloon to hire sailors, but once they see her, all of them take off in fright. Popeye finds an anchor and throws it over his shoulder for good luck, but it strikes The Sea Hag. Popeye apologizes and realizes who he accidentally hit. The sailor exclaims, "The Wicked Sea Hag!" The evil witch replies, "My mortal enemy Popeye. Oh, what am I saying? He's worth a thousand yellow-bellied sailors!" The Sea Hag convinces Popeye she has reformed and wants to make amends by harpooning Mobey Hick. She informs Popeye that the whale drowns poor sailor lads. That information enrages the sailor, and he decides to help her.

Mobey Hick encounters Popeye and kisses him. Popeye believes The Sea Hag has the friendly whale all wrong. Angered, the witch knocks Popeye out with a club. The vulture drops Popeye into Mobey Hick's spout. Inside the whale, Popeye finds The Seaman's Orphanage Treasure and realizes this is what The Sea Hag is after. Mobey Hick opens his mouth, and Popeye drags the treasure out but it is snatched away by the vulture. The sailor eats his spinach and socks the ugly bird. Popeye returns the treasure to the orphans and sings, "When I eats me spinach, there's a whale of a finich, I'm Popeye the Sailor Man." An exciting cartoon.

Mirror Magic (1960)

The narrator says, "Many years ago there was a little kingdom called Muscleona. That was ruled by whoever was the strongest man in the land." The King asked his mirror every day who was the strongest man of all. The mirror always said it was him until one day baby Popeye was born. As he grew older, the mirror changed his answer to the King, saying, "There is a lad who's so strong his muscles are like stone. He's a peasant named Popeye who'll soon seek your throne." The King mutters, "Methinks I'll have to rid myself of this Popeye threat!" Disguised as an old woman, the

King visits Popeye and attempts to kill him. He fails, and Popeye says to the faker, "Yer pretty spry fer an ol' lady, and I should belt ya one 'cepts I never smack old ladies." The King reveals himself and yells, "So you're not as strong as the mirror said you were!" Popeye is repeatedly punched, and the King walks away satisfied he is still the strongest. Popeye eats his spinach and socks the King into a well. The cartoon concludes with the mirror being asked who is the strongest. It replies with, "Why it's Popeye the Sailor Man."

It Only Hurts When They Laughs (1960)

Brutus is heading for Olive Oyl's house and growls, "If that runt Popeye is at Olive's house, I'll wring his neck." Popeye is also on his way to Olive's and says, "If that swab Brutus is visiting Olive, I'll lets him have me ol' twister punch." The pair end up at Olive's door. She asks them to come in, and they sit on her couch. Popeye and Brutus begin arguing, and Olive says, "Boys, boys, please! I want you both to behave 'till I finish washing the dishes." Naturally, they don't behave, and Olive declares, "Now I've got to finish the dishes, and to be sure you're not fighting I want to hear you both laughing while I'm in the kitchen." Both Brutus and Popeye begin to laugh while Olive goes back into the kitchen. However, the boys start to brawl again but this time laughing while they're beating each other up. When she's finished with the dishes, Olive comes out of the kitchen and sees the chaos caused by the boys' fight. Olive shouts, "Oooh, look what you roughnecks have done!" Popeye sings, "You're not a riff-raff." Brutus adds, "If ya fights and ya laugh." Popeye finishes the song, "…with Popeye the Sailor Man." This episode is based upon a *Thimble Theatre* Sunday page from 1937 by E.C. Segar.

Wimpy the Moocher (1960)

Popeye tells Olive Oyl, "Oysters on the half-shell are the specialty of the day at Rough House's diner, Olive." Olive would love to have some, and they go into the diner. When Popeye inquires if Wimpy has been in yet, an angry Rough House barks, "Don't mention that scallywag's name to me. He's a moocher and lives by his wits! But I'm wise to him, he'll get only what he pays for. He can't gyp me. I'm too smart for Wimpy, and he knows it!" Wimpy has been listening to Rough House and enters the diner. He tries to get free food from Popeye, Olive, and Mr. Geezil. He fails each time and, with a dime, buys one raw oyster. As Wimpy is about to consume the oyster, he says, "Well, bless my soul, I do believe it's a pearl! Just think, friends, poor little Wimpy has struck it rich!"

Rough House gives Wimpy thirty hamburgers in exchange for the pearl. The cook then dashes off to Geezil's hock shop. Rough House asks Geezil how much can he get for the pearl. Geezil examines it and says, "Phooey, I sell these pearls for ten cents a handful. In fact, it was only this morning that I sold Wimpy a fist full." An angry Rough House's face turns red! Popeye says, "arf! arf! arf! Rough House can't be gypped by Wimpy! arf! arf! arf!" This episode was based upon two *Thimble Theatre* Sunday pages from 1939 by Tom Sims (writer) and Doc Winner (artist).

Voo-Doo To You Too (1960)

Returning home from a long sea voyage, The Sea Hag and her vulture choose Olive Oyl's house to reside in. Olive sees the wicked pair and wants them out of her home. The Sea Hag decides to cast a spell over Olive and chants, "Zoola Kazu, Zoola Kazay, you are now my zombie slave!" Olive suddenly becomes obedient to the witch's every wish. Popeye arrives and tries to snap Olive out of her trance. The Sea Hag utters, "I'll fix that swab for butting into me affairs! This wax candle I'll shape into a wax doll of Popeye! And with a hair to make the voodoo spell right, I tie the arms to the side real tight!" Popeye can't move his arms, and The Sea Hag throws the wax doll into a sea chest. The witch's vulture takes the chest and is ordered to lose it. Popeye is searching for someone to help him break the voodoo spell. Suddenly Eugene the Jeep appears, and Popeye explains his problem. The magical creature already knows what happened and locates the sea chest. The Jeep tries to remove the hair tied to the doll's arms but can't do it. Eugene feeds Popeye his spinach which fails to break the spell. Popeye says, "Gorsh I still cants move me arms, 'dat voodoo spell is stronger than the spinach." Eugene feeds spinach to the wax doll of Popeye. The doll swallows the vegetable and breaks free of the hair. Popeye exclaims, "Me arms are as good as new! Thanks, Eugene!" The sailor heads towards Olive's house, and The Sea Hag orders her vulture to take care of him. A fight ensues, and the vulture flies out of the house with The Sea Hag clinging to its claws. Popeye snaps Olive out of her trance. She's angered by the mess the sailor's battle with the vulture created. Popeye is given a broom and ordered to clean up the mess. Popeye sings, "It may sound amusin', but women are confusin' to Popeye the Sailor Man. An exciting adventure!

Popeye Goes Sale-ing (1960)

Popeye and Olive Oyl are out for a drive. Olive notices a department store window that says, "Sale, half off on everything." She can't pass up the sale and drags Popeye into the store. Olive buys a left-handed monkey wrench but decides not to keep it. She tells Popeye to get back her money. The sailor goes to the refund department with the wrench and says, "I wants to exchanges this for money." A woman gives him a lot of paperwork and asks, "Just fill out these forms in triplicate, please." Olive tries to get a new pair of shoes but purchases too small a size. Meanwhile, Popeye is trying to answer questions to get a refund. The befuddled sailor reads aloud, "What does you usually eats for breakfast? Oh, s-p-i-n-a-c-h." Olive is seen trying to walk in a pair of new shoes. The footwear is much too small for her. She mutters, "The nerve of them selling me shoes that shrink so fast!" Olive wants Popeye to get the money back for the shoes. The befuddled sailor is back to filling out more paperwork in triplicate. On it goes until Olive sees a bunch of greedy women fighting over dresses. Olive says to Popeye, "Popeye, catch these dresses for me!" The sailor catches bargain dresses, which angers the women shoppers. They run over Popeye, and Olive shouts, "Popeye, Popeye, get the money back for those dresses! I just saw some gloves, which are a real steal!" An angry Popeye growls, "Tha's all I can stand, I can't stands no more!" Popeye eats his spinach, and his legs turn into propellers. He flies over the mob of women fighting over the gloves and pulls Olive out of the fray. Olive pleads, "Popeye put me down! I just saw some hats that they're practically giving away; put me down, put me down! The cartoon ends with Popeye and Olive continuing their drive. However, Olive is now wearing a visor. A fun story.

Popeye's Travels (1960)

Popeye is fishing in his boat when he suddenly gets a bite. The fish drags the sailor out of his craft and through the ocean. The fish pulls Popeye through the seven seas. The waterlogged sailor is finally set free when he hits the eighth sea. He lands on an island with trees no bigger than his foot. The sailor falls into a deep sleep and is tied up by the inhabitants of Lilliput. A tiny man wearing a crown climbs on top of Popeye and asks, "And whom may I ask are you, Mr. Giant?" When Popeye says he's a sailor, the tiny man replies, "A likely story, who ever saw a sailor so huge! Why the sailors in Lilliput are no bigger than me." Popeye breaks free of his ropes and convinces the townspeople he's friendly. Popeye is made head of Lilliput's navy and is ordered to stamp out the people from Bletuscu with his big feet!" Popeye replies, "Stamps out them little people! Why that would be inhuman!" Suddenly arrows, being propelled from three ships, fly through the air. When the King from Bletuscu sees Popeye, he shouts, "They've got a monster with them! Abandon ship! Jump for your lives!" Popeye plucks the panicked King out of the ocean. The King from Bletuscu pleads, "Puts me down, monster! I gives up. I'm too young to die!" Popeye picks up the King of Lilliput and declares he'll step on both of them unless they shake hands and make peace. The two Kings do what he asks, and Popeye sails home singing, "Whether you're a giant or a mite, that's no reasons ta fight, says Popeye the Sailor Man." A take-off on *Gulliver's Travels*.

Incident at Missile City (1960)

Popeye receives a telegram from King Blozo which reads, "Trouble come quick!" Olive Oyl and Popeye travel to Spinachia to visit the King. While traveling to the palace, missiles fly through the sky. King Blozo explains to the pair, "Spinachia's being invaded! There are missiles all over the place!" The trio hops on a missile and meet the Mad Leader of Missile City. The leader's vice missile takes Popeye, Olive, and King Blozo on tour. They're shown a launching pad full of rockets that will attack Spinachia. King Blozo says, "Oh yeah, well, I'm King Blozo, and you can't attack us without going through the proper diplomatic channels." After Blozo's outburst, the trio is thrown in prison.

The Mad Leader explains his people need spinach to live because of the iron it contains. He opens a safe to reveal one can of spinach. The leader says, "All the spinach that we have left in the entire city is in this one can." The King then zooms off to begin the invasion. Olive shouts, "Look, Popeye, he left the safe door open." Olive uses her big foot to reach the can of spinach. Popeye eats the spinach and busts out of jail. He reaches the Mad Leader and punches him! The injured leader mutters, "I'm sorry about the invasion, but we need spinach to live." Popeye feeds spinach to the King, who gets revitalized. Popeye promises the King he'll teach him how to grow spinach if there will be no more invasions. King Blozo, Olive, and Popeye fly home on a rocket while the sailor sings, "When ya aims for a pile a missile good as a mile, says Popeye the Sailor Man." An exciting adventure.

Dog Catcher Popeye (1960)

Popeye runs after a little puppy with a can tied to its tail. Popeye helps the pup who keeps following the sailor. Popeye says, "Oh youse cants go wit' me, I has ta gets back to me ship, and they doesn't allow doggies on it." The pup continues to follow Popeye, who can't seem to lose it. The dog catcher captures the pup, and Popeye mutters, "Oh, that poor li'l puppy is going to the dog pound!" After hearing the puppy cry out, Popeye rescues him. Each time the dog catcher snares the pup, Popeye performs a rescue. Finally, the angry dog catcher socks Popeye, who gets stuck inside a cannon. Popeye eats his spinach and sails into the air. The sailor socks the dog catcher who lands on top of his truck. This creates a hole in the vehicle, and all of the dogs escape. As the cartoon concludes, Popeye is on his ship and says, "Ahoy there matey!" The pup is in a dog house on a raft tied to Popeye's ship. Popeye names the dog "Pupeye." The plot of this episode closely follows that of another Paramount cartoon, *Dawg Gawn* (1958), featuring Little Audrey.

What's News (1960)

Popeye and Olive Oyl are traveling on a train. Olive asks Popeye, "But how do you expect to run that newspaper you bought, The Puddleburg Splash? You ain't got no book learning." Popeye explains the people in the town are lazy and uneducated. The train arrives in Puddleburg, dubbed "The Laziest Town on Earth." Later Olive moans, "Oh, Popeye, we've been here a month and haven't sold one single paper." Popeye tells Olive he's hired a comic artist to draw funny pictures for readers who can't read. An artist with a long, sad face arrives, calling himself B. Loony Bullony. Popeye reads one of his drawing samples which says, "Why does a chicken cross the street? Ta get to the other side." Popeye quickly closes the door! The sailor man decides to build a schoolhouse and have Olive teach the townspeople how to read. However, The Bruiser Boys arrive to tear the new school down because they want the townspeople to remain "stupid." Popeye declares, "I'll have to show the people of Puddleburg that even a woman can stands up against them big bullies." The three bruiser boys tear up the school. Popeye, dressed as an older woman in a wheelchair, confronts them. One of the brutes shouts, "Listen, granma, you old hag, if you were a man, I'd belt ya one." Popeye replies, "Ya mean like this!" The disguised older woman belts the bruiser to the amazement of the townspeople. The other two bullies also meet Popeye's fist. The school is opened, and Popeye drags the three brutes to class and says, "Olive, ya can starts class now; here's your first three pupils." The townspeople are now reading the newspaper as Popeye sings, "Now since ya can reads get the newspapers ya needs from Popeye the Sailor Man." This episode is based on a *Thimble Theatre* daily storyline from 1934 by E.C. Segar.

Spinach Greetings (1960)

Popeye, Olive Oyl, and Wimpy are waiting for Santa Claus's arrival. The Sea Hag mutters, "Christmas, nah, everyone is happy at this time of the year, and it's all Santa Claus's fault. Now, if we could capture Santa, it would fix everything to our liking, wouldn't it, dear vulture? Well, off to it. Get him before he can make his first delivery!" The Sea Hag's buzzard grabs Santa from his plane. The empty plane crashes near Popeye's house. The sailor man looks at the plane and discovers a vulture's feather. The sailor says, "The Sea Hag must be at the bottom of this." The Sea Hag ties up Santa in her lair and starts smashing the presents in his sack. Popeye arrives and sneaks in, and begins to untie Santa. The vulture spots Santa's rescuer and slugs him. Popeye pulls out his spinach and says, "The spirit of Christmas will be saved." The Sea Hag yells at her vulture, "Stop him before he eats that spinach!" The spinach pours into Popeye's mouth as the vulture carries his captive through the skies. The sailor comes back seconds later, holding a massive plate with a cooked vulture on it. Popeye gleefully says, "Oh Sea Haggy! Do ya likes yours with or without stuffing?" The witch pulls a lever, and Popeye nearly falls through a trap door. The sailor hangs on for dear life as waiting below are two hungry alligators. The Sea Hag stomps on Popeye's hands, and he falls in the alligator pit. However, Popeye emerges with four suitcases declaring, "Alligator luggage always makes a nice Christmas gift." The Sea Hag begins crying, and Santa resumes his deliveries.

The Baby Contest (1960)

Swee'pea needs cheering up, and Olive Oyl decides to enter him in a baby contest. The tyke has his eye on the prize, which is a loving cup. The trio arrives at the competition and hear judge Wimpy shout, "The winner of two out of three events gets the golden loving cup." Brutus approaches pushing a baby carriage and asks Popeye, "Is that scrawny brat in this contest?" Popeye replies, "Ya better take the mask orf that monster of yours! It ain't Halloween yet." The first event is the potato sack race, and Brutus places magnetized horseshoes in Swee'pea's sack. Popeye spots the dirty trick and uses a magnet to draw Swee'pea towards him. The lad wins the first event. The second event is the egg rolling race. Brutus substitutes Swee'pea's egg with one containing a chicken wearing boxing gloves. The egg hatches and bops Swee'pea in the nose, and his competitor wins. The final event is the crawling race, and Brutus tries to lure Swee'pea away from the finish line by tying a lollipop at the end of a fishing pole. Popeye sees what's happening and says, "Brutus is fishing fer trouble."

Brutus pulls up the pole but discovers his tyke, Bully Boy, with the lollipop. Aghast Brutus says, "Holy Mackerel! The wrong Mackerel!"

Swee'pea wins both the event and the loving cup. Brutus tries to bribe Wimpy into giving Bully Boy the loving cup. The brute holds a plate of hamburgers in front of the wide-eyed judge. Popeye witnesses the bribe, and Brutus socks the sailor who gets stuck in a tree. Brutus repeatedly punches Popeye's face, and his spinach can pops out of his pocket. Olive says, "Oh, Popeye's caught with his spinach down!" The can lands near Swee'pea, who eats the spinach and wallops Brutus so hard he lands in Bully Boy's baby carriage. Swee'pea pushes Popeye home in his baby carriage, singing, "I'm strong to the finish when I eats the spinach of Popeye the Sailor Man."

Oil's Well That Ends Well (1960)

Olive Oyl wins ten thousand dollars on The Get Rich Quick Show. Brutus wants her money and disguises himself as a representative of the Gusher Oil Corporation. He plans to sell Olive phony oil well stock. Olive and Popeye go to inspect the oil fields before the sale is made. Brutus says, "These wells have been bone-dry for over fifty years. But this one is gonna have just enough oil for me to land that ten grand." The swindler plants an oil can near a dried-up well. When Olive questions whether there is oil in the well, Brutus says, "Ma'am, every well is guaranteed. Just stand back, folks, while I turn on the machinery." Out of Popeye and Olive's sight, Brutus bangs on pans to simulate a well about to go off. A gusher occurs, and Olive hands Brutus her money. Popeye discovers the oil can and confronts Brutus, who runs over the sailor with his car, twice. Popeye puts his hand in his pocket and says, "Well, I guess it's about time for this!" Popeye eats his spinach, and when Brutus tries to run over him again, the sailor destroys his car. Popeye socks Brutus, and he lands on one of the oil wells which erupts. Olive shouts, "Oh, Popeye, look! A real gusher! Now I am rich!" She kisses Popeye, who then sings, "Oils well that ends well with Olive Oyl's oil well says Popeye the Sailor Man."

Motor Knocks (1960)

Popeye is taking Olive Oyl for a ride when the sailor says, "Uh, oh! The gas tank's empty." Olive spots Brutus's garage, and Popeye heads for it. Brutus says, "Ah, a sucker, I mean a customer!" Brutus fills up Popeye's car with gas while also filling his truck. The double filling rings up the gas price to ten dollars. Brutus flirts with Olive, and Popeye pushes him away. The bearded crook squirts oil on Popeye's face, who laughs it off and says, "Oh well, there's nothing like an oily start."

While the sailor goes to the washroom, Brutus tells Olive his real ambition is to be a songwriter. Brutus says, "Here's a few of my latest song titles: lover's lane, a flooded carburetor and you. I saw your vision in a three-car collision. You be my hubcap, and I'll be your wheel." Brutus tells Olive that with her as his inspiration; he could become another Gilbert & Sullivan. Popeye arrives and puts a stop to the conversation. Brutus secretly cuts wires under the hood of Popeye's vehicle and takes all of his money for repair costs. Popeye's car can't make it up to suicide hill, and Brutus drives by in his tow truck. The sailor sees Brutus with Olive in his arms. The bearded gas station owner says, "I'm gonna have to tow you back, and Olive will be safer with me in the tow truck." Popeye's car, with the sailor in it, is tied to Brutus's tow truck. However, Brutus unhooks the vehicle, and it goes speeding down a hill. When it finally comes to a stop, Popeye eats his spinach. The angry sailor races his car towards Brutus's tow truck with Olive in the front seat. Popeye snatches Brutus from the truck, and they end up inside a bridge. When the tow truck emerges, a bruised Brutus is hooked to the back of it while Popeye sings, "When it comes to jippers I clobber them clippers, I'm Popeye the Sailor Man."

Amusement Park (1960)

Popeye, Olive Oyl, and Swee'pea are spending the day at the amusement park. Brutus, who runs the freak show, spots Swee'pea and says, "That kid is just what I've been looking for to take the place of the midget that drowned in the saltwater taffy." Swee'pea goes into the funhouse alone, and Brutus captures him. Brutus has Swee'pea wear a giant top hat and calls him the baby midget. Popeye and Olive see Swee'pea, but Brutus scoops the lad up and runs off. A wild chase ensues throughout the amusement park until Popeye and Olive crash into a vegetable wagon powered by a horse. The horse, carrying Popeye and Olive, runs wild. The angry sailor says, "This calls for drastic measures!" Popeye eats his spinach, and the horse runs in the direction of Brutus's freak show. Brutus announces, "Step right up folks, and see the greatest show on earth! The bearded lady, skinny man, and the only baby midget in captivity!" Brutus sees the oncoming horse with Popeye and Olive aboard. The kidnapper grabs Swee'pea and heads into the funhouse. Popeye and Olive race inside the funhouse, and loud crashes are heard. When the loud noises settle down, Swee'pea is back with Popeye and Olive. However, Brutus is pulling the trio with his teeth, and Popeye announces, "Step right up folks and see the only human horse in captivity!" An exciting cartoon.

Duel to the Finish (1960)

Popeye and Olive Oyl are sitting on the couch. A disgusted Olive says, "Popeye would you stop playing with that yo-yo and look at me for a change?" Olive is angry at the lack of attention she's getting from Popeye and decides to make him jealous. She cooks up a batch of hamburgers to attract Wimpy, who lives close by. Wimpy sniffs the air and says, "Ah, that delicious odor is like music to my nostrils." Olive keeps feeding hamburgers to Wimpy, and in return, he says romantic things to her. Popeye says, "arf! arf! arf! I cants gets jealous of Wimpy."

When Wimpy says Olive's hair is like delicious strands of spaghetti, she kisses Wimpy on the nose. Hearing the kiss Popeye zooms into Olive's kitchen, and he grouses, "Why that two-timing no good chowhound! Look here, Wimpy Olive is my girl, and I don't like ya makin' love to her!" Wimpy explains he's infatuated with Olive and suggests they duel for her love. Popeye puts up his fists, but Wimpy decides to have an eating duel. Olive is frazzled cooking several hamburgers which Wimpy chomps down, but Popeye can't keep up. The weary sailor announces he can't eat anymore. An exhausted Olive declares she can't cook another thing. Upon hearing Olive's words, Wimpy announces Popeye, the winner. A fatigued Popeye says to Olive, "The next time ya decides to make me jealous, gives me some notice so I can diet for it." When Wimpy and Popeye discuss dueling, the scene keeps changing from a long shot of Popeye to a close-up. In the close-up, he has his pipe but not in the long shot. A fun cartoon with a unique premise.

Gem Jam (1960)

Popeye and Olive Oyl are in India, along with The Sea Hag. The old witch says to her vulture, "You'll be proud of your wicked Sea Hag, dear vulture, when I pull the greatest crime of my career and steal the sacred emerald from the crown of the jaded idol." The Sea Hag explains whoever steals the idol is cursed. She hypnotizes an unsuspecting Olive to do her dirty work. Olive puts the gem in her purse and snaps out of The Sea Hag's spell. When the witch tries to steal Olive's purse, Popeye intervenes. The Sea Hag says, "I can wait; yes, that idols 'curse will finish her off, and then I grabs the gem." The angry idol causes the top of a building to fall near Olive, but Popeye pushes her out of the way. The idol creates a hole in the ground, and Olive falls into it. Popeye removes Olive from the hole but gets trapped instead. As the hole gets smaller and smaller, the sailor says, "I'll needs me spinach to gets me outta here." The Sea Hag uses a slingshot to knock the spinach can out of Popeye's hand. The witch grabs Olive's purse and takes possession of the gem. Olive feeds Popeye his spinach, and the sailor snatches The Sea Hag, who tries to escape on her vulture. Popeye orders her to give up the gem, but she refuses. Popeye mutters, "I'm in a quandary. I can't hit a female woman even if she is the wicked Sea Hag!" Olive eats the rest of the spinach and beats up The Sea Hag. Popeye grabs the gem and tosses it back onto the idol's crown. The idol lets out a bolt of lightning, and Popeye remarks, "Is that gratitude?" The idol winks at Popeye and Olive. The sailor says, "Olive, you're my idol!" An exciting adventure.

The Bathing Beasts (1960)

Olive Oyl is very excited and can't wait to try out her new car. She asks both Popeye and Brutus to drive with her. The men brawl over who will ride in the front seat. Olive sees a sign which says, "Men Enter Now! Mr. America Contest." Olive says to the brawlers, "Alright, the one that wins the contest will ride in the front seat with me." Judge Wimpy announces the first event is the bathing suit contest. Brutus strides on stage wearing a one-piece bathing suit. Popeye is also wearing a one-piece bathing suit, but a thread is sticking out from the back. Brutus pulls the thread, and Popeye's suit starts coming off. Olive, in the audience, shouts, "Popeye! Your suit!" A nearly naked Popeye jumps in a barrel and utters, "Oh my gorsh! This is embarrassing!" The next event is the acting contest, and Popeye does a love scene with a French accent. When Popeye talks about a burning desire, Brutus sets his foot on fire. Brutus performs a Greek monologue with a skeleton's head as a prop. Popeye puts artificial teeth into the skeleton's mouth, which frightens Brutus. The following contest is the musical talent test. Brutus plays a harmonica without using his hands. Popeye slaps Brutus's back, and he swallows the harmonica.

Popeye can play music without an instrument. Instead, he just taps his head. Wimpy announces, "And now the last and most difficult category: feats of strength!" Brutus puts a sleeping pill in a glass of water. The cheater offers the drink to Popeye before he lifts a barbell. Despite his best efforts to stay awake, Popeye falls asleep. Before lifting a barbell, Brutus pushes Popeye out of the way. This causes a spinach can to roll in front of the sleeping sailor. Brutus slams the barbell on the can causing it to pop open. Spinach falls into Popeye's mouth, and he lifts Brutus, who is holding onto a barbell, in the air. Wimpy declares Popeye the winner, and it's the sailor who will sit in the front seat of Olive's car. Popeye says, "Ya can drives now, Olive." Olive replies, "Ooooh, I don't know if I can,

Popeye. I've never tried before." Popeye zooms out of the car and hides in a tree. The scared sailor sings, "I'd rather be alive than with a woman learning to drive, says Popeye the Sailor Man." A fun cartoon.

The Rain Breaker (1961)

Popeye, Swee'pea, and Olive Oyl are on an outing. Olive says to Popeye, "Now that we've had our lunch Popeye let's play games with Swee'pea." Popeye decides to sit the games out as he's too filled with food. Olive and Swee'pea go off by themselves while Popeye snoozes. Suddenly a thunderous rainstorm occurs, and Popeye decides to find out where it's coming from. Popeye climbs a mountain and lands amid a gray rain cloud. There he finds a castle in the clouds and hears a cry for help. Popeye says, "A female woman in the brig?" The woman explains, "I am Iris, the goddess of the rainbow, sunshine and sunny weather. I am the prisoner of Thor, god of the rain, thunder, and lightning. And it won't stop raining until I am free." Thor sends a lightning fist to knock Popeye down, but all it does is tickle him. Thor and Popeye brawl until the thunder god flattens the sailor with his fist. Popeye is hung like a dartboard while Thor throws lightning bolts at him. Popeye says, "Tha's all I can stands, I can't stands no more!" With the aid of his pipe, Popeye manages to get his spinach. Charged with the vegetable Thor's lightning bolts no longer hurt him. Popeye says, "I'll learn ya manners not to put nice dames in the brig!" The sailor socks Thor and his castle vanishes. Iris is freed from her prison, and Popeye slides down on a rainbow back to the picnic grounds. Olive returns and says to the sleeping sailor, "Popeye, wake up; you've slept long enough!" Popeye mistakes Olive's voice for Iris and mutters, "Oh Iris, youse followed me down the rainbow." Olive bawls Popeye out for dreaming about another woman. A colorful cartoon.

Messin' Up the Mississippi (1961)

Olive Oyl's showboat docks in a harbor to an enthusiastic crowd. Olive says, "Welcome to Olive Oyl's showboat folks, where you will see the finest entertainment on the driven Mississippi. And here is the star of our show, the greatest actor this side of the Mason-Dixon Line, Popeye the Sailor." Popeye announces the box office is open and Olive orders Brutus to start selling tickets. A disgruntled Brutus says, "Brutus sell the tickets, Brutus swab the decks, Brutus haul the trunks, and that squint-eyed runt takes all the bows. I should be the star of the show! And that's just what I aim to be." Brutus fowls up Popeye's juggling, weight-lifting, and high wire act. Finally, Brutus clobbers Popeye with sandbags and takes his place on stage. Olive gasps, "I've got to save the show," and plays the piano while Brutus lifts weights. Popeye, off-stage, says, "Shiver me timbers that swab Brutus stole me act!" He eats his spinach, lifts up Brutus by his feet, juggling him. The crowd cheers at the sight of Popeye's feat of strength.

Love Birds (1961)

Olive Oyl is dusting her house, thinking about springtime's beauty. She finds her pet bird Juliet sulking in her cage and says, "What makes a love bird so sad on a gorgeous spring day? Of course, she needs a boyfriend." Olive calls on Popeye to help, and the sailor goes to a pet store. Popeye tells the store owner, "I wants ta gets a romantical boy love bird for a female goil love bird that is very lonely." Popeye selects a love bird and brings it to Olive's house. The two birds get into a fight, and the boy flies out the window. Olive barks at Popeye, "You men are all alike! It's your fault Juliet's heart is broken, and if you don't get that Romeo back here pronto, I'll never speak to you again in my life!" Popeye discovers the love bird being chased by a hawk. The sailor eats his spinach and with the aid of his pipe launches himself skyward. He bops the hawk. When Romeo and Juliet are together once again, another fight ensues. Popeye says to Romeo, "I knows ya feels just like a dead duck. Here take a li'l bit of me spinach. It will give ya courage." The spinach-fed Romeo tweets loudly back at Juliet, and Olive says, "Popeye, they're just like love birds again." Popeye sings, "When I aims me arrows, it makes love birds of sparrows, I'm cupid the lovin' man!" A cute cartoon.

Sea Serpent (1961)

Olive Oyl uses a typewriter and explains to Popeye that being a reporter is exciting. She is called into her newspaper editor's office, and he says, "Miss Oyl, there's a rumor that a sea serpent has been seen at Loch Ness. Would you please cover the story?" Olive zooms out of the office, promising pictures of the creature. Popeye explains to Olive, "In all the times I've sailed the seven seas, I ain't never see-ed a sea serpent." The sailor decides to go with Olive just for laughs. Brutus claims to be an Official Guide whose sign reads a sea serpent appears every hour on the hour. Brutus sighs, "If business doesn't pick up soon, I'll just have to get meself another racket." Olive arrives and tells Brutus she wants a picture of the monster. Brutus charges her ten dollars an hour and five dollars for every photo she takes. Popeye suspects a hoax, but Brutus shows them phony footprints and a fake serpent egg. Popeye discovers Brutus's tricks and uses the crook's mechanical serpent to go after him. Brutus runs away, panicked, and Olive asks Popeye why he scared her to death. Popeye replies, "I said I was coming along for laughs, and it was really funny."

Bordering on Trouble (1961)

Popeye and Brutus own The Golden Lasso Hotel. Popeye wants to specialize in fine food, while Brutus feels it should be great entertainment. Popeye uses a paintbrush to create a dividing line and says, "This line divides the hotel in half. You runs your half your way, and I'll runs my half my way!" Olive Oyl arrives at the hotel, and both owners compete for her business. Brutus begins strumming a guitar, and Olive heads for his half until Popeye brings out shish kabob. Olive says, "What a delightful aroma!" She heads towards Popeye until Brutus squirts the shish kabob with ink! Brutus entertains Olive with some juggling. Popeye lifts up the hotel causing Olive to slide back onto his side. Popeye plans on serving Olive ham and eggs. Brutus, with a cloak, mask, and knife, plans to scare her to his side. Olive pulls out a gun and says, "Alright, Louie drop that knife." Brutus thinks the weapon is a water pistol, but Olive shoots him. The charred-faced bandit says, "Some water pistol!" Popeye checks the dangerous weapons in the safe. Brutus, thinking Popeye defenseless, picks up the sailor and sticks him in a pot. The bearded brute repeatedly pounds on Popeye. The sailor's spinach can appears, and after eating the vegetable, he punches Brutus, along with his half of the hotel, onto a mountain top. Olive is now seated eating a lot of food while Popeye sings, "Entertainments, not best fine foods gets the guests, says Popeye the Sailor Man." A fun cartoon.

Aladdin's Lamp (1961)

The Sea Hag uses her crystal ball to discover the great Aladdin's lamp's location. The witch learns Olive Oyl has won the lamp at an auction and goes after it. Olive says to Popeye, "It's a real old antique, Popeye, and I bought it at an auction for only five dollars!" Suddenly the lamp flies out of Olive's hands and gets stuck on a magnet held by The Sea Hag. The witch cackles, "At last! Aladdin's lamp is mine!" The witch takes off with Popeye in pursuit. On her ship, The Sea Hag rubs the lamp and summons a genie. The witch says, "Genie ol' fella, I want you to fill my ship with all kinds of treasure and riches!" The genie produces solid gold, precious stones, and genuine pearls. Popeye is headed for The Sea Hag's ship, and the genie gets back in the lamp. Popeye says to the witch, "I'll takes that lamp now." The Sea Hag tells Popeye she couldn't help borrowing the lamp as she is also a lover of antiques. She offers to clean the lamp before he takes it. The genie appears, and The Sea Hag commands, "Quick Genie 'fore he can get the spinach from his blouse, shrink Popeye down to the size of a mouse." Popeye is shrunk, and The Sea Hag chases him around her ship. She finally traps the sailor in what turns out to be his spinach can. Popeye eats the remaining contents and grows back to full size. The scared witch orders, "Quick genie, we've got plenty to fear if you don't hurry up and make him disappear!" Popeye sucks the genie up with his pipe and blows him into a big jar. Popeye plugs up the jar and tosses it into the vast ocean. The Sea Hag cries, "The spell is broken! All my riches are gone. Oh! I've got to get that genie back again! Where is he? Where is he?" She dives into the ocean in search of him. Popeye returns home with Olive's lamp only to discover she doesn't want it anymore. She prefers a combination lamp and coffee grinder. An exciting cartoon.

Butler Up (1961)

Olive Oyl is anxious for Popeye's help. She explains to him, "Well, an old schoolmate of mine is coming over to pay me a visit, and I want to make an impression. Would you please act as my butler?" Popeye agrees but is embarrassed by his butler's uniform. He welcomes Olive's old school mate, Brutus, who says to his hostess, "Olive, baby, you look gorgeous. Just the same when you were voted the prettiest girl in the class." Olive responds, "Oh, Brutus! You always were a flatterer." While at the dinner table, Brutus attempts to kiss Olive, but Popeye intervenes. Brutus mutters, "I'll never get anywhere with that butler butting in." Brutus asks Olive if she remembers the football game he won single- handedly. Brutus demonstrates one of his plays by grabbing Popeye and rolling him up into a ball. The brute then kicks him out the window. As Popeye flies through the air, he eats his spinach and zooms back to Olive's house. Olive says to an approaching Brutus, "Now, now you keep yourself to you! That's what you are!" Popeye dashes in and punches Brutus, who lands behind a screen. After a battle behind the screen, Brutus now wears Popeye's butler uniform. Popeye sings, "He may be a hero as a butler he's zero, says Popeye the Sailor Man."

The Leprechaun (1961)

The Sea Hag is sailing on a ship and says to her vulture, "You see we'll capture a leprechaun and force him to lead us to his crock of gold." Popeye, in a lighthouse, spots The Sea Hag and decides to investigate what she's up to. Popeye overhears The Sea Hag plotting to capture a leprechaun, and tries to stop her. However, the vulture knocks him out with a club.

A leprechaun discovers an unconscious Popeye and brings him around with some Shamrock juice.

Meanwhile, the head leprechaun explains to his followers they must only use their gold to help the poor and needy. They're also honor-bound, never to lead anyone to their crock of gold. The Sea Hag, pretending to be an impoverished old lady, tricks one of the leprechauns to give her a gold coin. In appreciation, she invites him for a cup of hot tea. The Sea Hag mutters, "Truth serum! One drop in his tea, and he has to tell me of his crock of gold." The leprechaun drinks the tea and reveals the gold's location. The head leprechaun says, "On account of you, our crock of gold is gone. Until it is returned, you are banished from the leprechauns forever!" Popeye hears of the leprechaun's plight and goes after The Sea Hag. The sailor knocks out her vulture, and the ol' hag says, "I'll put the evil-eye whammy on him!" Popeye, carrying the leprechaun's gold, begins to stagger, but he pulls out his spinach and sends the witch's' whammy right back at her. Both The Sea Hag and her vulture are down, and Popeye returns the gold. The head leprechaun says, "And because our gold was returned, we hereby reinstate you to the society of leprechauns. And we make Popeye an honorary leprechaun because he is our friend. Popeye, dressed as a leprechaun, sings, "A friend I am told is worth more than pure gold, says Popeye the Leprechaun." An exciting adventure.

County Fair (1961)

A farming contest is being held, and judge Wimpy announces, "Farmer Popeye and Farmer Brutus will compete in a series of contests for the best of show and the blue ribbon." The first event is for the juiciest watermelon. Brutus cheats by pumping a phony watermelon with air. He switches Popeye's watermelon with the phony one. When Wimpy sticks it with a fork, the melon explodes. Brutus attaches a hose in his melon, and it spouts water. Brutus wins the event, and Popeye wonders if he mixed too much spinach with the watermelon seeds. The next event is for the tastiest beef burger, which Wimpy will sample. Brutus sprinkles red hot pepper on Popeye's burger.

The one-eyed farmer notices what Brutus did. The farmers go back and forth, switching the bad burger for a good one. Finally, Wimpy arrives and eats Popeye's burger. He says it's very good but spits out Brutus's entry as that one contained the red hot pepper. Popeye wins the second event, and the third contest is the lamb with the strongest wool. Brutus shaves off part of Popeye's lamb's wool, putting it back with glue. Wimpy pulls Brutus's lamb and says, "Yes sir, that's pretty strong wool." When

Wimpy pulls Popeye's lamb, the wool comes off in his hand. Brutus wins this event, and Popeye mutters, "Looks like Brutus pulled the wool over me eyes." The next event is for the cow with the most milk.

Brutus thinks he's won until he sees Popeye's cow surrounded with nine full milk buckets. The next event is for the best rooster crowing contest. Brutus's bird lets out a loud crow, and Popeye tells his rooster to do his stuff. Brutus, however, lets the rooster see him suck on a lemon. Instead of crowing, the rooster squeals and faints. The next event is the hog calling contest, and Brutus calls a little pig, which jumps in his arms. Popeye does a hog call and is declared the winner when his arms become filled with hams. The final event is the spinach-eating contest and the test to prove its strength. Brutus says to Popeye, "What do you say, Popeye, let's keep this contest fair." Popeye agrees and shakes his competitor's hand only to be flung away. Popeye is slammed to the floor, and Brutus looks at the audience admitting, "You didn't think I was gonna play fair with that runt and take a chance against his spinach." Brutus eats some of the spinach on Popeye's plate and tosses it away. The plate conks Popeye on the head, and he uses his pipe to get the rest of the spinach. Wimpy is about to give Brutus the blue ribbon for lifting two horses until Popeye punches his cheating competitor. Popeye now raises two horses and Brutus. Wimpy awards him the blue ribbon, and Popeye sings, "Brutus was beaten because he was cheatin', says Popeye the Farmer Man." A fun cartoon.

Hamburgers Aweigh (1961)

Popeye and Olive Oyl count the boxes of canned hamburgers being loaded onto the sailor's ship. Wimpy offers to guard the cargo, but Popeye says, "Sorry, Wimpy, but it wouldn't be fair to put that temptation in your path." Wimpy pleads with Popeye, so the sailor whistles for the Magical Wiffle Bird. Popeye rubs the bird's head feathers and makes a wish that Wimpy hates hamburgers. Soon Wimpy is guarding the hamburger cargo when The Sea Hag and her vulture appear. The witch cackles to Wimpy, "How would you like to split the cargo of those heavenly hamburgers with me, eh?" Wimpy replies, "Madam Sea Hag, you speak of an edible which thoroughly disgusts me." The Sea Hag realizes he's under a spell and casts her own on Wimpy. The ex-hamburger fiend is now her slave. The Sea Hag orders Wimpy to throw all the spinach cans overboard. Wimpy is then commanded to hoist The Sea Hag's flag and tie Olive to a mast. The witch's vulture picks up Popeye and drops him into the sea. Wimpy sees The Wiffle Bird and rubs its head feathers, pleading, "Please, Mr. Wiffle Bird, break all the spells over me, especially that hamburger one." Wimpy zooms off to where the hamburger cargo is stored. Underwater, Popeye discovers spinach cans and eats the vegetable. He emerges from the water in time to see The Sea Hag about to push Olive overboard. Popeye bends the plank Olive is on, and they both catapult skyward. Popeye says to Olive, "Here takes some of me spinach. I cants hit a woman, so you takes care of The Sea Hag, and I'll flick the feathers off that vulture." The pair bop their enemies off the ship. Olive remarks in another minute she would have made hamburger out of the witch. The word hamburger reminds Popeye of Wimpy. Popeye and Olive check on the hamburger cargo only to see Wimpy has opened and eaten the contents of each can. An exciting adventure. When the Sea Hag casts a spell over Wimpy her purple hood becomes black.

Popeye's Double Trouble (1961)

Popeye is on a park bench wondering where he will take Olive Oyl on their date. A little boy comes by and gives the sailor a flyer that reads, "Dance contest tonight, loving cup to the winners." Popeye exclaims, "Now that's an idea for me date with Olive Oyl!" Popeye wonders if they will be lucky enough to win the loving cup. The Sea Hag and her vulture overhear Popeye. The vengeful witch requests a bad luck coin from her vulture. She tosses it near Popeye, who picks it up. Popeye says, "See a coin and picks it up and all the day you'll have good luck...*hmm*...I wonder if that's true." Popeye wishes for a car and chauffeur to take Olive dancing. Suddenly, both Popeye's wishes come true, and The Sea Hag realizes the vulture gave her a good luck coin. The angry witch barks, "Bah, you stupid bundle of feathers! You gave me the wrong coin! He has my good luck coin, and it has three wishes that go with it. And he's used up one already. Oh, we must get it back before he has a chance to use the other two." The Sea Hag ties up Olive and changes herself to look precisely like Popeye's girlfriend. The Sea Hag, disguised as Olive, goes to the dance with Popeye. Pretending she's dancing, the phony Olive spins Popeye, and he smashes into a wall. The faker hopes to shake the coin lose. The real Olive manages to escape and heads to the dance.

Once again, Popeye is sent spinning, but he crashes into the real Olive. Popeye says, "I must be seeing double, which one is the real Olive Oyl?" The befuddled sailor wishes he knew who was the real one. Suddenly one of the Olives turns back into The Sea Hag. The angry witch grabs Popeye by his legs, bouncing him on the floor, hoping the coin will appear. Popeye, his face being pounded on the floor, mutters, "Ooh, I cants hit a female woman. I wishes there was a way to make her stops." When Popeye makes the wish, a spinach can falls out of his shirt, rolling towards Olive. The Sea Hag yells, "That's the third wish, and nothing can help you now!" The witch slugs Popeye and Olive eats the spinach, becoming a whirlwind. Olive gets closer and closer to The Sea Hag, punching her skyward. The dance's announcer says to Olive, "And the winner of the most original dance, the solar sock, is Miss Olive Oyl." An imaginative plot showcasing Olive Oyl's resourcefulness.

Kiddie Kapers (1961)

Popeye promises to buy Olive Oyl anything she wants for her birthday. Olive looks at a wedding gown in a store window. She asks Popeye if he'll buy her that. Popeye says, "Why, ya getting married or something? Olive becomes angry and yells, "No, I'm not getting married, especially not to you. We've been going together for so long you're, you're, you're an old man!" Popeye doesn't believe he's an old man and gets upset when a boy scout offers to help him across the street. Brutus was the one who told the boy scout to help Popeye. Olive decides she wants a boyfriend who is young and handsome. Brutus visits The Sea Hag and asks for a way to become young and handsome. The witch cackles, "You! Young and handsome, that's a pretty tall order." Brutus barks, "Never mind the wisecracks! You're no prize winner yourself." The Sea Hag gives him a youth potion but instructs him not to take more than one drop. Brutus becomes young and handsome. He visits Olive, calling himself Don Juan, which disgusts Popeye. As Don Juan talks, Popeye recognizes his voice. When the sailor claims this suitor is Brutus, Olive says, "Brutus is ugly, but Don Juan here, *ooooh*, he's handsome." Popeye spots the bottle of youth potion in Brutus's pocket and says, "If one drop can do that to Brutus, imagine what a good swig will do for me." After drinking the potion, Popeye turns into a baby, whom Brutus spanks. Upon seeing the spanking, Olive says, "Popeye was right; you are Brutus!" She puts spinach in a spoon and feeds it to baby Popeye. Suddenly the roles are reversed, and Baby Popeye is spanking Brutus. The little tyke socks Brutus and Olive declares, "Oh Popeye no matter how old you are, you're still my hero." She doesn't want anything to keep them apart. Olive takes a swing of the youth potion, and she becomes a baby. The cartoon concludes with the tykes playing patty cake.

The Mark of Zero (1961)

Olive Oyl is chasing Deezil around the house, trying to get her to bed. Popeye picks up Deezil and tells her a bedtime story about a brave swordsman known throughout the land as the mark of Zero. The hero stops two bandits from robbing an older man by carving the number 'zero' on their shirts. When the old man asks how he can repay his rescuer, Zero replies, "Thinks nothing of it. I'm really a cut-up by nature." Brutus, the robber band leader, was mad as a hornet upon hearing of the foiled robbery. Brutus attempts to stop Zero's next heroic attempt but fails. Finally, the bandit disguises himself as a dame and asks to hold Zero's sword. Zero says, "It would be my pleasure, ma'am." Once Brutus has the blade, he says to Zero, "The mark of goose-eggs." Zero is punched and ends up hanging on a tree.

The bandit leader says to the dazed hero, "Now, just to show you that Brutus the Bandit ain't all bad, I'm going to give you a last request. What will it be? Steak? Lobster? Pheasant?" All Zero asks for is a spoonful of spinach. Brutus laughs and tells one of his men to bring Zero spinach. Upon swallowing the spinach, Zero zooms around the criminals taking their swords. Now defenseless Brutus and his gang take off. Deezil goes to bed, and Popeye says, "This ol' salt can spin a corkin' good bedtime yarn." Olive calls Popeye into Deezil's room and discovers the tyke has painted white zeros on her room's wall. A fun parody of the Zorro legend.

Myskery Melody (1961)
Olive Oyl is serving a chicken dinner to Popeye and Poopdeck Pappy. Suddenly Pappy hears a weird tune that neither Popeye nor Olive hears. The Sea Hag's vulture appears at the window and snatches Pappy's hat. The old sailor wails, "Oh now, The Sea Hag will know it's me for sure." Olive asks why The Sea Hag is looking for him. Pappy explains, "I be ninety-nine years old now. But when I was a young swab of nineteen and 'fore was married, I met a Rose of the Sea." Pappy says he courted this beautiful woman until she changed into her true self, The Sea Hag. The young sailor grabbed his cap and fled in terror. Pappy tells Popeye and Olive the ol' witch has been waiting eighty years to get her revenge. Eerie music is heard, and Pappy walks out of the house in a trance. The vulture picks up Pappy and drops him in front of Rose of the Sea. Pappy yells, "Ya cants fool me again, Rose of the Sea. I knows you really be The Sea Hag!"

The angry witch drops Pappy into her cellar while Popeye goes searching for his father. Popeye mutters, "I bets I could find me Pappy with the help of Eugene the magical Jeep." The Jeep appears and helps Popeye locate The Sea Hag's castle. The vulture carries off Popeye. The witch spots a charging Eugene and says, "Eugene, the magical Jeep! My evil magic is powerless against him." While Popeye is being carried away by the vulture, he eats his spinach and bops the bird. Eugene is zapping

The Sea Hag with his tail while Popeye rescues Poopdeck Pappy. Popeye, Olive, and Pappy resume their meal, but eerie music is heard again. It turns out it's just the tea kettle. This episode was based on a storyline in the daily *Thimble Theatre*, comic strip from 1937 by E.C. Segar. An exciting adventure.

Scairdy Cat (1961)

Brutus is at the library reading a book called "Ye Ol' Reliable Witches' Cook Book". He's looking for a recipe for fear gas and locates it. Brutus reads from the book, "Just a whiff will change one, no matter how brave, to a cowardly weakling and make him your slave." Brutus whips up the brew and runs into Popeye in front of Olive Oyl's house. Brutus picks up Popeye and drops him to the ground. The angry sailor is about to sock Brutus but gets squirted with fear gas. A yellow streak goes up Popeye's back, and then he pleads, "Please don't hits me, Mr. Brutus, please don't, please." Brutus replies, "Just to show you I'm a right guy, I'm gonna let you off, but you better hand over your can of spinach." Brutus tosses the can of spinach on the roof. The brute asks Olive if he can come inside and watch the fights on television. Olive explains Popeye is coming over, and he's very jealous. While Brutus questions Popeye's bravery, the fear gas wears off, and the sailor is back to his old self. Olive tells Popeye that Brutus called him a coward. She wants Popeye to make Brutus eat his words. The brute sprays the sailor with more fear gas. Olive retorts, "*Hmph!* You are a coward." She invites Brutus into her house, preferring the company of brave men.

When Olive slams her door, the spinach can falls off the roof and lands in front of Popeye. Popeye exclaims, "Well, blow me down! Me spinach! I wonders if it can throws off that strange feeling." Popeye eats the spinach, which throws off the effects of the fear gas. The brave sailor bursts into Olive's house, and Brutus squirts him again with fear gas. The bully mutters, "Uh, oh, it ain't working." Popeye smashes Brutus into the television set, and Olive says, "Oh, Popeye, you are brave." Popeye sings, "Ya have nothing to fear when your spinach is near, says Popeye the Sailor Man." A unique story.

Operation Ice Tickle (1961)

Popeye and Olive Oyl are taking a stroll in the park when Brutus joins them. Naturally, Popeye and Brutus begin arguing until Olives says, "I'm getting sick, sick, and sick of all this childish arguing. Why don't you two big babies do something worthwhile and important? Make your stamp on eternity." They all come across a statue of Admiral Peary, who discovered the North Pole. Popeye and Brutus compete to bring back not only The North Pole but a date with Olive. Brutus travels by rocket ship while Popeye uses a balloon for transportation. Brutus's rocket ship punctures Popeye's balloon, and the sailor crashes to the ground.

However, Popeye pumps a giant inflatable tire-shaped balloon and fastens a motor to it. The sailor zooms in the air ahead of Brutus and discovers The North Pole. With the aid of his inflatable tire, Popeye grabs onto the pole. Brutus mutters, "That sailor shrimp beat me to it!" Brutus pretends to shake Popeye's hand but clobbers him with a "noggin-bopper." The sailor lands into the icy water and emerges frozen solid. Brutus is tinkering with Popeye's mode of transportation and turns on a heat valve. The heat melts part of the ice Popeye is trapped in. The sailor eats his spinach and punches Brutus on top of The North Pole. Popeye says, "That's a polecat who looks at home on a pole." Brutus freezes on top of The North Pole. Popeye flies himself, Brutus, and the pole home to Olive. Popeye puts the North Pole near the statue of Admiral Peary, who is looking through a telescope. Suddenly Peary comes to life and says of The North Pole, "Well scrub my deck, man, if that ain't the most."

The Cure (1961)

The Sea Hag owns a restaurant called Hamburger Heaven and tries to lure Wimpy to her establishment. Wimpy smells the aroma of the hamburgers but has no money. The Sea Hag says, "He's broke, but he'll get the money somehow because he's hooked. Ah, but he'll be back." Popeye is on his ship and flips a quarter to decide what chore he will do first. The quarter lands near Wimpy, who puts it under his hat. Popeye shouts, "Ahoy there, Wimpy! Did ya sees anything of a quarter I accidentally flipped down here?" Wimpy attempts to rush off, but the quarter falls out of his hat. Popeye accuses him of being a real hamburger addict and convinces Wimpy to stop eating them. The Sea Hag uses a fan to blow the aroma of hamburgers in Wimpy's direction. Popeye sees what's happening and says, "Gosh! Wimpy's heading for The Sea Hag's hamburger joint." The sailor stops Wimpy from munching on a burger just in time and takes him to Hamburgers Anonymous. The Sea Hag is angry and snarls, "He can't take away my best, my only customer! I'll go out of business." Disguised as a nurse, the old witch attempts to smuggle in a hamburger to bedridden Wimpy. Popeye mutters, "*Hmm*...that nurse looks just like The Sea Hag." Popeye switches the hamburger for a picture of muscle man Mighty Marty. When Wimpy sees the picture, he says, "Thank you, nurse. I'm sure this will be an inspiration to me."

Next, the Sea Hag sends her vulture, carrying a hamburger, to Wimpy's open window. Popeye, thinking the room drafty, slams the window shut on the vulture's head. The Sea Hag mutters, "My strategy has failed. I must resort to brute force." She sends one of her Goons in with a hamburger which Popeye intercepts. The Goon tosses Popeye down a garbage chute, and The Sea Hag carries off Wimpy. In her restaurant, the witch holds a hamburger just above Wimpy's reach. She won't give it to him until he signs over his life insurance policy to her. Popeye runs inside the restaurant, but the Goon slaps the sailor against a wall. Popeye's spinach can is shaken loose and falls to the floor. The stricken sailor falls on top of it, and the spinach flies into Wimpy's mouth. Now fortified with strength, Wimpy punches the Goon. The Sea Hag shrieks, "Oh, he's a mad man!" The witch takes off while Popeye revives, shouting, "Wimpy, don't stop!" Wimpy grabs Popeye by his shirt collar, lifting him while he gorges on hamburgers. Wimpy is missing the whiskers under his nose when Popeye escorts him out of The Sea Hag's restaurant. A fun story spotlighting Wimpy's addiction to hamburgers.

William Won't Tell (1961)

Popeye Tell is on his way to meet his true love, the Maiden Olive Oyl, when he sees the Queen's broken-down carriage. The Queen says, "Oh dear, I must be back at the castle before I am missed." Popeye uses his arrows to fashion a wheel from a tree. Popeye chuckles, "There you are, your majesty, an oaken-wheel for a broken wheel, arf! arf! arf!" The Queen is so grateful she kisses Popeye on his head but pleads with him not to let the King know about it. She explains the King is very jealous, and Popeye maintains so is the Maiden Olive Oyl.

The Queen's driver informs the King of the kiss. The King snarls, "Who is the nave! I'll have his head!" The driver explains he only saw the Queen's lip prints on Popeye's bald head. The King gets an idea and has his town crier announce, "His majesty the King proclaim-eth that all male subjects must pass-eth before him in review and remove their hats as a gesture of loyalty." A parade of male subjects goes by the King, but Popeye refuses to remove his hat. The angry King commands Popeye to either remove his cap or shoot an apple off Maiden Olive Oyl's head. Popeye still refuses, and the King places a tiny apple on Olive's head. Popeye's arrow shoots the apple off Olive's head and removes his hat, revealing the Queen's lip prints. The King orders the expert archer to the guillotine, but the Queen intervenes. She explains being on her way to get the King's birthday present when the carriage broke down. The Queen presents the King with a new crown. The King says, "All is forgiven, forgive this old fool."

When the Queen removes the King's old crown to put on his new one, the monarch's hair goes with it. The crowd shouts, "Oh! Our good King is bald!" Popeye Tell says, "Oh, stately cue ball!" Olive responds with, "Oh, regale bean." Everyone has a good laugh. This episode was co-written by Jack Mercer, who tried to avoid the spinach gimmick when possible.

Pop Goes the Whistle (1961)

Popeye visits Swee'pea and gives him a big teddy bear called Whistling Willie. The sailor explains squeezing the bear's stomach causes it to whistle every time. Swee'pea starts jumping on the bear, which makes the whistle inside of the toy fall out. The lad starts bawling, and Popeye looks around for the whistle. Swee'pea looks out the window and hears a policeman using his whistle. The baby crawls into the street with Popeye in pursuit. The sailor catches the lad but causes several cars to crack up. The angry policeman says, "Well, now 'tis a fine kettle of fish when an adult has to play with a child right in the middle of a busy intersection." While the policeman bawls out Popeye, Swee'pea crawls away. Popeye sees the lad climb a tall tower, tooting smoke at the very top. The frantic sailor chases Swee'pea and steps into a nest with two baby storks. Popeye says to the frightened babies, "Well, what do ya know, baby storks. It's alright little fellows; I ain't gonna hurt you any." The father stork appears and is angry! Popeye takes off his hat and says, "Oh hello, Mr. Stork, we're old friends, remember? Ya gives me foist ride on me birthday."

The stork slugs Popeye! Swee'pea climbs a rope to get to a boat whistle. Popeye flips the rope which flings Swee'pea onto a circus tent. The lad slides down the tent and sees a seal blowing a whistle. Swee'pea isn't tall enough to grab the whistle, so he climbs a tree. Popeye gets on the same tree, and the branch breaks. Popeye ends up on the seal's nose, and the sailor is tossed around. Finally, Popeye is thrown against a tree, and the seal's whistle falls into his mouth. An excited Swee'pea bounces up and down on a tooting Popeye! The sailor says, "A happy child is a healthy child, arf, arf, arf, arf!" A fun cartoon.

Autographically Yours (1961)

A little boy visits Marathon Cartoon Studios to get an autograph of his favorite hero, Popeye. When Brutus spots the little boy, he says, "Hi, Kid. Looking for me? Sure. All the kids want my autograph. You little fellas know a big star when you see one." The little boy kicks Brutus in the leg, claiming he wants Popeye's autograph. Brutus explains they write movies to make Popeye look like the hero, but in real life, he tops him. The boy wants proof, so they compete in a fancy shooting contest with Popeye victorious. Next is a fancy roping contest, but Brutus turns on a wind machine. Popeye's rope entangles him, and Brutus turns on the machine full speed. The wind blows Popeye against a cage holding a lion. Seeing Popeye defeated, the little boy says, "Well, Mr. Brutus, I guess you are the best. *Hmph*, you can sign my autograph book." Brutus responds, "Yeah, I think I'll sign it Brutus the Fearless." Before Brutus has a chance to sign the book, the beast approaches. The little boy shouts that the lion is loose and runs off. A terrified Brutus yells, "Gangway! Help! Help! Help! We'll be chewed up. Help! Help! Oh, Help!" Popeye awakens and realizes he has to do something quickly. He eats his spinach and uses a rope to swing in front of the lion. Popeye picks up Brutus and the little boy, bringing them to safety. Popeye turns back and punches the lion, who lands back in his cage. The little boy says, "Oh, Mr. Popeye, I always knew you were my hero. Won't you please sign my book now, huh, please?" Brutus offers his autograph book to Popeye and asks him to sign it. When we first see the lion, he has a black nose, but it changes to brown until he's back in his cage again. An interesting premise, and it's nice to see Brutus admit he's wrong for a change.

A Poil for Olive Oyl (1961)

Popeye takes Olive Oyl shopping for her birthday present. She would like a pearl necklace. The necklace is advertised as twenty percent off, and they go into the store to make a purchase. Popeye asks the salesman how much the necklace costs and is told four thousand dollars. Popeye gets angry and decides to pick pearls at the bottom of the ocean. The sailor and his girlfriend travel on a motorboat. Popeye explains, "Now all we have to do, Olive, is cruise around and keeps our eye on the underwater TV set." Olive asks how that will get her a pearl necklace? Popeye says when they see oyster beds, he'll dive for them. Soon Popeye and Olive spot a lot of oysters with pearls. The sailor dives into the water and takes the pearls. Suddenly The Sea Hag appears, yelling, "Get out of here and leave my pearls alone!" Popeye informs the witch the pearls are free in the deep sea.

The Sea Hag says, "Dogfish! Teach that squint-eyed runt to respect my property." A school of dogfish swims towards Popeye, but he sends a school of cat-fish after them. Angrier than ever, The Sea Hag orders several swordfish to attack Popeye. Olive is watching the action on the undersea TV screen and says, "Ooh, I'll take care of that evil Sea Hag!" She eats spinach and is propelled, fist first, in the water. The Sea Hag cackles, "That'll teach you to stay out of me oyster bed." Olive's fists slam the witch into the ocean floor! Popeye uses an electric eel to melt the sharp points off each swordfish. He sees Olive on the ocean floor and gives her a pearl necklace. The cartoon concludes with the pair on a rowboat while Popeye sings, "There's only one pearl, that's me goil Olive Oyl, says Popeye the Sailor Man."

My Fair Olive (1961)

Popeye and Olive Oyl are visiting the Museum of Antiques looking over a Brontosaurus skeleton. Brutus, the guard, walks over to Olive and explains more about the structure while tickling her chin. Popeye pulls her away, and they go to the King Arthur exhibit. Olive looks at the original armor and says, "Oh, Popeye! Just think how romantic it was in those days with knights fighting in shining armor for their lady love." Brutus wishes he had known Olive back then. Popeye gets mad at Brutus for butting in, so Olive suggests they settle their argument with a joust. Brutus says, "Okay, gorgeous, I'll do joust that for you." Popeye thinks it's silly but decides to wear, as he calls it, a tin suit. Both men emerge from Ye Olde Armour Shop dressed for battle. However, while Brutus wears typical armor, Popeye has on an old-fashioned stove. The embarrassed fighter mutters, "Oh, how mortifying! This is the best they can does for me. They makes no armor me size!" Olive drops her handkerchief, and the joust begins. Popeye can't get his donkey to start running. After a few comical twists and turns, Brutus picks up a pole. He uses the pole to smack Popeye and his donkey. The pair fall to the floor with a thud. Olive wails, "Oh dear, look what that brute did to my Popeye!" Brutus says Olive is now his personal fair lady and chases after her. Popeye feeds himself and the donkey spinach. The energized pair go chasing after the bearded knight. With his fist extended, Popeye crashes into Brutus, who lands in Marty's Junk Yard. Olive says, "Oh, Popeye! You're really my knight!" She kisses the sailor several times, who sings, "A knight should joust right when he aims to fight Popeye the Sailor Man. An exciting adventure.

Giddy Gold (1961)

Popeye and Olive Oyl are in the Tunnel of Love. Olive is spooked by all the weird creatures in the cave. Popeye explains to her, "Calms yourself, Olive. They ain't fer real. They're just made of paper, cardboard, paint, and stuff." Olive sees signs which read "Secret Diamond Mine," "Forbidden Gold Mine," and "To the Cave of Jewels." Olive wishes everything in the cave was real. The magical Wiffle Bird flies by, and Olive rubs its tail feathers to have her wish granted. The Wiffle Bird warns of three dangerous dangers before they're allowed to leave the cave with their wealth.

They run across two big stones with a pathway between them. One stone is painted with the message, "To Ye Boat." Popeye and Olive attempt to walk through the path.

Suddenly the stones slam shut, nearly crushing them. Popeye says, "So that's the first dangerous danger, eh. We'll has to be fast enough to beat this booby trap, just follows me." Popeye and Olive manage to be fast enough, but one of the rocks rip off Olive's skirt revealing her pink bloomers. Olive comes across a sign which states, "Beware of Medusa. One look at her weird face and you turn into stone." Popeye realizes this is the second dangerous danger and sees Medusa blocking their way to the boat. Olive doesn't believe Medusa can do what she claims and is turned into stone. Popeye is horrified but has an idea to break the spell. The sailor, wearing a blindfold, puts a sign around his neck which reads, "Venus Beauty Parlor, Free Beauty Treatment." Medusa says, "I've been waiting for this for thousands of years." When the old hag zooms off, Olive returns to normal. The pair come across a sign stating, "Beware of the Siren. She bewitches men with her magic harp."

Popeye mutters, "Now if that's the third dangerous danger, I thinks I'm goings to like it." Olive sees the siren sitting on a rock playing the harp. The music puts Popeye into a trance, and Olive declares, "This calls for drastic action." She removes Popeye's spinach can from his pocket and consumes the vegetable. Olive socks the Siren, and Popeye snaps out of her trance. They're both relieved they survived the three dangerous dangers, but all of their diamonds, jewel, and gold suddenly turn into pictures. The Wiffle Bird forgot to tell them the magic spell is broken once they hit daylight. Popeye says the joke's on Olive and sings, "Oh yes indeedy, doesn't pays to be greedy, says Popeye the Sailor Man.

Seer-Ring Is Believer-Ring (1961)

A sidewalk salesman attempts to sell genuine gold rings for one dollar. He is approached by a strange-looking man wearing a black hat and red beard. The man's name is Evil Eye, and he sticks his hands in the salesman's rings. Disgusted with the merchandise, he walks away bragging about his ring, allowing the wearer to foretell the future. Evil Eye goes to look at his ring and gasps. "Huh, it's gone! It must have slipped off my finger when I was handling those junky rings!" Olive approaches the sidewalk salesman and buys Evil Eye's ring. Evil Eye approaches the salesman looking for his ring. The salesman tells him, "A funny skinny-looking dame just bought a ring that I never saw before. Maybe it was yours?" Olive is at home trying on the ring and sees Popeye clearly in her mind. The sailor is bringing her a bottle of perfume called Evening in Persia. The doorbell rings, and it's Popeye with the bottle of perfume.

Popeye believes Olive knowing about the gift is just a coincidence. Olive sees a vision of Wimpy, holding money, who says, "Greetings dear friends, pray be my guests at Rough House's diner; it shall be my treat." Popeye laughs and says, "It's only in a vision that you'll find Wimpy doing the treating." Wimpy appears and says precisely what Olive saw in her vision. Olive gushes, "Oh, Popeye, I'm clairvoyant." Popeye responds, "You're not Claire Voyant; you're Olive Oyl and dis was just another one of those coincidental things." By using his evil eye, the owner of the ring tracks down Olive Oyl.

Olive has a vision of a strange, foreign-looking gentleman wanting to kiss her hand. This angers Popeye, and when Evil Eye approaches, the sailor sends him spinning. Evil Eye hypnotizes both Popeye and Olive so they will fall asleep. While he struggles to remove Olive's ring, a sleeping Popeye eats his spinach. Just as Evil Eye gets his ring back, Popeye bops him, and the ring falls into the sewer. Popeye and Olive awaken, believing everything which occurred was a dream. Olive sees Evil Eye using a fishing pole to try and get his ring out of the sewer. She asks Popeye what kind of a ring could that silly man be fishing for? Popeye says, "Maybe it's a herring." While Evil Eye is kissing Olive's hand during the vision, her hair's bun is colored red instead of black. Evil Eye's look and behavior are based upon the many spies employed by The Sea Hag seen in the comic strip and books.

Strange Things Are Happening (1961)

Popeye looks out his window and says, "Well, blow me down, a perfect day for fishing. And that's just what I aim to do. Take the day off and enjoy meself." Meanwhile, a sinister-sounding man says to The Sea Hag that he'll make it worth her while capturing Popeye and bringing him to a specific address. The witch dresses up as an old lady whom Popeye helps across the street. Suddenly she yells, "Grab him, my trusty Goons!" Two Goons grab Popeye, but he socks both of them. The Sea Hag takes off while Popeye thinks there's something fishy going on.

The man approaches Wimpy and offers him free hamburgers for a month, providing he can bring Popeye to the same address. Wimpy pushes Popeye into a diner, offering to buy him lunch. Suddenly the diner moves with Wimpy behind the wheel. Popeye realizes the diner is moving and uses his fishing pole to yank himself out of the vehicle. The sailor encounters Doctor WottaSnozzle. The doctor pulls out Popeye's tongue, saying, "It's a good thing we meet, Popeye. You look terrible. You must come to my office for a checkup." Once at the office, WottaSnozzle prepares to give Popeye knock-out drops to get him to the address.

However, a terrified Popeye jumps out the window. The man whispers in Olive Oyl's ear "...and that's all you have to do" before Popeye approaches. The sailor asks Olive to go fishing with him, but she declines. Olive would instead like to go to a movie with Brutus. Popeye yells, "But ya cants go out with him! I'm your boyfriend." Brutus threatens Popeye, and the sailor is going to punch him when a police officer stops him. Olive tells the policeman Popeye is trying to prevent her from going to the movies with Brutus. Popeye is led away in handcuffs and finds himself sitting in a chair with a light shining on him. The sinister-sounding man says, "Is your name Popeye the Sailor?" Popeye replies, "Yeah, but I'm innocent, I tells ya." The man continues. "Well, Mr. Popeye, you're such a modest man that this was the only way to get you here. Popeye, this is your day!" The man hands Popeye a book, and the lights go on. On a television stage are Olive, Wimpy, Swee'pea, Doctor WottaSnozzle, The Sea Hag, and Brutus, all applauding him. Popeye gushes, "Gosh, this is me most embarrassing day." A fun cartoon and another example of a script co-written by Jack Mercer, not involving spinach.

The Medicine Man (1961)

Olive Oyl says to a crowd of people, "Welcome to Popeye's medicine show!" Popeye is trying to convince the public to buy bottles of his spinach health juice. This angers Dr. Quack, who growls, "That runt is trying to ruin my racket. It's unethical! He's stealing my clientel. *Hmm*, let me see. I got to do something to prove him to be a fake." Dr. Quack mixes up a phony bottle of spinach health juice which contains Tabasco sauce, red pepper, ground horseradish, red hot mustard, and green horse liniment. Dr. Quack joins the crowd and asks Popeye to try his health juice to prove it works. However, Dr. Quack has switched bottles on Popeye. The sailor drinks the phony concoction and begs for water! The crowd boos Popeye who develops hiccups. Olive asks Dr. Quack, "Oh doctor, please can you stop Popeye's hiccups?" Doctor Quack agrees and gives Popeye Mexican jumping beans and says he'll bounce right back. Popeye swallows the beans and bounces in the air, hitting a tree limb. Next up is the scare treatment. Dr. Quack and Popeye are flying skyward in a plane. The doctor jumps out with a parachute, but the plane, still containing Popeye, crashes to the ground. The battered sailor survives the crash. Dr. Quack gives Popeye a sleeping pill and puts him in a wheelchair. He pushes the wheelchair, which smashes into the vehicle containing bottles of spinach health juice. The juice falls into Popeye's pipe, which revives him. The determined sailor punches the doctor, who lands on an operating table. When Popeye pretends to begin an operation, the doctor runs for his life. Popeye gives Olive an apple while singing, "An apple a day keeps the doctor away, says Popeye the Sailor Man."

A Mite of Trouble (1961)

The Sea Hag says, "We're going to be rich, my darling vulture!" She wants to snatch the treasure map Popeye has hidden in his house. Olive Oyl arrives at Popeye's home with Swee'pea and asks, "I was wondering if you would take care of Swee'pea while I go shopping?" Popeye agrees, which angers The Sea Hag because she can't look for the treasure map in his house while he's babysitting. The witch flies off to Tinagling Bros. Circus to speak with Major Mite, the Midget. To collect half of the treasure, the little person dresses up as Swee'pea. The Sea Hag snatches the real Swee'pea, and the phony one takes his place.

Popeye sees the disguised baby smoking and yells, "Swee'pea! Where in the world did you get that cigar! Throws it away!" The fake tyke puffs a large smoke ring at Popeye and starts looking for the treasure map. Popeye finds him in the kitchen and decides he needs a bath to wash off the cigar smell. A quick flip by the faker, and Popeye ends up in the bathtub. The sailor decides it's time for lunch and gives the midget a baby bottle. The bogus baby spits out the bottle, and while the sailor fetches it, the midget squeezes instant glue on Popeye's chair and table. While Popeye is stuck, the search for the treasure resumes. Popeye frees himself and takes Swee'pea for a stroll in a baby carriage. However, the crooked infant hurls Popeye into the carriage and pushes it away. Rushing back into Popeye's house, the treasure map is located on a lampshade. Major Mite gives it to his partner in crime and says, "Here it is Sea Hag, and now I can be myself again." The witch cackles, "Now that I have the treasure map, you can have your brat back again!" Olive returns and wonders what happened? Popeye explains The Sea Hag stole his lampshade with the treasure map. It turns out that the map was fake, and the actual treasure map is hidden in a safe place. Popeye lifts the back of Swee'pea's gown, and the map is written on the baby's diaper. While Popeye is stuck to the chair, his closed eye briefly disappears.

Who's Kiddin' Zoo (1961)

Popeye and Brutus visit the city zoo. The pair overhear Olive Oyl on the phone, saying, "I wish to place an ad in your paper. Wanted an assistant to the zookeeper. Must apply in person." Suddenly both Popeye and Brutus appear in front of her, wanting the same job. Olive only needs one person. She tests both to see who is the better friend and influence towards animals. Olive introduces the pair to Gloomy the Laughing Hyena. The one who makes the hyena laugh will get the job as her assistant. Brutus's joke fails, but Popeye has the animal howling. As the newly employed sailor strolls off, he says, "Bye Bye Brutus! Youse is a great swab, but yer jokes is awful!"

An angry Brutus vows to get the last laugh. Popeye has to water the elephant, and Brutus offers to help him. The bearded bully pours a weight-reducing liquid in the water, which shrinks the animal. Olive is shocked until Popeye blows into the elephant's trunk restoring his weight. Next, Brutus puts springs on the legs of a baby Kangaroo. When the animal snatches a carrot from Popeye, it flies out of his mother's pouch, but the sailor rescues it. Popeye says, "Ya sees it can be dangerous when ya runs away." Olive is delighted that Popeye is a lover of animals, so Brutus dresses up as a gorilla to woo her. The fake gorilla bops Popeye but loses his head while offering Olive a banana. The elephant, who Brutus harmed earlier, gives Popeye his spinach. Popeye zooms to Olive's rescue and punches Brutus in a cage. The sailor puts a sign on the cell calling Brutus half man, half ape, only one in captivity. The sailor sings, "When youse go to the zoo ya must knows who's zoo, says Popeye the Sailor Man."

Robot Popeye (1961)

Brutus uses a mechanical man kit to build a robot double of Popeye. He carries the tin man over his shoulder and sees the real Popeye approaching. The robot says, "Hello Matey," and the real sailor replies, "Hello Popeye." Brutus grabs the robot, and Popeye says, "I could have sworn I sees me-self walking down the street. But it couldn't be me 'cause I am me." Brutus watches Rough House give Wimpy a hard time about not paying his bill. The Popeye robot says, "Rough House, I wants ya to give me friend Wimpy here all the hamburgers he can eats and charges it up to me account." Rough House gives Wimpy a massive plate of hamburgers. Brutus says, "That's going to cost Popeye a pretty penny. Now to mess him up with Olive once and for all." Olive Oyl is making Popeye dinner, but the robot arrives to test her cooking. He chews on a wooden spoon with disgust and offers to do the serving. Olive is delighted until the robot pulls her chair out from underneath. Olive shouts, "Popeye! I'm burning mad!" The mechanical sailor tosses a glass of water in Olive's face. Brutus grabs the robot when Popeye approaches Olive's house. Furious with Popeye, Olive whacks him with an umbrella and slams the door! Popeye ponders,

"I jus' can't understand what happened to Olive." The mechanical impostor approaches Popeye, who hears Brutus's hearty laugh. Popeye grabs the robot's controls from Brutus and plays with the knobs. Suddenly the robot growls, "Get Brutus! Get Brutus! Get Brutus!" The frightened fat man runs off with the angry robot in pursuit. Later Olive, Popeye, and the Robot sit down to dinner. The robot is given empty spinach cans to munch on. Popeye sings, "I'm glad he's mechanical and not so romantical, says Popeye the Sailor Man." While Popeye is walking he doesn't have his pipe. It appears, however, in his close-up.

Sneaking Peeking (1961)

It's Swee'pea's birthday, and Olive Oyl has put his presents in the closet. Swee'pea gets into the closet, which causes Olive to say, "Oh, Swee'pea! How could you, you bad boy! Sneaking and peeking when you were told not to." Olive tells Swee'pea a story about a terrible thing that happened when someone else just had to take a peek. A long, long time ago, in a land far away, lived a Prince and Princess who had fun all day long. Not too far away lived an old King who had a servant named Mercury. Mercury had wings on both his hat and shoes. The King orders Mercury to take a box marked: "Danger do not open" and drop it into the sea. However, Mercury sees the happy home of the Prince and Princess. He stops for a visit and joins them for lunch. While Mercury heads for the kitchen, he says, "I'll just leave this box right here. I understand it contains something awful, so please don't open it." The Princess is curious and opens the box.

Out springs Mister Mischief and he thanks the Princess for letting him out. He says, "Fear me not; I will be your humble slave." Mister Mischief polishes the Prince's crown but puts bees in it! Mister Mischief pretends to clean the palace chimney but blows black smoke on The Prince, Princess, and Mercury. The trickster pours water, from a fountain, on the trio to clean them up. The Princess complains of being all wet, and she's shivering. To warm her up, Mister Mischief takes out all of the palace furniture. He then sets all of it on fire. The Princess is worried the palace will burn. Mister Mischief pushes the palace away, causing it to crumble. The Prince says, "There's only way to get rid of Mischief." He pulls out a can of spinach and eats the contents. The Prince flies into the air and uses his fists to push Mister Mischief back into the box. It turns out Swee'pea wasn't even listening to Olive's story and opens up one of his gifts. It's a jack-in-the-box containing a toy version of Mister Mischief. This causes Swee'pea to cry while Popeye says to Olive, "I still thinks it was a good story, Olive!" An exciting story!

The Wiffle Bird's Revenge (1961)
Wimpy approaches Popeye for money, but the sailor says, "Wimpy, you're a moocher, and you're not getting any more handouts from me!" A famished Wimpy grabs the magical Wiffle Bird with plans to eat him. Since Wimpy says he's hungry as a wolf, the bird casts a spell over him. Each time Wimpy says the word hamburger, he will turn into a werewolf. The moocher says hamburger to see if the spell really works, and he turns into a snarling beast. Popeye is in Rough House's diner, and they hear, on television, about a werewolf sighting. Popeye says, "Well, blow me down. I always thought that this happened in those horror moving pictures!" Rough House locks the door, but the werewolf appears outside of the diner. The beast growls, "Let me in! Or by the hair of my chinny chin, chin I'll huff, and I'll puff, and I'll blow your diner in." The beast fails to blow down the diner and leaves. Popeye tracks down the werewolf by studying the creature's footprints. The sailor encounters Wimpy, who explains about the Wiffle Bird's spell. Wimpy demonstrates what happens when he says hamburger and he again turns into a werewolf. The beast goes after Popeye, and the pair end up in the diner. Rough House feeds a plate of hamburgers to the angry monster. The werewolf turns back into Wimpy, but Rough House says, "That savage critter left a hamburger!" Wimpy exclaims, "A hamburger!" The beast again chases after Popeye, who encounters the Wiffle Bird. The sailor pleads with the bird to uncast his spell over Wimpy. The Wiffle Bird agrees but says to Popeye, "He'll have to hold still for me to do it." Popeye eats his spinach and punches the beast who lands on the ground. The Wiffle Bird flies over to the werewolf and says, "I break the spell, and then Wimpy can be himself again!" The moocher is back to his old self, and Popeye offers to buy him a hamburger.

Going...Boing...Gone (1961)
Wimpy runs into Brutus and says to him, "I was just saying to myself, Wimpy I said if there's anybody who's a prince of a guy it's that handsome, charming, brilliant fellow, Brutus." Brutus is smitten until the moocher asks for a buck or two for hamburgers. Enraged, Brutus chases after Wimpy, who manages to elude him in a drug store. Wimpy finds a jar of vanishing cream and puts it all over himself, and disappears. While walking, Popeye bumps into the invisible Wimpy, who explains to the bewildered sailor, "Brutus was chasing me, so I covered myself in vanishing cream to get away from him." Popeye whispers in Wimpy's ear a plan to get even with him. Brutus asks Popeye if he's seen Wimpy when suddenly the brute's hat levitates and he's kicked in the leg. Brutus is then punched

in the stomach and runs into Rough House's diner, with Popeye in pursuit. In the restaurant, Brutus orders a hamburger which the invisible Wimpy eats. Brutus asks Rough House what happened to the hamburger? The angry cook replies, "Brutus, are you trying to pull a Wimpy to get a free hamburger?" The brute is given another hamburger under Rough House's watchful eye. The invisible Wimpy pulls Rough House's chef's hat over his face and eats Brutus's hamburger. Brutus refuses to pay for the two hamburgers since he didn't eat them. Rough House chases after Brutus, holding a rolling pin threatening to make him look like a hamburger! Popeye tells Wimpy he can wipe off the vanishing cream. Instead, Wimpy decides to eat a lot of hamburgers off a hot grill. While munching away, he says, "I'll be seeing you, but will you be seeing me?"

Popeye Thumb (1961)

Popeye is visiting Olive Oyl and sees a tearful Swee'pea. Olive explains to Popeye he wasn't allowed to play baseball with the other boys and was called a quarter-pint. Popeye says, "Oh, fish-sticks! Being small is nothing to be ashamed of. Why I heard of another little fellow who was small and let's me tells ya about him." Popeye tells Swee'pea the story of an old farmer and his wife who were very, very poor. The couple dreamt of having a strong enough son to do all the farming and to have food to eat. The good fairy heard their wishes and blessed them with a son who was no bigger than someone's thumb. Though happy to have a son, the elderly farmers were upset because they knew he wasn't big enough to do the farming. Popeye said, "Although this Popeye Thumb was small in size, he was big in brains." The tyke asked his Pappy if he had any spinach seeds. The old farmer found one spinach seed, and Popeye Thumb planted it. Soon it grew into a nice healthy spinach plant, but Pappy said, "I'm afraid that's hardly a meal for even one of us 'cept you, Popeye Thumb 'cause you're so small." Popeye Thumb swallowed a piece of the spinach plant and grew enormous muscles. The lad was now able to plow all the fields and plant plenty of food. The family could rush all the food to the market and come home with a lot of money. Popeye Thumb bought lots of animals for the farm and rebuilt their broken-down house. Soon they were the riches farmers in the village. When a television announcer asked Popeye Thumb what the secret of his success was, the tyke replied. "I always eats me spinach!" Popeye concludes his story and says, "So ya sees Swee'pea, your size ain't something you should be ashamed of." Swee'pea digs his hand into Popeye's shirt pocket and pulls out the sailor's can of spinach. The tyke eats the spinach and hurries off to the baseball field. The energized lad grabs a bat and is pitched a baseball which he slams out of sight. One boy exclaims, "Wow! It's a home run!" Swee'pea finds himself in a tug of war, being wanted by both team captains. Popeye sings, "You can be small as a mite and have plenty of height, says Popeye the Sailor Man!" A fun cartoon.

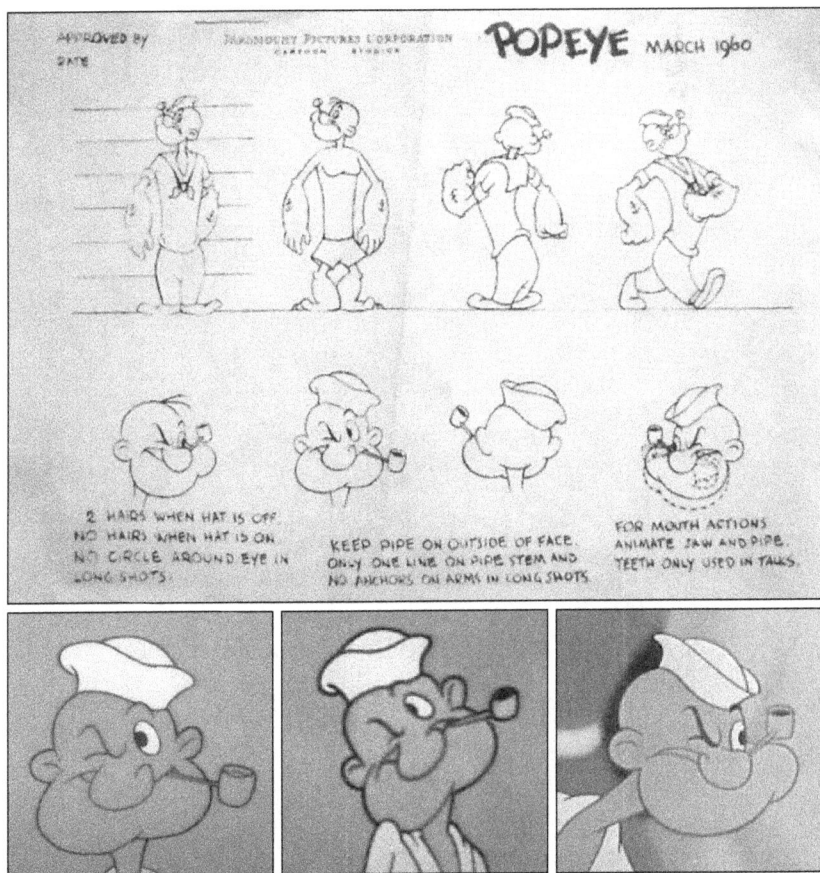

ABOVE: *an animation model sheet dated March 1960 of Popeye used by Paramount Pictures Corporation. The faces of Popeye were glimpsed in various cartoons including* Popeye's Picnic *(Jack Kinney, 1960),* Partial Post *(Gene Deitch, 1960) and* Disguise the Limit *(Gene Deitch, 1961).*

Jack Kinney's animation director's facial designs for Popeye varied. Clockwise from top left: Ken Hultgren, Rudy Larriva, Eddie Rehberg and Hugh Fraser.

Popeye's neighbor is about to clonk him in one of the pilot films for the cartoon series, Barbecue for Two *(Jack Kinney, 1960).*

Popeye serenades the comic strip design of Olive Oyl in Barbecue for Two *(Jack Kinney, 1960).*

Wimpy, Alice the Goon, Eugene the Jeep, The Sea Hag and Swee'pea all sing during Popeye's Testimonial Dinner *(Jack Kinney, 1960).*

Wimpy is about to be catnapped in Tiger Burger *(Jack Kinney, 1960).*

Sitting in a tree Deezil and Swee'pea learn how to play games the right way in Coach Popeye *(Jack Kinney, 1960).*

Wimpy shakes Popeye's hand while the sailor speaks gibberish at the conclusion of the poorly animated cartoon Popeye and the Giant *(Jack Kinney, 1960).*

Brutus and The Sea Hag are diamond smugglers in Private Eye Popeye *(Jack Kinney, 1960).*

The Sea Hag sells Popeye a magic can of spinach from Popeye and The Beanstalk *(Jack Kinney, 1960).*

Popeye loses both his mouth and pipe while reading a letter in Mississippi Sissy *(Jack Kinney, 1960).*

A ship's cabin is empty until Olive Oyl and Wimpy appear out of nowhere in a sloppy animated scene from Mississippi Sissy *(Jack Kinney, 1960).*

Popeye says to Olive, "Fat boy doesn't have a chance. If I gets in trouble I can always use me spinach gimmick." From After The Ball Went Over *(Jack Kinney, 1960). This is an example of a clever television cartoon marred with sloppy animation.*

Rip Van Popeye *(Jack Kinney, 1960). Sloppy animated scenes include green foam suddenly appearing and disappearing from the top of a mug.*

The Goons raise Popeye as one of their own in Popeye The Ugly Ducklin *(Jack Kinney, 1960).*

Alice the Goon is in love with Popeye in Frozen Feuds *(Jack Kinney, 1960).*

Olive Oyl grows an eyeball underneath her nose in Old Salt Tale *(Jack Kinney, 1960).*

The sequence of Popeye running was originally seen in Popeye and the Phantom *(Jack Kinney, 1960). A fireman's hat was plopped on the sailor's head so this same sequence could be reused in Jack Kinney's 1960 cartoon* Popeye the Fireman, *which was poorly animated.*

Popeye returns home after a trip through Professor WottaSnozzle's time machine in The Black Knight *(Jack Kinney, 1960).*

While talking to Popeye, Wimpy's mustache disappears then reappears in Camel Aires *(Jack Kinney, 1960).*

An animation cel of Popeye used in the production of Coffee House *(Jack Kinney, 1960).*

Olive: POPEYE, TAKE CARE OF YOUR GUESTS..

A storyboard featuring sketches of Popeye, Olive Oyl, and the neighbor used in the production of Barbecue for Two *(Jack Kinney, 1960).*

Apparently Swee'pea lost his arms while searching for The Sea Hag in Hag-Way Robbery *(Gene Deitch, 1960).*

Brutus says "This looks like a job for Popeye" as he feeds the costumed sailor his spinach to battle an alien invasion in There's No Space Like Home *(Gene Deitch, 1960).*

An angry space boy doesn't want to be friends with Popeye in From Way Out *(Gene Deitch, 1960).*

Popeye's wet suit becomes full of water in Sea No Evil *(Gene Deitch, 1960).*

The conclusion of Insultin' The Sultan *(Gene Deitch, 1960) had Popeye and Olive Oyl having a loud argument.*

Brutus enjoys Olive Oyl's new look in Weight For Me *(Gene Deitch, 1961).*

Olive Oyl is not impressed with The Sea Hag's Goons in Which is Witch *(Gene Deitch, 1961).*

Popeye punches Brutus who tried to sabotage his sculpture of Olive Oyl in Model Muddel *(Gene Deitch, 1961).*

A Police Chief and Popeye hope to hear news regarding a jewelry store robbery from Roger *(Gene Deitch, 1962).*

Olive Oyl is taken hostage by an alien spacecraft while out for a drive with Popeye in Ace of Space *(Larry Harmon, 1960).*

Popeye is handed his spinach by the Foola Foola Bird *(Larry Harmon, 1960).*

Olive Oyl and Popeye become involved in the Crystal Ball Brawl *(Larry Harmon, 1960).*

Popeye becomes Napoleon at the conclusion of Ski-Jump Chump *(Larry Harmon, 1960).*

Suicide McBride suddenly gains a long-sleeved shirt after kicking sheriff Popeye out of a saloon from Dead-Eye Popeye *(Larry Harmon, 1960).*

An animation cel of Baby Popeye and Brutus used in the production of Childhood Daze *(Larry Harmon, 1960).*

A storyboard used in the production of Muskels Shmuskels *(Larry Harmon, 1960). Notice how Popeye was drawn with his Captain's hat seen in print at the time.*

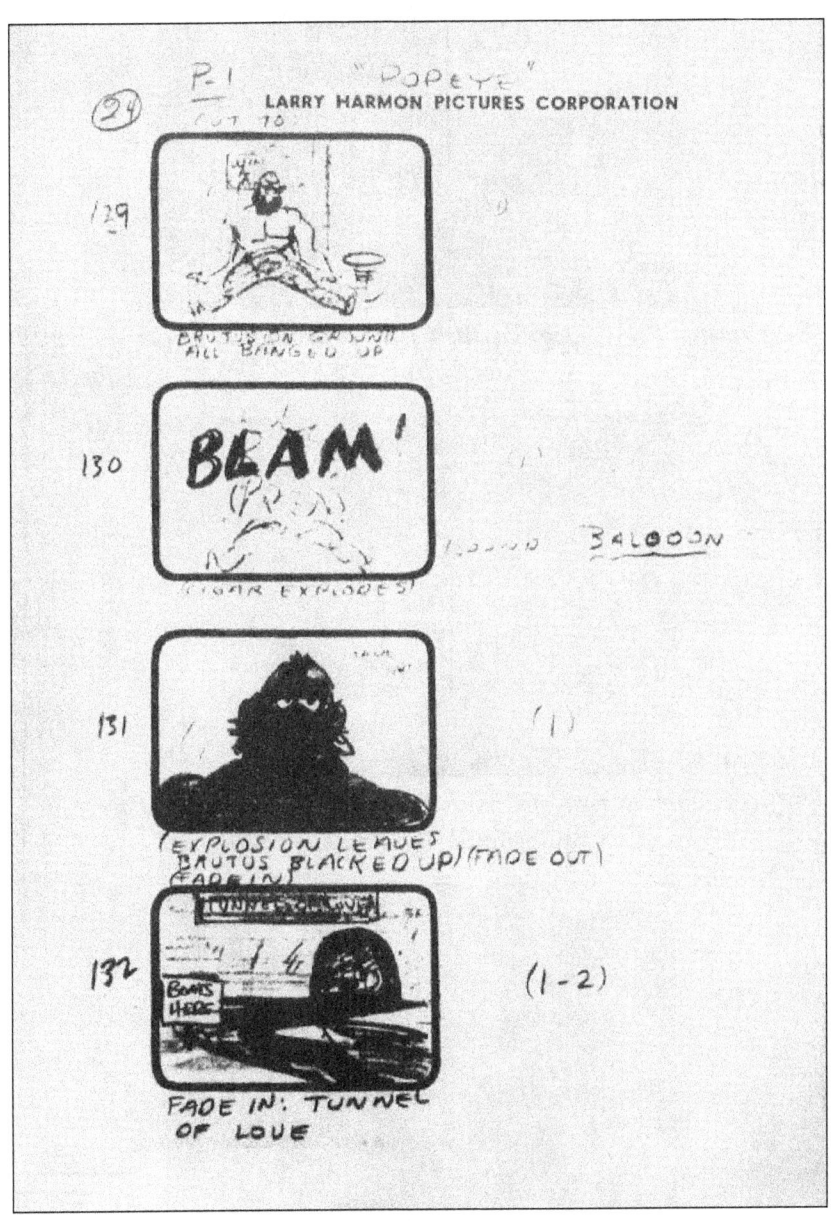

Swee'pea and Popeye enjoy Poopdeck Pappy's tall tales in Jeopardy Sheriff *(Gerald Ray, 1960).*

After consuming a can of spinach, Brutus proceeds to beat up Popeye in I Bin Sculped *(Gerald Ray, 1960).*

"It's bad to be tardy to a hamburger party says Wimpy the Burger Man" from Egypt Us *(Gerald Ray, 1960).*

Popeye and Olive Oyl discover The Sea Hag and Toar are producing "funny money" in The Last Resort *(Gerald Ray, 1960).*

Wimpy, Popeye and Olive Oyl (wearing a dress like the one worn in the Famous Studios' theatrical cartoons) listen to a Professor's lecture in Hits and Missiles *(Paramount Cartoon Studios, 1960). This was one of two pilot cartoons for the series.*

Brutus is about to beat the tar out of "Popeye Ye Pleasant Peasant" in Mirror Magic *(Paramount Cartoon Studios, 1960).*

The Goons say farewell to Popeye who helped them, with the aid of spinach, defeat a band of pirates after the creature's skins in Valley of the Goons *(Paramount Cartoon Studios, 1960).*

Popeye grabs The Sea Hag who has stolen a sacred emerald in Gem Jam *(Paramount Cartoon Studios, 1960).*

King Blozo, Popeye and Olive Oyl investigate an Incident at Missile City *(Paramount Cartoon Studios, 1960).*

"A friend I am told is worth more than pure gold says Popeye the Leprechaun" from The Leprechaun *(Paramount Cartoon Studios, 1961).*

Prince Popeye eats his spinach to stop Mr. Mischief in Sneaking Peeking *(Paramount Cartoon Studios, 1961).*

The Sea Hag plans a theft and requests Wimpy's aid in Hamburgers Aweigh *(Paramount Cartoon Studios, 1961).*

Popeye and Rough House are shocked when Wimpy becomes a werewolf thanks to The Wiffle Bird's Revenge *(Paramount Cartoon Studios, 1961)*.

Since Popeye's sailor code wouldn't allow him to strike a lady, Olive Oyl often ate the spinach to sock The Sea Hag. Olive consumes a can of spinach when The Sea Hag menaces Popeye in A Poil for Olive Oyl *(Paramount Cartoon Studios, 1961)*.

"Brutus was beaten because he was cheaten says Popeye the Farmer Man" from County Fair *(Paramount Cartoon Studios, 1961)*.

Swee'pea swallows the sailor's spinach after he's told the story of Popeye Thumb *(Paramount Cartoon Studios, 1961)*.

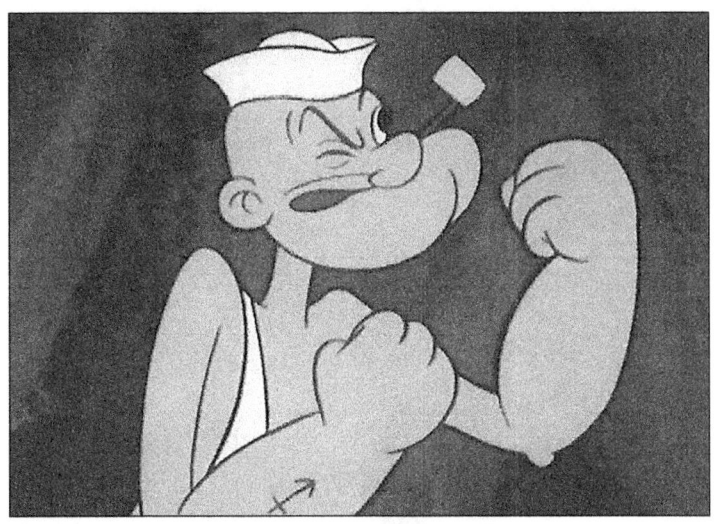

Stories, depicting Popeye's origins with eating spinach, were used in the sailor's theatrical cartoons. This episode has Popeye explaining to Olive Oyl how he started on his spinach diet. It began with Popeye's great, great, great, grandpappy, Pre-hysterical Popeye in Caveman Capers *(Larry Harmon, 1960).*

Jackson Beck gave Jolly Roger's voice a French accent in this cartoon where he woos Olive Oyl and battles Popeye in Irate Pirate *(Larry Harmon, 1960).*

Brutus kidnaps Swee'pea when the tyke is the recipient of a million dollars. While Popeye is being beaten up, Swee'pea spells out the letters on a can; "S-P-I-N-A-C-H, Popeye". This cartoon depicts Brutus at his meanest; a baby kidnapper. It also has an eerie and haunting instrumental music score in Interrupted Lullaby *(Gene Deitch, 1960).*

Popeye is being spied upon by sea creatures while searching for treasure in this colorful adventure. This cartoon was selected as the Popeye entry for Ideal's Pocket Flix movie viewer. The Lost City of Bubble-Lon *(Gene Deitch, 1960).*

Popeye is tricked into applying a lotion to his face. When people sniff it they have the urge to sock the sailor. This is used as a diversion by Brutus and his gang when they rob a bank. A clever story! Potent Lotion *(Gene Deitch with animation by Halas & Batchelor, 1960).*

Popeye gives Olive Oyl a million dollars. She buys a beauty salon which totally makes her over! Popeye laughs at the 'new' Olive explaining, "I likes ya ugly!" This cartoon was influenced by the popular television series, "The Millionaire" *which aired on CBS from 1955 to 1960.* The Billionaire *(Gene Deitch with animation by Halas & Batchelor, 1961).*

When Popeye and Brutus return from the sea, they discover an overweight Olive Oyl. She made a pig of herself waiting for the boys. This pencil sketch was used during the production of the film. It is courtesy of Heritage Auctions. *Quite possibly the animators had yet to be given a Brutus model sheet. He is doodled looking like Bluto, wearing his sailor's uniform, worn in the theatrical cartoons from* Famous Studios *in* Weight For Me *(Gene Deitch with animation by Halas & Batchelor, 1961).*

Popeye and Brutus are named in Barnacle Bilge's will. The brute becomes furious believing all he was left is one can of spinach. Brutus beats up Popeye and tosses the can in the sailor's direction. Suddenly the spinach eating theme plays. Brutus looks at the audience and says, "Whoops, I shouldn't have done that." The episode was released as a "Musical Story" by Peter Pan Records *(below).* Where There's A Will *(Gerald Ray, 1960).*

An elephant is one of the captives released from a dog catcher's truck during Popeye's search for his trained fleas. This entry was the basis for a "Musical Record" *from Peter Pan (below). The vocals on these adaptations was performed by Harry Welch. Welch was given permission by* King Features Syndicate *to be their "live" Popeye at events. He also did the sailor's voice in some of the theatrical cartoons. The picture of Popeye playing his flute was originally used in the comic strip.* Fleas A Crowd *(Gerald Ray, 1960).*

Kasimoto, the Halfback of Notre Dame steals Olive Oyl's raccoon coat to keep warm in this amusing cartoon. The stories from Gerald Ray's studio were witty and fun to watch. The Big Sneeze *(Gerald Ray, 1960).*

Popeye punishes Swee'pea and dreams he's run away to become the world's greatest juggler performing at The Bungling Bros. Circus. As in the theatrical cartoons, Swee'pea is seen either in the care of Popeye or Olive Oyl. In print he has always been the sailor's adopted son. Baby Phase *(Gerald Ray, 1960).*

A baseball smashes a television screen representing the set viewers are watching this cartoon on. Popeye explains, "Sorry folks, pardon the interruptions. Due to mechanical difficulties..." An exciting episode with excellent animation in Battery Up *(Jack Kinney, 1960).*

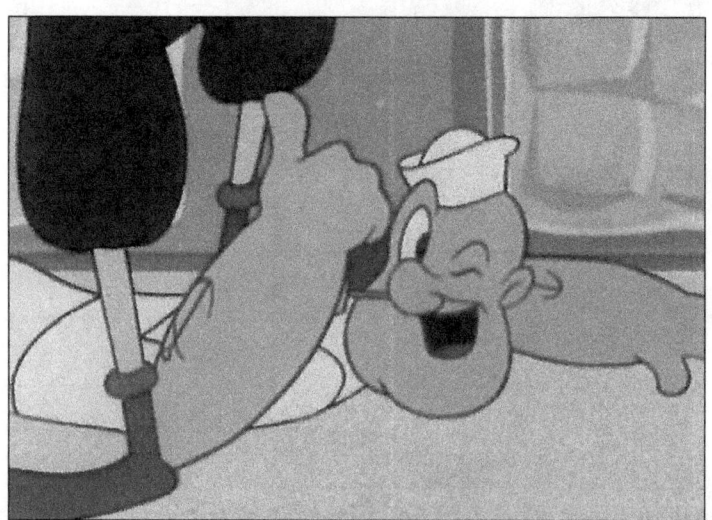

Olive Oyl twists Popeye's foot at the conclusion of this fun cartoon. He says to the audience, "I guess I teaches 'em too good!" Jackson Beck's regular speaking voice is heard as the television announcer in Popeye's Pep-Up Emporium *(Jack Kinney, 1960).*

Brutus has cornered the world's spinach market leaving Popeye in search of his favorite vegetable. The weakened sailor repeatedly tries to get into the brute's warehouse but is constantly thwarted. A unique story in Spinach Shortage *(Jack Kinney, 1960).*

Popeye and Olive Oyl are haunted by a ghost. The sailor can't seem to defeat him. Instead, he remarks, "I always say if you cants lick 'em ya joins 'em." The trio decide to play bridge in Popeye and the Phantom *(Jack Kinney, 1960).*

Brutus hires Popeye to work on a construction site with Wimpy as supervisor. The one-eyed sailor's ineptness causes chaos in Skyscraper Capers *(Jack Kinney, 1960).*

Brutus hypnotizes Olive Oyl to love him. He also makes Alice the Goon fall head over heels for Popeye. An inventive story with excellent animation in Popeye's Hypnotic Glance *(Jack Kinney, 1960).*

Popeye tells Swee'pea a story about his great grandpappy when he was the captain of a prairie schooner. This cartoon had Pappy battling the Cleveland Indians *and* Milwaukee Braves. *It is a pun-filled cartoon laced with amusing baseball related humor featuring excellent animation in* Westward Ho-Ho *(Jack Kinney, 1960).*

Because it's so hot during the summer, Olive Oyl and Swee'pea beg Popeye to build a swimming pool. When Brutus isn't invited to use it, he steals the pool from the sailor's yard. A humorous cartoon. Popeye's Cool Pool *(Jack Kinney, 1960).*

Popeye is guarding a valuable painting which Brutus wants to steal. The sailor is aided in this colorful episode by Eugene the Jeep. Popeye's Museum Piece *(Jack Kinney, 1960).*

Popeye is watching over Wimpy's diner. Brutus forcibly tries to install a juke box in the establishment. A fast-paced episode with excellent animation in Wimpy's Lunch Wagon *(Jack Kinney, 1960).*

Wimpy Weatherbee reports inaccurate forecasts reported by Popeye. Brutus takes advantage of these mishaps to get Popeye fired so he can get his job. A creative story. Weather Watchers *(Jack Kinney, 1960).*

Popeye tangles with Brutus the Magician who uses his wand to humiliate the sailor on stage. A fun cartoon! Popeye and The Magic Hat *(Jack Kinney, 1960).*

Brutus the Kid socks Popeye for humiliating him in public following a gun battle. An action filled cartoon with fine animation in Bottom Gun *(Jack Kinney, 1960)*.

Princess Olive Drab's father tells his daughter to look for Prince Popeye. He is needed to find out why ships are vanishing. The father, in this fun cartoon, resembles Cole Oyl, Olive's dad in the comic strip. Olive Drab and the Seven Sweapeas *(Jack Kinney, 1960)*.

Popeye tells Swee'pea a tale about his great, great, grand pappy's first experiment building steamboats. The Sea Hag and Brutus, sailing in their ship called The Blackhawk, believe the sailor will be competing for their business! A nice look back at sailing history found in Popeye's Folly *(Jack Kinney, 1960).*

An interesting cartoon dealing with Japanese culture. A Samurai tries to rescue a Princess from an evil bandit. This cartoon showcases Mae Questel's singing voice. In 1961, The St. Louis Globe Democrat *noted about Questel; "The success of these films (phenomenal and seemingly interminable; only recently she completed recordings for* King Features *of 220 new Popeye cartoons) has made her rich."* Spinachonara *(Jack Kinney, 1960).*

The Wiffle Bird is sad the square egg she produced is broken. However, it will hatch an adorable creature. This cartoon was based upon the story, Square Egg Island, from the daily Thimble Theatre *comic strip published in 1951. It was written by Tom Sims with art by Bela Zaboly.* The Square Egg *(Jack Kinney, 1960).*

LEFT: *Two panels from Square Egg Island published on September 21, 1951.*
RIGHT: *A photograph of Tom Sims circa 1954. Sims wrote the daily* Thimble Theatre *comic strip from 1939 to 1954. He continued with the Sunday page until 1958.*

Brutus admires wall paper for the playroom consisting of comic strips from Thimble Theatre *published, August 4th and 5th, 1954. Written by Tom Sims with art by Bela Zaboly.* Paper Pasting Pandemonium *(Jack Kinney, 1960).*

  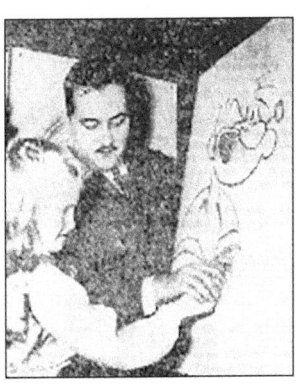

LEFT: *Two panels from the August 4th, 1954* Thimble Theatre *comic strip.*
RIGHT: *Bela Zaboly is pictured showing a student how to draw Popeye. This was published in the December 4th, 1941 edition of The* Punxsutawney Spirit *(Punxsutawney, Pennsylvania).*

Popeyed Fisherman *(Jack Kinney, 1960)*. *This is an amusing cartoon where Popeye teaches Swee'pea and Olive Oyl how to fish. All of the Jack Kinney directed Popeye cartoons were scored by Ken Lowman (pictured at right).* The Akron Beacon Journal *(Akron, Ohio) wrote an article on Lowman for its April 23, 1987 edition. It stated "Lowman scored the background music for the first 101 Popeye cartoons made for TV. Thus, every time Popeye pops the top on another can of spinach, Lowman pockets another $4.20. Add up all the times Bluto has been punched out on TV sets all over the world during the past quarter-century and Lowman has collected more than enough to lend Wimpy a couple of bucks for another hamburger. The checks keep coming in every three months, Lowman, who is 70, said with a smile." Originally Lowman turned down Jack Kinney's offer to score Popeye's television adventures. The money wasn't good but Kinney promised him royalties which were sent to Lowman since 1963. Lowman was an accomplished musician and played the bassoon with the Baltimore Symphony in the late 1930's. Later, he played for the orchestra of movie mogul* Samuel Goldwyn. *Lowman also played music for* Disney *films. It was while working with* Disney, *Lowman met Jack Kinney. Due to the royalties from the Popeye cartoons, Lowman was able to own the* Bowling News.

As of April, 1987, Lowman received as much as $80,000 a year. Another testament to the popularity of these made for television Popeye the Sailor cartoons.

Popeye tells Swee'pea stories about bad drivers. When this episode was distributed to schools for educational purposes, a new ending was added. A safe driving related song was performed by Popeye. It was animated by Paramount Cartoon Studios. *The song is usually not heard in the print airing in syndication.* Uncivil War *(Jack Kinney, 1960).*

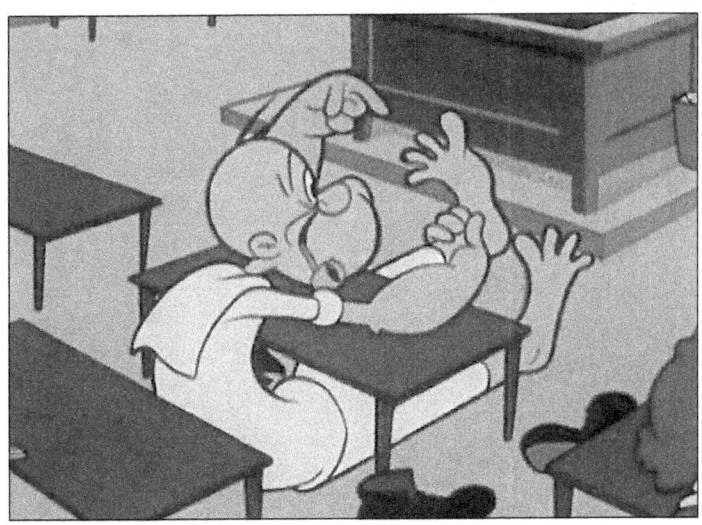

Olive Oyl refuses to date Popeye until he gets an education. The sailor goes back to school but humiliates himself. He goes from one grade to the other ending up in kindergarten. However, as he tells Olive, "I went through the whole school in one day!" A delightful cartoon. The Spinach Scholar (Paramount Cartoon Studios, *1960).*

Brutus disguises himself as Ed Shrinker, a psychiatrist. He makes Popeye believe it is his spinach consumption which causes him to fight. A fun cartoon! Psychiatricks (Paramount Cartoon Studios, *1960*).

Wimpy inherits a fortune and tries to double his money by betting against Popeye in a boxing match. As referee Wimpy tries to revive Popeye's flattened opponent, Kid Nitro. In the end Wimpy's loyalty to Popeye wins out though he loses all of his money in Rags to Riches to Rags (Paramount Cartoon Studios, *1960*).

Hair Cut-Ups (Paramount Cartoon Studios, *1960*). Swee'pea is reluctant to get the one piece of hair on his head cut. Popeye tells the lad about another fellow who didn't want his hair snipped; Sampson! Sampson believed it was his hair which gave him strength!

The music in this adventurous cartoon, as in all of the sailor's television episodes from Paramount Cartoon Studios, *was provided by composer Winston Sharples (pictured at right). His music cues were also heard in the theatrical Popeye films and utilized in episodes of several television cartoon series. They included Felix the Cat, Beetle Bailey, Snuffy Smith, King Leonardo, Tennessee Tuxedo, Batfink and Milton the Monster. His music cues originated in animated cartoons, from* Paramount Pictures, *first seen on theatre screens. He remained with Paramount's animation unit until its closing in 1967.*

A doctor informs Olive Oyl, as one did in the Thimble Theatre *Sunday page from October 3, 1937 by E.C. Segar (below), her boyfriend has Melankonkus. This causes Popeye to act strangely. It was caused, in the strip, because Swee'pea was taken away by his mother. In the animated cartoon a phony father does the same. Swee'pea manages to run away and return to Popeye in both versions. All ends happily in* Poppa Popeye (Paramount Cartoon Studios, *1960).*

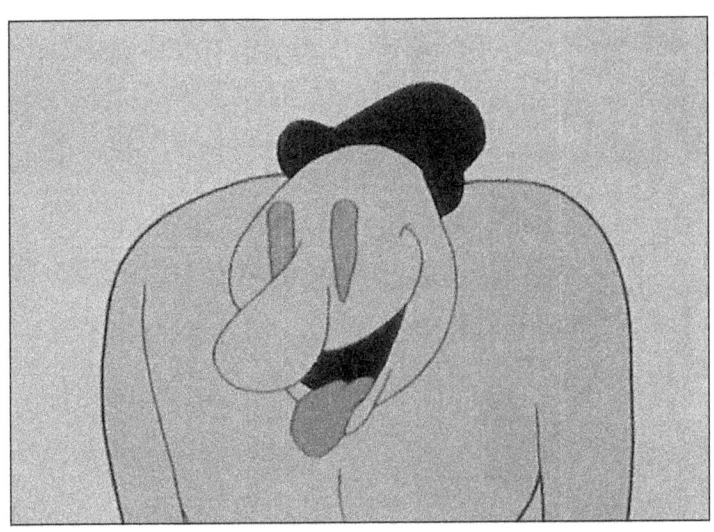

Valley of the Goons (Paramount Cartoon Studios, *1960). Carrots are used as bait to capture Goons! Pirates want the creatures for their skins. The plot of this exciting cartoon was based upon a* Thimble Theatre *daily storyline from 1937 originated by E.C. Segar. The comic strip panels (below) are from December 9, 1937. When Segar became ill, during this story's run, it was drawn by* King Features Syndicate's *bullpen artist, Doc Winner. Winner worked on several comic strips, eventually taking over* The Katzenjammer Kids *Sunday page.*

Me Quest for Poopdeck Pappy (Paramount Cartoon Studios, *1960*). *Popeye finds his long, lost father on the island of Goona. When Popeye asks his father if he's glad to see him, the ol' sailor replies "Well what do ya want me to do, Kiss ya?" Popeye received a similar response in the daily* Thimble Theatre *strip, by E.C. Segar (below), on October 28, 1936. Seymour Kneitel (pictured at right) was head of Paramount Cartoon Studios, and worked on many of the companies' animated films for theatres. Kneitel often used Popeye's comic strip adventures as source material for stories.*

It Only Hurts When They Laughs (Paramount Cartoon Studios, *1960*). *Olive Oyl tells the boys to laugh while she's doing the dishes. In this way she knows they're not fighting with each other. They brutally beat on each other while laughing. This clever story was originally read in the October 4, 1936* Thimble Theatre *Sunday page by E.C. Segar (below). In the strip Popeye's rival was named Curly.*

Wimpy the Moocher (Paramount Cartoon Studios, *1960*). *This delightful cartoon had Rough House believing Wimpy discovered a pearl in one of the chef's raw oysters. The storyline was based upon two similarly written Sunday pages by Tom Sims (writer) and Doc Winner (artist). Rough House was fooled by Wimpy on February 19, 1939 while Geezil was later tricked on November 26 within the same year (below). George W. Geezil was created by E.C. Segar. He hated Wimpy and wanted him dead! Rough House gives Wimpy thirty hamburgers for the pearl. Geezil, at his hock shop, tells Rough House he sells those pearls for "ten cents a handful."*

The Sea Hag is at her wickedest when she ties her hair around a voo-doo doll of Popeye! Many of the episodes from Paramount Cartoon Studios, *though not ignoring humor, were more all out adventure stories.* Voo-Doo To You Too (Paramount Cartoon Studios, *1960).*

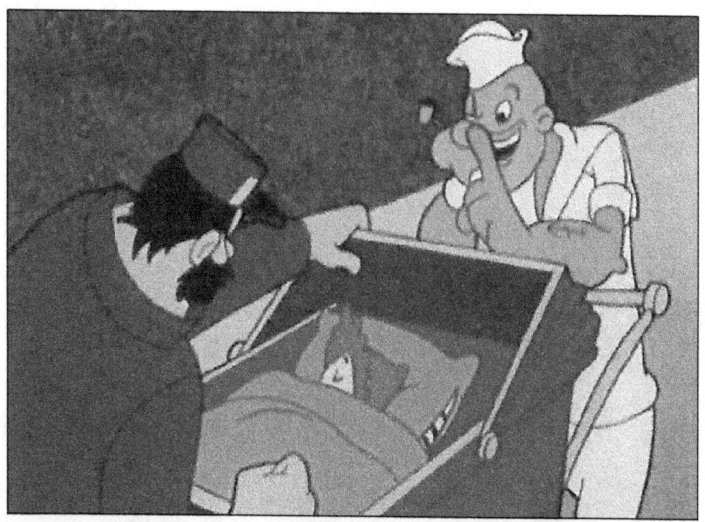

Dog Catcher Popeye (Paramount Cartoon Studios, *1960*). *This cartoon highlights Popeye's tender side as he protects a little puppy from Brutus the dog catcher. The plot of this episode was previously utilized in a Little Audrey animated theatrical film (below), called* Dawg Gawn *(1958). Both cartoons came from Paramount Cartoon Studios.*

Popeye buys a newspaper called the Puddleburg Splash. *In both the cartoon and daily* Thimble Theatre *strip, dated January 3, 1934 by E.C. Segar (below), he hires B. Loony Bullony, a comic artist. Neither the print or animated version of the cartoonist impresses Popeye in* What's News *(Paramount Cartoon Studios, 1960).*

Popeye enters Swee'pea in a baby contest to win a loving cup in this exciting cartoon. Brutus brings Bully Boy to compete against the lad. What relation Bully Boy is to Brutus is not revealed in The Baby Contest (Paramount Cartoon Studios, *1960).*

Popeye is accidently given a coin, belonging to The Sea Hag, which gives three wishes to the owner. The witch masquerades as Olive Oyl to get the coin back. When this fails, she repeatedly pounds Popeye on the floor which reveals his can of spinach. The can rolls towards Popeye's girlfriend who, after consuming the spinach, gives the ol' witch "The Solar Sock!" An exciting story written by Joseph Gottlieb. Popeye's Double Trouble (Paramount Cartoon Studios, *1961).*

Popeye tells Olive Oyl's *niece, Deezil, a bedtime story about Zero the Hero. The one-eyed swordman cuts a zero, with his sword, on the clothing of criminals including Brutus, the Bandit Leader in* The Mark of Zero (Paramount Cartoon Studios, *1961).*

This episode is based upon a Thimble Theatre *adventure from the dailies titled* Mystery Melody *by E.C. Segar. Pictured, at right, is a panel from the strip published on December 28, 1936. In both versions, The Sea Hag plays a magic flute to get Poopdeck Pappy in her power! The old sailor courted the witch when she was disguised as Rose O' the Sea. When he discovered her true identity, the sailor fled away in terror. This cartoon is another example of writer Seymour Kneitel's ability to present a long* Thimble Theatre *storyline in a little over five minutes.* Myskery Melody (Paramount Cartoon Studios, *1961).*

Brutus whips up some fear gas and sprays it on Popeye. The sailor becomes terrified of the bearded brute in this unique story in Scairdy Cat (Paramount Cartoon Studios, *1961).*

This interesting premise portrays Popeye and Brutus as movie actors competing for a little boy's autograph. When Brutus' tricks cause the brute and the lad to be chased after by a lion, it's Popeye to the rescue. Not only does the little boy want Popeye's autograph but Brutus does too! Autographically Yours (Paramount Cartoon Studios, *1961).*

Olive rubs the tail feathers of The Wiffle Bird (called the Whiffle Hen in print) and wishes for diamonds, jewels and gold. This magical creature originally made Popeye indestructible in the Thimble Theatre *comic strip. When E.C. Segar dropped the character, spinach became the source of Popeye's strength. Pictured below is a panel from the daily strip from June 11, 1929, by Segar, where Popeye rubs the bird's feathers for luck after being shot fifteen times!* Giddy Gold (Paramount Cartoon Studios, *1961).*

Seer-Ring Is Believer-Ring (Paramount Cartoon Studios, *1961*). *A foreign looking and sounding man, Evil Eye, accidently loses his special ring. Whomever wears it can foretell the future. This is something Olive Oyl discovers when she puts it on. Evil Eye attempts to woo Olive to get the ring off her finger. The character design of Evil Eye was based upon the look of the Sea Hag's spies from the comic strip and books. Pictured below, he is drawn by Bud Sagendorf. Another example of Paramount Cartoon Studios using Popeye's printed adventures as source material.*

A mysterious man plots with Brutus and Olive Oyl to get Popeye at a certain address. Turns out the sailor is being honored on the television program, "This is Your Day!" This episode, as with others from Paramount Cartoon Studios, *was written by Carl Meyer and Jack Mercer. Mercer, Popeye's voice, often co-wrote or solely scripted the sailor's adventures and eliminated spinach for broader story ideas.* Strange Things Are Happening (Paramount Cartoon Studios, *1961).*

Popeye drinks a spinach concentrate turning hims to a genius. However, it's only a shared dream between Popeye and Olive Oyl. This cartoon was obviously produced outside of the United States. The title card reads "By King Features Sindicate (instead of Syndicate) Inc. All Rights Reserved. Intellectual Interlude *(Gene Deitch, Sources site this episode's date as both 1961 or 1962).*

The Sea Hag wants Poopdeck Pappy's teeth as she has none. A cartoon with a creative story offering lessons in hygiene. Children are reminded to, "Brush your teeth twice daily, see your dentist twice yearly." Pappy adds, "If you take care of yer teeth, yer teeth will always take care of you." Tooth Be Or Not Tooth Be *(Gene Deitch, 1962).*

BLOW ME DOWN ... HERE HE IS ... E. C. SEGAR, THE CREATOR OF POPEYE, IN KANSAS CITY TODAY ... "I YAM WHAT I YAM."

King Features Syndicate's *publicity for the television cartoons acknowledged Popeye's creator, E.C. Segar (at left from a 1936 photograph):*

"When the late E.C. Segar created Popeye over thirty years ago, he could hardly have envisioned the tremendous, world-wide impact his indomitable sailor man would have on children of all ages. Popeye, star of the (name of program) *beginning* (date) *on* (station and channel) *has become one of the world's best known personalities, a leading figure in the entertainment world, the world's greatest spinach booster and a health symbol of rough, tough righteousness of millions of children".*

About the Author

FRED M. GRANDINETTI has been chronicling Popeye's career in newspapers, magazines and the internet since 1983. His articles have appeared in *The Big Reel, Filmfax, Animato, Entertainment Magazine, Hollywood Then and Now, Movie Collector's World, Antiques and Collecting Magazine, CBR.Com, Searchmytrash, Skwigly Online Animation Magazine, The Film Detective, Animated Views, i.Italy, Bleeding Cool,* and *Boomer Magazine.*

Additionally, he has written about *I Dream of Jeannie, The Avengers* Television series, *The Mighty Hercules,* television's version of Batgirl and Kathy Kane, the original Batwoman.

Since 1992 he has been the host and producer of the award-winning cable access series, *Drawing With Fred.* Fred's public relation skills kept the critically-acclaimed anthology series, *The Popeye Show,* in production. The program, featuring restored theatrical Popeye cartoons, aired for three years on The Cartoon Network. He helped get these same Popeye films on DVD.

Bear Manor Media

Classic Cinema.
Timeless TV.
Retro Radio.

WWW.BEARMANORMEDIA.COM

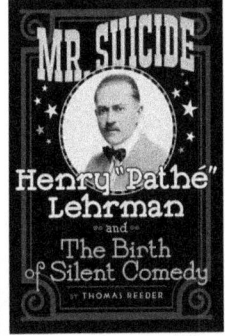

www.ingramcontent.com/pod-product-compliance
Lightning Source LLC
Chambersburg PA
CBHW060115170426
43198CB00010B/899